Community Lost
The State, Civil Society, and Displaced Survivors of Hurricane Katrina

Neither government programs nor massive charitable efforts responded adequately to the human crisis that was Hurricane Katrina. In this study, the authors use extensive interviews with Katrina evacuees and reports from service providers to identify what helped or hindered the reestablishment of the lives of hurricane survivors who relocated to Austin, Texas. Drawing on social capital and social network theory, the authors assess the complementary, and often conflicting, roles of the Federal Emergency Management Administration (FEMA), other governmental agencies, and a range of nongovernmental organizations in addressing survivors' short- and longer-term needs. Although these organizations came together to assist with immediate emergency needs, even collectively they could not deal with survivors' long-term needs for employment, affordable housing, and personal records necessary to rebuild lives. *Community Lost* provides empirical evidence that civil society organizations cannot substitute for an efficient and benevolent state, which is necessary for society to function.

Ronald J. Angel is Professor of Sociology at the University of Texas, Austin.

Holly Bell is a Research Scientist with the Center for Social Work Research in the School of Social Work at the University of Texas, Austin.

Julie Beausoleil is an Affiliate Research Associate with the Center for Social Work Research in the School of Social Work at the University of Texas, Austin.

Laura Lein is Dean and Katherine Reebel Collegiate Professor of Social Work and Professor of Anthropology at the University of Michigan.

Community Lost

The State, Civil Society, and Displaced Survivors of Hurricane Katrina

RONALD J. ANGEL

University of Texas, Austin

HOLLY BELL

University of Texas, Austin

JULIE BEAUSOLEIL

University of Texas, Austin

LAURA LEIN

University of Michigan

CAMBRIDGE
UNIVERSITY PRESS

CAMBRIDGE UNIVERSITY PRESS
Cambridge, New York, Melbourne, Madrid, Cape Town,
Singapore, São Paulo, Delhi, Mexico City

Cambridge University Press
32 Avenue of the Americas, New York, NY 10013-2473, USA

www.cambridge.org
Information on this title: www.cambridge.org/9781107002951

First published 2012

Printed in the United States of America

A catalog record for this publication is available from the British Library.

Library of Congress Cataloging in Publication data
Community lost : the state, civil society, and displaced survivors of
hurricane Katrina / Ronald J. Angel ... [et al.].
p.   cm.
Includes bibliographical references and index.
ISBN 978-1-107-00295-1 (hardback)
1. Hurricane Katrina, 2005.   2. Emergency management – Gulf Coast (U.S.).
3. Disaster relief – Government policy – Gulf Coast (U.S.).   4. Disaster
victims – Gulf Coast (U.S.).   I. Angel, Ronald.   II. Title.
HV551.4.G85C66   2012
976'.044–dc23   2011032289

ISBN 978-1-107-00295-1 Hardback

Contents

Acknowledgments

This research was supported in part by the National Science Foundation grant No. 0555113.

The work reported here was accomplished by a large team of researchers, and we are grateful to them. Faculty from several universities who contributed to this project include Dawn Fowler, Roberta Greene, Johnnie Hamilton-Mason, Barbara Jones, Shanti Kulkarni, Elizabeth Mueller, Beth Pomeroy, Loretta Pyles, Michele Rountree, and Cal Streeter. Students, postdoctoral Fellows, and research associates who contributed to the project included Tuti Alawiyah, Michael Balliro, Anna Bauer, Megan Becknell, Melissa Biggs Coupal, Elisa Borah, Rachel Brown, Beth Bruinsma Chang, Sara Elizabeth Campbell, Annette Cerda, Cati Connell, Cristina Coupal, Daniela de los Angeles, Donna Del Bello, Monica Faulkner, Amy Felker, Courtney Fitzgerald, Anjali Fleury, Griselda Flores, Stephanie Gajewski, Angelica Gonzalez, Melissa Haney, John Huggins, Tenisha Hunter-Cleveland, David Johnson, Kristie Kimbell, Rebecca Kuipers, Leslie Landwehr, Ashley Lemell, Monica Lenker, Letti Lopez, Elissa Madden, Pam Malone, Ginger Mayeaux, Emily Miller, Jennifer Karas Montez, Coleen Moreno, Tammy Peacock, Allen Pittman, Lisa Pokorny, Julie Ramirez, Diane Rhodes, Megan Reid, Laura Romsdahl, Ratonia Runnels, Dolores Saenz, Sara Siegel, Amanda Rowe Tillotson, Laura Texera, Bernice Tostado, Emily Wade, Georgeanne Wilkins, Mary Williams, and Emily Ybarra.

We also received considerable assistance from the Center for Social Work Research, the Population Research Center, and the Office for Research Support at the University of Texas at Austin, which made this work possible.

This project would have been impossible without the collaboration and participation of the many service workers who answered our questions, provided documentation, and offered their interpretations. They have our gratitude.

And finally, we appreciate deeply the willingness of so many Katrina survivors to share their stories with us. Their struggles, trauma, and resilience are at the core of this work.

Introduction

In the Shadow of T. H. Marshall – Social Capital, Social Rights, and Sources of Vulnerability among Low-Income and Disadvantaged Groups

HURRICANE KATRINA AND THE SOCIAL CONSTRUCTION OF DISASTER

After living through one of the largest storms of the century, on the morning of August 29, 2005, the residents of New Orleans, Louisiana, appeared to be safe. Within hours, though, the seriousness of the situation became clear as the storm surge breached the levee system that protected the city and submerged large areas, including many low-lying and low-income neighborhoods. More than a million individuals were forced from their homes, many never to return. Many lost family members, and many more lost their homes, their possessions, and all ties to their old neighborhoods and communities. The human tragedy that unfolded in the media riveted the nation's attention. In response to the massive suffering, communities in Texas and elsewhere responded generously. By September 4, more than 250,000 hurricane victims had evacuated to Texas (Embry, 2005). Houston provided shelter and emergency services to approximately 150,000 evacuees (Berger, 2006). Other large cities, including San Antonio, Dallas, and Fort Worth, hosted additional thousands. During the weekend of September 2, the Austin Convention Center opened its doors to between five thousand and seven thousand evacuees, and many others were sheltered elsewhere in the city (Humphrey & Fitzsimmons, 2005; Wynn, 2006). Many of these survivors of the storm began a long diaspora during which they attempted to rebuild their lives in the new city. In this book, we tell the story of those victims of the storm who remained in Austin for long periods and their attempts to return to normal and build new lives in a new and strange city.

As their stories reveal, the challenges they faced were daunting. Most of those who did not return had lived in low-income communities in New Orleans, and many had not owned their homes. Between 2005 and 2007, half of the population of New Orleans consisted of renters (U.S. Census Bureau, 2005–7). For renters and owners alike, though, the storm destroyed the very basis of their daily security. Disasters exacerbate problems of housing affordability because they reduce the inhabitable housing stock (Comerio, 1998). Estimates suggest that more than 140,000 housing units were damaged or destroyed in New Orleans, including more than 73 percent of all low-rent units (National Low-Income Housing Coalition, 2005). Before the storm, approximately 5 percent of the population of New Orleans, or nearly twenty thousand individuals, lived in more than five thousand public housing units (Katz, 2008). Nearly two thousand additional public housing units lay vacant. Two years after the storm, only twelve hundred units had been reopened and occupied (Katz, 2008; Rose, Clark, & Duval-Diop, 2008).

As the story we tell in this book shows, although nature's fury may be largely random, the vulnerability of the most seriously affected victims of disasters is not. Rather, that vulnerability reflects historically based structural disadvantages that give individuals few choices but to live and work in the disaster-prone areas that the more affluent can escape. As we will also see, that vulnerability is closely tied to race as well as social class. In the following chapters, we reveal the race-based sources of that vulnerability and recount the stories of the victims of Hurricane Katrina who did not immediately return to New Orleans and describe the difficulties of their efforts to rebuild their lives in a new city. We also examine the roles of the major governmental actors, including the Federal Emergency Management Administration (FEMA) and nongovernmental actors, in responding to crises. Although many critics of big government look to local nongovernmental organizations as an alternative form of service delivery and social organization, our study reveals the central role of effective government in facilitating disaster recovery and empowering local nongovernmental organizations to function effectively. As we show, rather than being representative of big government, FEMA's clear failure resulted from years of political tinkering and underfunding. In the end, FEMA was inadequate to the task, and local government and nongovernmental organizations were in no position to compensate for its inadequacies.

THE 2008 ECONOMIC TSUNAMI

In December 2007, the citizens of the world, much like the residents of New Orleans early in the summer of 2005 who were unaware that Katrina would dramatically change their lives in just a few weeks, were happily unaware of the serious economic collapse that the subprime mortgage crisis in the United States, in addition to unsustainable levels of consumer debt, would soon unleash on the planet. Within a year, Iceland would be bankrupt, Spain's decade-long economic boom would be over, unemployment rates would soar everywhere, and the nations of the world would learn a hard lesson on just how interdependent their economies had become. A bubble had clearly burst, and the economic miracle of previous decades came to an abrupt and painful end. During the miracle years, China experienced almost unbelievable economic growth as long as Americans bought the products it produced. In the new economic environment, Americans, who had become used to spending far beyond their means, stopped buying and a world economy based on the assumption of endless growth ground to a halt. The speed of the downturn was breathtaking. As manufacturing giants such as General Motors and Chrysler, which had seemed too big to fail, neared bankruptcy, and as the major financial institutions of the United States and Europe, which had seemed invulnerable just a year before, neared insolvency, the neoliberal economic experiment of the 1980s and 1990s reached a point of crisis that left the world peering into a frightening and unpredictable future. As the developed nations implemented economic stimulus packages to increase aggregate demand, one might well have imagined that the ghost of John Maynard Keynes was stalking the planet. At the very least, the crisis made it clear that the state is a necessary participant in the market in modern economies.

The crisis also gave greater urgency to the ongoing debate concerning the nature and extent of the welfare state, which since the 1970s had been dominated by a minimalist social welfare ideology. The election of Margaret Thatcher in Britain in 1979 and Ronald Reagan in the United States in 1980 marked the beginning of an assault on the post–World War II social agenda that focused on ensuring the material welfare of citizens. Thatcher and Reagan became the standard-bearers for a new philosophy of less government intervention in the market and in all areas of social life. According to the new supply-side economics that had come into fashion, lower marginal tax rates, free markets, and entrepreneurship would result in economic growth that would eliminate the need for an extensive welfare state. The force of the Thatcher philosophy gained such momentum that in 2002 Labour MP Peter Mandelson proclaimed that in terms of economics, "we are all Thatcherites now" (Charter, 2002).

Of course, we were not all Thatcherites then, nor are we now, but the new economic and political realities of the day required some rethinking by defenders of the traditional welfare state. In a globalized world with highly interdependent economies and instantaneous communication, the Keynesian macroeconomic controls of the post–World War II years had clearly become less effective (Giddens, 1994; Pierson, 2001a; 2001b). Governments were increasingly unable to maintain full employment and provide the full range of social benefits while maintaining high rates of economic growth. The result was somewhere between compromise and a genuine transformation that redefined the traditional Democratic philosophy in the United States and that of Labour in Britain. In the United States, the Personal Responsibility and Work Opportunity Reconciliation Act (PRWORA) of 1996, more commonly known as welfare reform, was signed into law by Democratic president Bill Clinton, and in Britain a new "Third Way" was introduced by Labour Prime Minister Tony Blair and elaborated by sociologist Anthony Giddens (Giddens, 1998, 2000).

The previous use of the term "Third Way" referred to Sweden's social democratic model, which represented a reformist compromise that combined aspects of capitalism and socialism. The term took on a new life as a political response to the neoliberal right, which many liberals saw as representing a genuinely new way of viewing citizenship rights and responsibilities (Giddens, 1994). Many critics of the traditional welfare state, including those on the left, faulted the old policies for creating dependency. In the United States, which had a far more limited welfare state than Britain to start with, the "New Democrats" represented the trans-Atlantic variant of the new approach (Faux, 1999; Hale, Leggett, & Martell, 2004). The more recent debt crises in Greece, Spain, Portugal, and other European nations, as well as the mounting federal, state, and municipal government debt in the United States, have made the need for greater controls on public spending clear.

The core principle of the new approach, which was adopted with variations in other nations, can be summarized in the proposition of "no rights without responsibilities." This phrase, which is frequently cited by both supporters and critics, affirms the belief that social benefits should be contingent on responsible prosocial behavior (Hale et al., 2004; Havemann, 2001). Rather than individuals and families being entitled to cash assistance, health care, housing, and the rest of the benefits of the welfare state solely on the basis of need, the new philosophy tied an individual's and family's receipt of benefits to work. "Self-sufficiency" became the new catchphrase. Welfare reform in both the United States and Britain introduced policies based on the new expectation that rights to social welfare benefits do not exist except in conjunction with responsibilities, primarily the willingness to take whatever job is available (Barrientos & Powell, 2004).

The new philosophy was sold to the developing world as a guaranteed method of fostering development. In Latin America, neoliberal economic policies imposed by the United States and major international lenders such as the World Bank and the Inter-American Development Bank placed the market at the center of a new social contract (Bebbington, Woolcock, Guggenheim, & Olson, 2006; Hammer & Pritchett, 2006). Free markets, deregulation, privatization, and reductions in social expenditures formed core components of the new approach that was adopted to varying degrees in all Latin American countries. As with the new Third Way in Britain and welfare reform in the United States, the philosophy replaced notions of entitlement and public good with the principle of individual responsibility. In nations with low levels of education, massive inequality, few job opportunities, and minimal social supports, cuts in public programs only increased the misery of low-income citizens and, as in Europe, the neoliberal experiment was soundly criticized and resulted in oppositional movements and a new debate over the rights of citizenship and the meaning of good governance (Delgado & Nosetto, 2006; Peruzzotti & Smulovits, 2002; Vanden, 2004).

The impact of neoliberal reforms in Latin America and other parts of the developing world made the tragedy of the unqualified notion of responsibility over rights obvious. The region's notoriously high rates of inequality persisted even as the free market generated great wealth, and access to such basic needs as health care for low-income citizens did not improve (Armada, Muntaner, & Navarro, 2001; Hoffman & Centeno, 2003; Homedes & Ugalde, 2005). In most of Latin America, new, more social democratic governments are replacing governments that embraced a narrow neoliberal agenda, and a new post-neoliberal philosophy with a focus on social welfare is drawing increasing attention (Riggirozzi, 2010; Sader, 2009).

In the absence of even minimal opportunities to behave responsibly in terms of finding gainful employment, destitute individuals have little opportunity to do so. The desperate attempt by impoverished street people in developing nations to eke out a living however they can unmasks the inhumanity of inflexible neoliberal policies. Even in the developed world, though, the call for responsibility in terms of economic self-sufficiency presumes an adequate set of opportunities and sufficient human capital. For many, and especially for minority group members, human capital and opportunities are limited. The retreat from the old left's focus on redistribution and greater economic equality places the most vulnerable members of society at a major disadvantage. Even if the top-heavy Keynesian welfare state proved to be inefficient, the moral imperative to ensure the material basics of a dignified and productive life remains.

The New Democratic and Third Way approaches can be seen as pragmatic compromises that were necessary to respond to the politically powerful neoliberal movement that preceded them and that still exerts great economic and political power. Conservative critics of the welfare state do not believe that individuals have broad social rights. Many political theorists reject in principle the proposition that material security is a right (Etzioni, 1993, 1995, 2000; Mead, 1986, 1997; Murray, 1994, 1996, 1999, 2006). Communitarians, libertarians, and others on the right reject social policy based on the concept of social rights not only on moral grounds, but because of the belief that such policy creates welfare dependency and contributes to the growth of an underclass. These critics hold that basic political rights, consisting primarily of protections from interference by others or the state in carrying out one's wishes, are the only basic rights. Material welfare is in effect a commodity that one can purchase on the open market to the extent that one is able, but which one has no right to at public expense. Critics on the left object to the concept of social rights for very different reasons; they see the focus on a minimal level of material well-being as an incomplete or partial solution to the problems of the working class that require more radical solutions (see Dwyer, 2004, for a useful overview).

In the following chapters, we examine aspects of the modern welfare state and relate the concept of "social rights" that it embodies to the reality of powerlessness among low-income and minority Americans. We focus on a particular event, a natural disaster, to expose the social sources of the vulnerability of specific groups – in this case, minority individuals and impoverished communities. A natural disaster such as Hurricane Katrina exposes long-standing historical and structural vulnerabilities that affect specific groups and that can remain invisible in normal times. As we will show, the vulnerabilities of those who suffered the most serious losses as the result of the storm were the result of long-standing, racially-based social policies that made it difficult for individuals and families to evacuate and that undermined their capacity to recover. A disaster of the magnitude of Hurricane Katrina clearly illustrates the limitations of the devolution of federal governmental responsibilities to local governmental and nongovernmental agencies. Our data illustrate the inability of local agencies and organizations to deal with large-scale human need. In the end, the disaster clearly revealed the vital role of an effective central government in responding to crises and in creating an environment in which local governmental agencies and nongovernmental organizations can operate effectively.

THE WELFARE STATE AND CITIZENSHIP

The welfare state represents one of the major social and political developments of the twentieth century. To varying degrees depending on their unique histories and political cultures, all developed nations today embody basic welfare state principles that ensure education and health care, protect against unemployment and disability, and provide old-age pensions and often much more, to their citizens (Baldwin, 1990; Esping-Andersen, 1990; Esping-Andersen et al., 2002). In times of crisis, citizens have come to expect that the state will respond immediately and effectively to alleviate human suffering and return things to normal. The modern welfare state evolved as part of the capitalist system and serves to humanize what in its absence would be potentially inhumane and politically destabilizing market outcomes (Baldwin, 1990; Esping-Andersen, 1999). Despite their near-universality, though, welfare state principles have always been contested. Many traditional liberals, as well as contemporary conservative critics, see fundamental conflicts among core principles related to political and economic freedoms, individual responsibility, and a paternalistic state (Barry, 1999; Hayek, 1976; Mead, 1986; Murray, 1994; Nozick, 1974). In addition, welfare states today face serious revenue and debt crises that will inevitably require significant reductions in state support and in many countries result in profound changes in the post–World War II social contract (Giddens, 1998; Padgett, 2008; Pierson, 2001a; 2001b; Somers & Block, 2005).

The highly developed role of the state in ensuring the material welfare of citizens since the nineteenth century reflects the emergence of the expectation that citizens are entitled to more than just basic civil and political rights. Social rights include the right to the basic material and social requirements of a productive and dignified life, including education, health care, housing, retirement security, and more. The concept of social rights is fairly new in historical terms, confined largely to the latter part of the twentieth century. The term is often attributed to T. H. Marshall, who characterized the evolution of social rights in England in terms of three approximate historic periods in which civil and legal rights were extended to larger segments of the population during the eighteenth century, political rights during the nineteenth century, and the social rights during the twentieth century (Marshall & Bottomore, 1950).

Marshall's account of the evolution of social rights is clearly an idealization and has been criticized for its focus on England and for the fact that it ignores the situation of women and other excluded groups (Holmwood, 2000). Social rights are far from universal, and individuals in many parts of the world still lack even the most basic civil and political rights. Yet in developed nations the belief that the state should provide a minimal level of security against material want is generally accepted. The ongoing debate centers on what that minimal level of security consists of, who is eligible to receive it, and what responsibilities those who accept publicly funded support bear. There is almost universal consensus that the victims of disasters have the right to at least short-term emergency assistance, but there is far less agreement on what right to public support longer-term impoverished groups have.

We examine these issues in the context of the states' and civil society's response to a natural disaster and the human crisis that it provoked. Hurricane Katrina, which struck the Gulf Coast on August 29, 2005, represented the most serious humanitarian crisis of recent memory in the United States and revealed the basic structural sources of the vulnerability of the victimized population. That vulnerability was not the result of individual or group failings or even exceptionally bad luck; rather, it was the result of deliberate and racially tinged policies that limited the economic and social resources of local communities, increased their exposure to harm, and undermined the capacity of federal and state governments to carry out their basic responsibilities (Burby, 2006; Duncan, 2001; Elliott & Pais, 2006; Greenbaum, 2008; Henkel, Dovidio, & Gaertner, 2006; Landphair, 2007; Langsdorf, 2000; Lavelle & Feagin, 2006; Lopez & Stack, 2001). These same forces that placed the victims of Hurricane Katrina in jeopardy operate daily to undermine the capacities of people experiencing chronic poverty to get ahead.

Our examination of the roles of government and nongovernmental actors in the response to Hurricane Katrina is based on a study of survivors who were evacuated or voluntarily relocated to Austin, Texas, where they remained for varying periods. In time, some returned to New Orleans, but for others, the move was long-term or permanent, and in the public eye their identities transformed rather quickly from that of deserving victims of a disaster beyond their control to that of long-term disadvantaged groups who represent a burden and even a threat (Berger, 2006). This transformation was a replay of long-standing historical and political processes that have shifted explanations of poverty from structural and economic factors to individual failure (Marshall & Rossmann, 2011; Somers, 2008; Somers & Block, 2005). Although our analysis focuses on a select group of survivors and their unique circumstances, the issues that we deal with are general and relate to debates concerning the sources of the vulnerability of specific groups, usually racial and ethnic minorities, and the role of the state and civil society in mitigating that vulnerability.

The hurricane was clearly an act of God, but the suffering that followed it was very much a function of governmental and political decisions made long before the storm struck. The vulnerability of the victims was greatly increased by the anti–welfare state sentiment of recent years that cast suspicion on big government and the paternalistic state and romanticized the capacity of local governments and nongovernmental actors to address nearly all human needs. Ultimately our conclusion is that civil society actors, including faith-based organizations, nongovernmental organizations, and other local-level entities, can only complement state efforts in dealing both with emergencies and longer-term social problems. Despite claims that the welfare state can be greatly reduced in scope, the aftermath of Hurricane Katrina showed that a strong and efficient state remains central to our collective welfare and well-being.

Although we deal with very practical issues related to poverty, race, and social service delivery in a crisis, our discussion addresses core theoretical issues related to the structural sources of individual and group agency, resources, and power. The concepts of *social capital* and *civil society* are central to our discussion, and we develop and criticize both concepts further in the course of our presentation. Social capital is a concept that has gained wide usage in multiple domains in recent years (Bebbington et al., 2006; Duncan, 2001; Hero, 2003; Putnam, 1993, 1995, 2000; Saegert, Thompson, & Warren, 2001; Stanton-Salazar, 1997; Temkin & Rohe, 1998). Its appeal results from its potential focus on non-market aspects of group power and influence. Yet the term and the concept have many detractors who see social capital as at best an empty label and at worst a mask for predatory neoliberal market forces

(Portes & Landolt, 2000; Somers, 2008). Part of the problem of defining and operationalizing the concept of social capital has to do with the lack of clarity associated with the individual or collective nature of the benefits that the concept conveys. As we discuss, although social capital by definition emerges from networks, its benefits are often individual. How social capital is related to group advancement in a nontautological way is often not clear.

Given its wide use, we must confront the concept of social capital and point out its strengths as well as limitations in dealing with poverty generally and with the survivors of Hurricane Katrina in particular. Although social capital can refer to individuals' social embeddedness, we are more interested in its collective nature. At the level of neighborhoods and communities, high levels of social capital are indicated by complex networks of informal and formal organizations and high levels of positive interaction and trust. Low levels of social capital are reflected in a lack of such networks and organizations; low levels of trust; and the physical decay, social disorganization, and crime that a lack of citizen involvement brings about. As we will illustrate in later chapters, the members of communities with low levels of social capital tend to have low levels of human capital, as measured in terms of education and job-related skills. Whether what we think of as social capital is really a proxy for collective human capital remains a question for discussion. One of our core questions relates to the extent to which the concept of social capital is useful in understanding the economic and political vulnerability of certain groups and whether nongovernmental civil society actors might mobilize to increase the social and material capital of those who lack such capital.

For purposes of this study, civil society refers to the wide range of organizations that are neither governmental nor purely market-oriented. These include well-known responders to crises, such as the Red Cross and other emergency-focused nongovernmental organizations (NGOs), as well as many others that are less well-known. From our perspective, the potential usefulness of the concept of social capital relates to aspects of group membership that can be used for political and economic gain. The common saying, "It's not what you know, but who you know," captures the notion that social networks and contacts can be useful in very practical ways. For Robert Putnam, group and associational activity is the key to the formation of trust and civic commitment. In addition to fostering greater community involvement, it leads to better governance and ultimately to increased prosperity (Putnam, 2000; Souza, 2001). Even Putnam, though, realizes that not all groups increase their participants' social capital and that some groups promote socially undesirable ends. Racist organizations, street gangs, and old-boy networks may be highly cohesive with high levels of trust among members, but from the perspective of nonmembers, they do not further socially desirable ends nor extend their benefits to outsiders. The objective, then, is to identify groups and associations and potential collective action that foster positive outcomes, including the material welfare of disadvantaged groups.

Pierre Bourdieu elaborates the concept of social capital in a way that emphasizes its potential utility for our purposes. He notes that social capital makes little sense other than in terms of its association with cultural and material capital (Bourdieu, 1986). For our purposes, the focus is on the aspects of social capital related to economic and political power. Without that connection, the term and concept are vacuous and one might well ask what utility the use of the term entails. The use of the term "capital," a preeminently economic term, to characterize certain qualities of social interactions may seem inappropriate and perhaps even counterproductive. Some critics, primarily economists, find the concept of social capital to be seriously misleading given the very specific economic definition of capital as a stock that is the result of deliberate investment (Arrow, 2000; Farr, 2004; Sobel, 2002; Van Deth, 2003). One's social capital largely reflects the circumstances of one's birth rather than specific investments intended to increase that capital. In addition, although material capital can be alienated – that is, sold – social capital cannot.

Additionally, although the meaning of social capital at the individual or family level, primarily operationalized in terms of educational and other individual attainments may be clear, the meaning of social capital at the level of neighborhood or community is less so (Portes & Landolt, 2000; Woolcock, 2002). Critics of the term may be right in their observation that the label itself is of less use than a truly detailed understanding of the dimensions of economic and political power to which it refers. In the following chapters, we use the term to refer to the entire package of economic, political, and cultural knowledge and power that individuals and groups can draw upon either individually or collectively to further their own interests. Ultimately, though, the concept must be operationalized in terms of specific social class and historical factors that determine minority groups' economic and political disadvantage in particular.

The ultimate objective of our attempt to deconstruct the concept of social capital and its origins is not solely to identify the sources of the vulnerability of the survivors of crises like Hurricane Katrina or that of longer-term disadvantaged groups; it is to identify civil society organizations that might foster political action and social movements that could enhance social, cultural, and material capital and help eliminate the most serious sources of vulnerability experienced by specific groups. That is, of course, a tall order in a world in which inequalities between the rich and the poor remain huge and continue to grow and history tempers any undue hope for self-help by those with little power. In the United States, inequality has increased significantly since the Second World War, with particularly serious consequences for minorities and women (Danziger & Haveman, 2001; Lawrence, 2008). Although economic crises may diminish the wealth of the richest among us, they have devastating effects on minority group members, those in poverty, and those with little human capital. Ultimately we are interested at both the theoretical and practical levels in whether civil society organizations, including NGOs, faith-based organizations, and other collectivities can foster the development of effective social capital that can be leveraged into political and economic gains, as well as provide the material resources necessary to ease the trauma of a catastrophic disaster.

DEMOCRATIC PARTICIPATION AND ACTIVE CITIZENSHIP

A core question that remains unanswered for those concerned with greater equity, less poverty, and more opportunity for vulnerable groups relates to the potential organizational and institutional sources of change. Certain theoretical traditions base their core ethical systems on the possibility that civil society, or perhaps a more effective civil society, could address problems of political and economic marginalization and enhance individual and group social capital, as well as economic status. For Antonio Gramsci, perhaps the first to employ the term "civil society," the term refers to venues in which groups can interact to overcome the ideological hegemony of the dominant classes in order to bring about a more equitable distribution of power (Gramsci, 1971). Jürgen Habermas and others, including proponents of what has come to be known as "deliberative democracy," propose normative ethical and political systems that ensure that all citizens, or even all residents of a country, have the capacity for and the right to unimpeded personal expression and the opportunity to participate in the open public discussion of social matters that affect their lives (Benhabib, 2002; Braaten, 1991; Fishkin, 2009; Habermas, 1984).

Such theories place great emphasis on what is termed "communicative competence," or the effective command of all participants in a debate of language and the other necessities of effective argument. Such requirements clearly assume an open political forum in which everyone possesses the right to unimpeded expression. Critics, of course, find such idealized situations in which the rich and the poor are on equal footing in terms of their capacity to defend their own interests unrealistic (Langsdorf, 2000). The focus on communication and debate and the possibility of such egalitarian communication opportunities would require that everyone have the necessary education and other capacities, in addition to the personal freedom, to participate effectively in public discussions. For this reason, such idealized normative systems often appear to take as prerequisites the practical outcomes of the deliberative process. Nonetheless, the proposition that ultimately democracy and an equitable economic and political system require open and equal communication remains appealing.

Practical attempts at a more inclusive involvement of all social classes in public discourse and decision making – such as the public budgeting experiments in Brazil and elsewhere, in which citizen groups are involved in setting municipal priorities – have met with some apparent success in certain places (Baiocchi, Heller, & Silva, 2008; Cabannes, 2004; Novy & Leubolt, 2005; Souza, 2001). Yet the extent to which such deliberative democratic processes can actually improve the situations of previously excluded groups or the extent to which they can be introduced into communities in which they do naturally occur remains unclear (Kay, 2006; Saegert, Thompson, & Warren, 2001; Silverman, 2004). The term "social enterprise" refers to formal attempts to foster social capital and probably describes what we are dealing with in the following chapters (Kay, 2006; Silverman & Patterson, 2004). Again, though, the sources of social capital remain elusive. Certain communities naturally and spontaneously develop high levels of social capital, while others do not. The challenge appears to be to alter the institutional basis of the latter in such a way as to enhance the trust, reciprocity, and cohesion that one finds in the former. Whether that can be done effectively by outsiders is the question. In the following chapters, we employ the experiences of survivors of Hurricane Katrina who arrived in Austin to ask whether community can be reconstructed in a new place after a disaster.

A NEW INSTITUTIONAL ORDER

Normative theories of communicative competence and deliberative democracy can too easily focus on ideals that do not conform to what most practical observers would consider realistic. Spontaneous democratic communication might emerge among individuals who are equal in terms of education, wealth, and social position. They rarely occur spontaneously among groups that differ significantly in these characteristics. What is lacking from discussions of deliberative democracy for those with more empirical agendas and objectives is an understanding of the conditions under which communicative competence or deliberative democracy could even be approximated. Such an approach calls for a theoretical and empirical understanding of the institutional context within which individuals and groups interact.

A more useful conceptualization would be informed by traditional interest group political theory, as well as institutional theory (Campbell, 2004; Campbell & Pedersen, 2001). Several observers note that although organized social capital is a necessary condition for enhancing the effectiveness of low-income communities, it can do so only through connections with traditional political parties and other interest groups such as unions (Cohen, 2001; Fuchs, Shapiro, & Minnite, 2001). The practical utility of theories of communicative competence and deliberative democracy can seem limited even in highly developed democracies given the reality of interest-based decision making. When and where are individuals motivated to participate in the sort of discourse that requires a complete and unconditional respect for the other and a willingness to be convinced by the force of an argument? That sort of open-mindedness and willingness to act on the basis of a stronger argument is rare even in university seminars.

Culture and society consist of and are transmitted through institutions. Institutions provide opportunities for change at the same time that they constrain individual consciousness and freedom of action. Recent work in institutional theory focuses on the role of ideas, in addition to interests, in determining institutional evolution (Campbell, 2004). Social institutions and their key actors help define and redefine social reality by providing cognitive frames in terms of which social actions are interpreted both by institutional actors and outside observers. Today NGOs and other civil society institutions represent major organizational actors in most areas of social life. Their efforts to reframe specific social problems and change the social agenda in ways favorable to excluded groups are in direct opposition to the frames promoted by the far right. What is clear is that discussions of the major social issues of the day, such as multiculturalism, immigration, and poverty, are dominated by interested parties who institutionalize various political perspectives. The Tea Party movement is only one recent example. Understanding the role of such institutions and social movements in determining the direction and content of cultural change represents a major intellectual, as well as practical, agenda.

COMMUNITY AND INTERPERSONAL TIES

Our hope is that this introduction serves to situate our presentation theoretically. In the following chapters, we address practical questions concerning the experiences of the survivors of Hurricane Katrina who evacuated to Austin, Texas. We present their accounts of their social capital before the storm and its sources in their neighborhoods and communities in New Orleans. We also document the loss of those sources of social capital as a result of the evacuation and document the consequences of that loss for their potential return to New Orleans or their permanent relocation to Austin. The literature on social capital distinguishes between what are termed "strong" and "weak" ties, also known as "bonding" and "bridging" ties (Granovetter, 1973; Putnam, 2000). Ties refer to relationships with other people that can vary in terms of intimacy, support, and information. Bonding or strong ties are those that define close relationships, such as those with family members and close friends. They are the relationships on which one can rely in times of crisis or that low-income families rely on for daily survival. When one needs money for food or some other immediate assistance, one usually calls upon a close family member or friend.

Bridging ties, on the other hand, are less intimate, and include relationships with teachers, employers, coworkers, colleagues, and other more limited contacts. Bridging ties characterize professional relationships that one can call upon for professional purposes. Although bonding ties are useful for immediate support, bridging ties are information-rich and can further economic, political, or professional ends. One's brother-in-law might know of a job at the local sawmill, but a member of one's professional association can provide information on jobs in other parts of the country. Low-income families and communities tend to rely heavily on bonding ties for basic survival, but they have few bridging ties to individuals in positions of power who might help improve their lot (Edin & Lein, 1997; Stack, 1974).

To varying degrees, the survivors of Hurricane Katrina who evacuated to Austin, Texas, lost the bonding social ties that they had developed in New Orleans. Even the networks of those who evacuated with family and friends were fragmented. This meant that they arrived in Austin with weaker networks, or often none at all. As a result, they had to rely on FEMA, the Red Cross, and other formal aid agencies for basic survival. Those agencies and organizations operate very differently than informal networks, and the survivors were forced to learn new bureaucratic procedures and ways of obtaining the assistance they needed. They were often unsuccessful or succeeded only on an episodic basis. Although NGOs and other civil society organizations were very active, and often quite effective in providing temporary shelter, food, and health care, they faced serious challenges in providing assistance with employment and longer-term housing that was necessary in order for the survivors to get back on their feet.

In the following chapters, we examine the situations of the survivors and characterize the differences among them in terms of their social capital. We examine the role of governmental and municipal agencies, as well as that of civil society organizations, in providing short- and longer-term assistance. The core question that we address relates to the extent to which civil society organizations are effective in helping families rebuild their social capital or the extent to which such organizations themselves represent sources of social capital that can be leveraged into material and social gains. In New Orleans both before the storm and after the evacuation, certain families had more social capital and had better outcomes than others. Whether such social capital can be restored where it was lost or never existed remains a vexing social question. Our study suggests that the social capital of low-income communities may be location-specific and that without bridging ties and real economic and political power, it cannot be easily transferred or rebuilt in a new city. Ultimately, our study clearly demonstrates the importance of the welfare state and the inability of civil society to guarantee the social rights and basic welfare that the state alone can provide. Civil society and social capital are potentially useful ways of describing the world and of dealing with certain individual and group needs, but they exist effectively only in the context of an equitable and effective state.

I

After the Storm

The State, Civil Society, and the Response to Katrina

CASE STUDY: JUSTINE BETTS, A TALE OF TWO CITIES

Justine Betts,[1] a thirty-nine-year-old African American female, remembered her life in New Orleans, where she was born and had been raised, as "beautiful." The shared routines of daily life, the familiar places, and her family and neighbors were central to her fond memories of the old city. During our first interview, she bordered on the romantic as she characterized life in New Orleans by saying that. "...you get up in the morning, the birds are singing, the sun is out. Your husband [is] going to work; you going to work; your son going to school. [You] come home from work, sit on your porch with your neighbors, laughing, talking. It was just like a big family." Yet despite her optimism and the positive attitude she conveyed in our initial interview, it was clear that life in the old city had not always been easy or beautiful. One suspects that Justine's memories of New Orleans had been made fonder by the contrast to an unfamiliar and sometimes foreign-seeming city and the hardships that she encountered there.

In New Orleans, both Justine and her husband worked at the same restaurant. For many years, the couple had lived in the same rental house close to Justine's family. The support system and the routines that structured Justine's life became particularly important when tragedy struck. About three months before Hurricane Katrina, Justine lost her son. The unexpected loss thrust her into a severe depression. Her family was vital in bringing her out of her despair. During our initial interview,

---

[1] All of the names of survivors and individual service providers and certain aspects of their stories have been changed to pseudonyms to protect their identities.

Justine reported that just before Katrina struck, she had begun to enjoy life again. Unfortunately, more difficult times and more tragedy were in store.

Like many other survivors, Justine reported that the relatively low cost of living in New Orleans made it easy to get by. Many of the survivors we spoke to were shocked by how much more expensive rents and other costs were in Austin, Texas. In New Orleans, the family lived comfortably on the couple's wages and tips, and Justine went out of her way to make it clear that they were not living "from paycheck to paycheck." In her words, they were able to "...do little things, [we] went out, [we ate] dinner out sometimes...then go shopping and buy a little outfit...we still had our bills paid. We still had everything we needed in our home."

The couple was able to live a comfortable life on a low income in part because of their familiarity with local institutions. They were able to get Medicaid, which they both needed because of medical problems, and they also received food stamps. Both Justine and her husband were paid in cash, which as we will see caused problems when they moved to Austin. In addition to the family's knowledge of New Orleans, Justine had substantial social capital in the form of a large extended family that provided assistance in times of need. When the storm struck, Justine and her husband went to her mother's third-story apartment, which was located on higher ground. About ten of Justine's relatives sought shelter there. When their food ran out, Justine's husband and other men waded through deep water to an abandoned local grocery store to recover what they could. Residents of the apartment building acted as a community and shared meals and provided mutual assistance.

After a few days, though, Justine, her husband, and her daughter decided that they would leave the apartment and seek help because rescue did not seem to be on the way. They paid a man with a boat to ferry them to the Carrolton Bridge, which was visible from the apartment. They hoped that from there they would be able to escape the flood and send help to the other family members. Instead of a route of escape, though, the bridge became a trap, where they were forced to stay for four days. At the end of that ordeal, they were taken from the bridge by bus and evacuated to Houston by air. Justine's mother and other family members were rescued from the apartment by helicopter, and Justine lost track of them for some time.

In Houston, Justine and her immediate family received assistance and eventually found temporary housing from a local church. They did not know where the rest of the family was. While in Houston, the family received a $2,000 relief check from the Federal Emergency Management Administration (FEMA), which they used to buy clothes, linens, a television, and other household necessities. All the while, they desperately searched for the rest of the family through the Internet and with the help of whomever they could ask. From Houston, they contacted Justine's brother-in-law, who lived in another Texas city. He invited them to stay with him for a while. The family took the bus there, where they spent what Justine called "a very long week." Justine received a call from her sister who, with other members of the extended family, had settled in Austin. Justine decided to move to Austin; the family used their remaining FEMA money for bus tickets. In Austin, they stayed at a hotel and at a transitional housing facility until they were able to find housing in a complex where they were reunited with members of their extended family who had also ended up there.

The arrival in Austin began a series of bureaucratic encounters and difficulties with FEMA that we heard repeated many times by survivors. The fact that the family had registered for assistance with FEMA in Houston caused problems when they attempted to apply for rental assistance in Austin. As Justine recounted, "FEMA was paying our rent in the hotel, well, the hotel [subsidy] was getting ready to run out so we had to sign up for an apartment before a certain date...we went to FEMA, and they said we [were not] eligible...because...we didn't sign up at Austin." At first, the family was told that they would have to return to Houston for an apartment, but eventually they discovered that they could get FEMA assistance because they had relatives in Austin.

It became clear fairly soon that the family would not be able to reestablish the routines that had structured their lives in New Orleans. A year after our first interview, neither Justine nor her husband had been able to find anything but temporary part-time work, despite applying for all available jobs. As she told us, "I've tried everything...everything that someone...told me about...a job here, a job there, I go for it." Justine told us that before the family managed to buy a car, she had had to ride to interviews on the handlebars of her husband's bicycle. Despite their best efforts, though, neither had been able to find permanent full-time work. The couple's employment difficulties were made more serious by delays in replacing her husband's social security card, which had been lost. Justine also felt that their plight had been made worse by competition from Mexican workers, whom Austin employers seemed to prefer. Justine put it this way: "...the problem is, is they [are] hiring more

Mexicans than anything. You go there, the job is filled. You come back it is a Mexican or something."

Because of differences in state welfare programs, the family lost their food stamps and Medicaid coverage when they relocated to Texas. This left Justine without resources to deal with serious dental problems. Her frustration was evident when she told us about her dental problems. As she said, "...I still need [Medicaid] for this [tooth] right here...[it's] killing me. Can't get no Medicaid, can't get nothing down here. It's just like I said, it is hard right now. When I say hard, I mean *hard*." Although her husband managed to obtain food stamps for the family for a short period, these were cut off because of problems with paperwork. Because they had been paid in cash in New Orleans, Justine and her husband found that they were ineligible for unemployment benefits since they could not document the fact that they had been employed.

As was the case for many survivors, bureaucratic complexity, unclear rules, and confusion about disaster assistance benefits caused serious problems. Justine received what she thought was a personal property settlement from FEMA and used it to purchase a car and furniture because her rent was being paid by another program. FEMA later demanded that the family repay the money, which had apparently been intended for rent. The matter had not been resolved by the time of our last interview. In part because of this bureaucratic confusion, Justine's assessment of FEMA was negative despite the assistance the family received. As she said, "...you know...most of us have to fend out here for ourselves. They put us out here like wild animals, fend for yourself, and this is not fair."

Justine had clearly lost a great deal in the move to Austin. In our final interview a year after she had arrived, she contrasted her situation in New Orleans with that in Austin in a way that made it clear that her natural enthusiasm was strained and that she was exhausted. As she said, "I am not used to living like that. Every time I wonder where we are gonna get tissue paper and where we are gonna get soap from. It is hard down here and I'm not used to living like this. It is getting miserable." Justine reported that in Austin she was forced to wash clothes in the bathtub to save money; she worried about how to pay for food and household items; and she feared eviction because piecing together part-time work made it difficult to pay the rent.

Although the family received much support from the Austin community, they felt unwelcome at times. Justine told us about her suspicions that some people were hostile. As she said, "...you know, they have some good [people] here, but [there are] some that look at us and treat us like nothing but dirt. You know, like we're nobody. We didn't ask to come here. We had our own city, we [were] happy and everything. We [were] doing well for ourselves. We [were] going to the doctor, getting my nails done, working…." As the recipient of charity, Justine sometimes felt that she was being treated as a pauper. She told us about a couch that the family had been offered. The fact that it was in bad condition undermined the charitable intent and made the offer insulting. She said of the gift that, "…they [were] trying to give us a…sofa with a big hole in it. Well, when I was in New Orleans I didn't have a sofa with a hole in it, so what do I want that for? I'm not being ungrateful, but I'm not going to take nothing that I didn't have when I was in New Orleans. If I can't get better, I don't want it."

During our time with the family, it became clear that adapting to a new city with a very different culture and economy would be difficult, if not impossible, and that the life they left in New Orleans was gone forever. The community and networks they had relied upon in the old city could not be transplanted to the new city, and voluntary organizations, although helpful, were no substitute. Over time, Justine had also lost part of the limited family network she had been able to bring with her to Austin, as some of her relatives returned to New Orleans. Justine and her husband discussed moving back, but they lacked the resources for the move and were not sure how they would support themselves if they were to return. Their lives had clearly taken a new turn and what the future would hold was uncertain.

THE STORM

On Wednesday, August 24, the twelfth tropical depression of the 2005 hurricane season, which was originally thought to be a remnant of the tenth tropical depression, strengthened to hurricane force as it passed over the Bahamas and was officially named Katrina. For the population of New Orleans, the threat must have seemed remote since the storm appeared headed toward southwestern Florida. On Thursday, August 25, the storm struck Florida and killed nine people. Florida's Governor Jeb Bush declared a state of emergency as the storm moved over the warm waters of the Gulf of Mexico. By that point, the people of New Orleans had far more to fear as the storm moved northwest, gaining strength by the hour. By Friday, August 26, with the storm's wind speed at seventy-five miles per hour, the White House ordered FEMA and the Department of Homeland Security (DHS) to prepare. Ten thousand National Guard troops were deployed along the Gulf Coast.

By Saturday, August 27, Katrina's wind speed had reached 115 miles per hour and the storm was expected to reach category four or even possibly category five intensity by the time it made landfall somewhere on the Gulf Coast. A hurricane warning was issued for southwestern Louisiana. Max Mayfield, the director of the National Hurricane Center, called Mayor Ray Nagin to recommend a mandatory evacuation of New Orleans. The mayor declared a state of emergency and ordered a voluntary evacuation. As the storm approached the Gulf Coast, Governor Haley Barbour of Mississippi declared a state of emergency and ordered a mandatory evacuation of Hancock County.

By Sunday, August 28, Katrina had reached category five strength and was headed directly toward the Louisiana coast. The situation was clearly grave and DHS Secretary Michael Chertoff and FEMA Director Michael Brown were briefed by the National Hurricane Center on the possibility of levee breaks in New Orleans. As the storm approached, the Superdome was opened to receive individuals seeking sanctuary in New Orleans. Mayor Nagin ordered a mandatory evacuation of the city and established ten shelters, including the Convention Center, for those unable to leave. Highways out of the city were gridlocked. Ten thousand individuals who could not leave sought safety in the Superdome.

At approximately six in the morning on Monday, August 29, the storm made landfall as a category three storm with winds of 125 miles per hour and record storm surges. The worst possible scenario followed. By nine in the morning, the Lower Ninth Ward levee was breached and floodwaters poured in. By two in the afternoon, City Hall confirmed that the Seventeenth Street levee had failed. President Bush declared an emergency disaster for Louisiana and Mississippi as the Coast Guard rescued twelve hundred individuals from the flood and the National Guard was called upon to ensure public order. By Wednesday, August 31, the levee situation was deteriorating and water covered nearly 80 percent of the city. FEMA activated the National Response Plan while as many as fifty thousand to sixty thousand individuals fled to rooftops to escape the flood. The mayor called for anyone with a boat to help the stranded.

As the days passed, the waters continued to rise and reports of looting were widespread despite the presence of the National Guard. In the aftermath, it was difficult to determine whether the reports reflected actual looting or families foraging for food in the absence of alternatives. Governor Kathleen Blanco of Louisiana ordered the evacuation of the Superdome, where poor planning and inadequate facilities had created a nightmare scenario. Stories of violence, including rape, filled the information vacuum and fed on the inevitable fears of people experiencing the near-total collapse of social order. With the situation deteriorating rapidly, other states responded with offers of assistance. Texas Governor Rick Perry offered the Astrodome in Houston, Texas, as a temporary sanctuary for those in the Superdome. A federal health emergency was declared throughout the Gulf Coast, and medical supplies and professionals began to arrive, as did buses to begin the evacuation of the Superdome and Red Cross shelters. That same day, the first evacuees arrived at the Astrodome in Houston. In New Orleans, the police focused on looting and violent crime rather than search and rescue, as fears of violence and crime escalated and the media continued to report incidents of looting and criminal behavior. Meanwhile, tens of thousands remained in desperate circumstances. As time passed, more levees failed and the military sent transport aircraft to evacuate the most seriously ill to Houston. FEMA deployed more medical teams to deal with the emerging health crisis.

By Thursday, September 1, the National Guard deployment reached thirty thousand, as violence and looting remained a central focus of attention. Mayor Nagin pleaded for more buses to help with the evacuation of the forty-five thousand individuals still trapped in the Superdome and the Convention Center. In a televised interview, FEMA Director Brown told television host Paula Zahn that he had become aware of the situation at the Convention Center only a few hours before the interview. On Friday, September 2, President Bush toured the Gulf Coast from the air and acknowledged that the government's response had been inadequate. Relatively quickly, Congress approved $10.5 billion for rescue and relief efforts, and fifteen airlines began flying evacuees to cities in Texas and elsewhere.

The diaspora that followed created additional trauma and loss as families were separated and as individuals were put on airplanes with no knowledge of where they were going. Within a few days, individuals and families who had been members of dense social networks in New Orleans found themselves separated and alone in strange cities. As in all disasters, those who were most seriously affected were low-income citizens, and, in this case, mostly African American. Although most of the evacuees came from families that had been disadvantaged for generations, their New Orleans neighborhoods were familiar and long-standing communities with complex systems of mutual aid and support. For people living on low incomes, such social capital is vital for basic survival. However, the evacuees had lost those vital support networks.

Some evacuees, largely by chance and occasionally by choice, arrived in Austin, Texas, where they were initially received as the helpless victims of events beyond their control. In Austin, as in Houston, San Antonio, and other cities across the southern United States where the evacuees were sent, state and municipal agencies sprang into action. Churches and other nongovernmental organizations also shifted their focus to the needs of the evacuees. Given the number of those displaced and their desperate condition, the challenge was huge, and as the story we tell in the following chapters reveals, the outpouring of assistance, funds, and supplies was a testament to the civil society response. However, a lack of coordination among governmental and nongovernmental organizations represented a major hurdle to the long-term recovery of the victims of the storm. In many cases, there was no coordination at all and efforts at assistance were duplicated, resulting in the waste of precious resources. FEMA and other funds were probably wasted or inequitably distributed, meaning that some of the most desperate survivors did not receive what they needed while others received an oversupply.

Although some of the evacuees returned to New Orleans, for many others Austin became their new home, or rather, their new place of residence. Many, if not most, remained in a social and economic limbo throughout the period of our research, and we ended the study with little hope that the new city would become a real home. As we have mentioned, in many host cities the deserving victims of the days immediately following the disaster joined the ranks of the long-term disadvantaged who make up the lower echelons of our economy and society. Without their old networks and lacking knowledge of the new social and cultural environments, many individuals never managed to establish new identities or become part of the economic, cultural, or social life of the new city. Despite the best efforts of governmental and civil society organizations, many remained strangers in a place that was largely foreign, and they remained socially marginalized. Although they might have had limited incomes in New Orleans, they at least enjoyed aspects of community. That was lost when they came to Austin.

The stories we tell in the following chapters reveal the real precariousness of the survivors' situations even before the storm. They also illustrate serious limitations in the capacity of civil society organizations to deal with major crises to which only the state has the resources and authority to respond. The lesson we take away from this research is that the rejection of big government and the belief that civil society can address the major social welfare needs of the nation's low-income citizens must be seriously questioned. Ultimately, our study reaffirms the centrality of the welfare state in dealing with the manifold risks of life. Let us return briefly to a consideration of the welfare state and its role in dealing with risks such as Hurricane Katrina before we move on to a discussion of the survivors' experiences.

THE WELFARE STATE AND RISK

In the mid-nineteenth century, Chancellor Otto Von Bismarck oversaw the unification of Germany and introduced sickness and accident insurance, as well as old-age benefits to protect citizens against the risk of poverty when they could no longer work (Esping-Andersen, 1990; Sigerist, 1999). Bismarck's programs marked the beginning of the modern welfare state (Palier, 2010). Later, in 1942, English economist William Beveridge's report "Social Insurance and Allied Services" set out the agenda for the National Health Service and the rest of the British welfare state (Beveridge, 1942). The fact that a conservative aristocrat such as Bismarck was one of the founders of the welfare state may seem ironic, but it clearly underscores the fact that the social welfare state is vital to the success of capitalism (Baldwin, 1990). Bismarck's motive in introducing protections against poverty was to blunt the appeal of socialism, but his perhaps cynical actions underscore the fact that the welfare state protects capitalism from the political instability that would result from having a large number of starving citizens.

Since Bismarck's day, the essence of the welfare state has consisted of protections against risk, including illness, disability, unemployment, and destitution in old age. The welfare state's protection against risk is partially embodied in the concept of "social rights," introduced by T. H. Marshall, which we mentioned in the introduction (Marshall & Bottomore, 1950). Social rights go beyond basic civil and political rights and include rights to the material basis of a healthy and dignified life. More than a hundred years after Bismarck's death, the welfare state has expanded greatly and represents a major expense for most nations. Demographic realities, including the aging of the populations of developed nations and the serious global fiscal crises that have affected nearly all mature welfare states, have led to attempts to decrease the state's role in social insurance (Palier, 2010). Yet despite the growing cost of social insurance, the belief that the state should provide a minimal level of security against material want persists. The ongoing debate centers on what that minimal level of security consists of and what responsibilities those who receive it bear. There is almost universal consensus that the victims of large-scale disasters such as Hurricane Katrina have a basic right to emergency assistance. What additional longer-term assistance they have a right to is less clear and remains a source of heated debate.

In the following chapters, we employ the concepts of social rights and responsibilities in reference to the experiences of the predominantly low-income African American and powerless victims of a specific catastrophic event. Our objective, though, is broader and focuses on the fact that risk is not borne equally by all members of society and that for minority Americans it is structured by a history of systematic exclusion. In a system characterized by great inequality, those individuals and families with economic resources are better protected against risk and have far greater security than those without such resources. Social factors that restrict a group's access to social and material resources increase the vulnerability of the group's members to crises. In the following chapters, we investigate the social sources of individual and group vulnerabilities and also ask whether and how nongovernmental voluntary organizations and action can compensate for long-standing structural disadvantages in order to empower individuals and groups and enhance their ability to act as effective agents in furthering their own interests.

CIVIL SOCIETY, SOCIAL DIFFERENCES, AND THE WELFARE STATE

Nongovernmental organizations – such as the Red Cross, Oxfam, the Louisiana Disaster Recovery Foundation (which was established to provide assistance to the victims of hurricanes Katrina and Rita), as well as churches and other civic groups – provide vitally important assistance to the victims of disasters. This is especially the case in the immediate aftermath of a disaster, when basic needs must be quickly met. International and local nongovernmental organizations have been active in most countries for more than a century, but their number exploded after the Second World War and today there are thousands that operate in nearly every nation of the world (Boli & Thomas, 1997; Edwards & Sen, 2000). Taken together, the voluntary nongovernmental sector employs a significant fraction of the labor force and accounts for a substantial component of gross domestic product in most developed nations (Amendola, Garofalo, & Nese, 2010; Anheier & Salamon, 1999; Salamon & Wojciech, 2004; Tennant, 2009).

The sheer size of the voluntary nongovernmental sector leads one to wonder about its potential for bringing about significant social change and providing opportunities for effective political action. In the absence of a vibrant civil society, nations remain closed and citizens have few venues in which to express their opinions. An open civil society holds out the hope of greater democracy and effective opposition to authoritarian regimes (Edwards, 2009; Edwards & Sen, 2000). Global civil society, often in the form of movements that focus on major social issues such as the abolition of slavery and female suffrage, allows individuals and groups to coordinate collective action that can have major cultural and social consequences (Keck & Sikkink, 1998). In the case of disasters such as that brought about by Hurricane Katrina, the question remains as to whether civil society activity can go beyond the basic alleviation of short-term suffering to a greater social and political empowerment of those who were the most vulnerable to the disaster. As we discuss in later chapters, disaster case management focuses on short-term needs with the objective of returning individuals and families to their pre-disaster status. For those most vulnerable to crises, a return to what was normal often means a return to marginality. Potential civil society responses to disasters and the vulnerability of specific social groups also raise questions related to the relative roles of outside intervention and self-help. Whether major social change depends on autonomous and spontaneous political action by communities themselves or whether it can be fostered by NGOs and other outside groups remains a major question.

Investigations of where, when, and how civil society organizations, and especially NGOs, can empower their clients and the circumstances in which they can effectively complement governmental efforts to further specific social agendas or address specific crises form part of an old but important research agenda. Despite the theoretical potential for civil society organization to bring about positive social change, the objectives and structure of the nongovernmental organizations that make up civil society differ greatly, and the objectives of specific groups can be exclusive and even negative. These do not reflect a common social or political agenda. Highly cohesive but exclusive organizations may further their own ends at the expense of others. In addition, as we will see in later chapters, even among organizations with similar objectives, a lack of communication and coordination can limit their effectiveness. As voluntary organizations, NGOs, churches, and grassroots movements have their own agendas that do not always reflect more general societal interests or even the true desires of those they attempt to help (Shefner, 2008).

Yet the focus on smaller groups and their potential for political action, as well as their potential for asserting the rights of groups that have traditionally been excluded, is clearly part of the appeal of the concept of civil society, even if the initial enthusiasm has been somewhat tempered by political realities (Edwards, 2009).

From our perspective, the theme of civil society organization as providing a voice and potential venues for political action for marginalized groups relates to recent debates on multiculturalism that have important implications for the core issue dealt with in this book. The new multiculturalism is concerned with the vulnerabilities associated with minority status and focuses on the extent and nature of the social rights of those individuals and groups that are culturally and socially different from the majority (Benhabib, 2002; Fraser & Honneth, 2003; Kymlicka, 1995, 2007; Kymlicka & Norman, 2000a, 2000b; Taylor, 1994; Valadez, 2001).

An active civil society provides the opportunity for expressions of important social and cultural differences, including those related to differences in religious beliefs and practices. Because of colonization, slavery, and immigration, modern nation-states are made up of individuals from very different cultural and social backgrounds. Rather than assimilating into an undifferentiated cultural mass, a process that traditional assimilationist theory envisioned, many groups retain their unique identities, often as a political statement. As we will document in later chapters, the Hurricane Katrina survivors who arrived in Austin were often seen as culturally different and many of their problems were attributed to aspects of their culture and behavior. The survivors themselves often experienced cultural barriers related not only to social class but language and local practices. While some individuals and groups choose to reaffirm and maintain their group identities, others, as in the case of racial and ethnic minorities, have the fact of difference forced upon them as the result of exclusion from and discrimination by the majority group. Given the history of race in the United States, the African American Hurricane Katrina evacuees shared many of the characteristics of immigrant groups whose assimilation and economic incorporation experiences are affected by ethnicity and culture.

A NEW SOCIAL CONTRACT

The new Third Way in Europe and the New Democratic philosophy in the United States that we discussed in the introduction reflect the rejection of the proposition that the state should closely control the economy for the purpose of redistributing resources from the rich to the poor. Welfare reform in the United States and attempts to reduce the size of the welfare state elsewhere place greater emphasis on individual responsibility and market solutions rather than state-led redistribution. Big government solutions to the problems of unemployment and poverty provoke much political opposition, create bloated bureaucracies, and in the end leave many individuals and families in poverty. The new philosophy, though, also rejects neoliberal economic theories, which overemphasize the free market and reject all but the most minimal state regulation of the economy. The most potentially positive aspect of the Third Way and New Democratic approaches is that their rhetoric places a major emphasis on increasing the human capital of those with low levels of education and few job skills and equalizing life chances by eliminating structural barriers that create and maintain an underclass (Giddens, 1994, 2000). In practice, of course, such principles can turn out to be empty, and the practical obstacles to the implementation of any new Third Way agenda remain daunting (Reich, 1999).

Critics of the new focus on individual responsibility also point out the danger implicit in the emphasis on the philosophy of "no rights without responsibilities," which ignores the fact that equality of opportunity still does not exist for many individuals because of their race or social background. Nearly fifty years after the passage of the Civil Rights and Voting Rights Acts of 1964 and 1965, the African American population of the United States still faces serious challenges to economic security and social mobility. The public is far less accepting of programs aimed at equalizing educational and occupational opportunities than it was during the civil rights movement, when the economic pie was growing (Sterba, 2009). Negative attitudes toward affirmative action programs are fueled by the race of those whom they benefit (Wilson, 2006). Today, assuring equality of opportunity, however it is defined, generates massive resistance, often accompanied by accusations of reverse discrimination. An ongoing criticism of Third Way approaches from the left is that they do not give sufficient weight to the unequal distributions of wealth and power that maintain both differences in opportunities and inequities in outcomes. Many critics see the Third Way not as a positive compromise between the political left and right, but rather a politically expedient retreat from welfare state principles (Andrews, 1999; Charter, 2002; Faux, 1999).

We are left to ask where we are at this point in our nation's and the world's history in terms of the emerging social contract. The economic tsunami of 2008, like Hurricane Katrina, radically changed the economic and political reality upon which the current social contract is based. The neoliberal experiment that was largely responsible for the crisis still has many defenders and it has restructured much of the world's economic order, but a new historical moment has clearly arrived. We may not be ready to adopt a centrally controlled economy with massive state bureaucracies, but the clear need for regulating financial and commodity markets, as well as the global interconnectedness that characterizes modern life, means a greater level of state involvement at all levels, perhaps focused more on coordination and regulation than on direct command and control. Internationally, governments are responding to the new economic order by discussing new mechanisms for coordinating the global economy. As of yet, what those mechanisms might be remains unclear. The experience of the European Union in creating a European economic order reveals the challenges that exist. The rejection of a European Constitution by several nations and the serious differences in levels of economic development between regions make true continental unification difficult, if not impossible (Hooghe & Marks, 2006; Rae, 2011; *Washington Post*, 2011). The citizens of rich countries often resent the economic burden of bailing out poorer nations that have accumulated massive debt. Such resentment is often accompanied by a resentment of immigrants (Meuleman, Davidov, & Billiet, 2009). In the aftermath of Hurricane Katrina, resentment of the financial cost of assistance to survivors quickly turned into resentment toward survivors.

Race, ethnicity, and group differences in wealth, in conjunction with fiscal crises and a resurgent anti–welfare state sentiment, clearly place impediments in the way of a new, more egalitarian social contract. The experience of the European Union reveals that even in highly developed welfare states, a contract that is based on transfers from the rich to the less well-off creates increasing resistance among those who must pay. If we were to invent a new Fourth Way, or reform the Third Way approach in ways that guarantee social rights, what might such a new or reformed approach look like? Is there some organizational possibility for a new social movement focused on broader inclusion and social rights? Along with the rejection of neoliberal approaches, the renewed interest in civil society and nongovernmental organizations as means of involving individuals in the decisions that most influence their lives is clearly relevant, as is the focus on the human need for community. The question, then, is how best to develop cohesive, yet politically effective, communities and the vibrant and vital civil society that sustains them.

As we discussed earlier, many critics find the concept of civil society ambiguous and imprecise and think that it offers little by way of opportunities for meaningful economic or political change. Some see the rejection of the welfare state and the idealization of the local, especially as it is portrayed by conservatives, as little more than a rejection of contemporary liberal Western culture at the same time that they embrace the most powerful engine for cultural change, the free market. The massive growth in nongovernmental organizations, though, leads us to believe that something important is going on and that if one goes beyond a simple concern with self-help, collective action holds the potential for greater empowerment of marginalized groups. In any case, there seem to be few options to an effective and new political discourse. Some institutional form, separate from the state and perhaps political parties, is required.

The chapters that follow represent an attempt to examine some of these issues in the context of a massive human disaster that tested, sometimes to the breaking point, the family, communities, and formal organizations that form the foundation of our contemporary social contract. The narratives and other information we draw upon reveal the failures of federal and state governments in responding to the crisis, but they also illustrate the limitations of civil society organizations, including NGOs, churches, and other groups, to provide what the state could not or would not. The narratives illustrate the noble efforts of volunteers to make a difference in the lives of the survivors, but they reveal little by way of political action or effective attempts to change the basic rules of the game. Volunteers and caseworkers, though, were vitally important in optimizing survivors' ability to deal with complex bureaucracies. What it all amounted to is a topic we will return to at the end.

It would be possible, of course, to focus solely on the massive failure by all parties, and especially FEMA, in responding to this enormous disaster. Failures were common and serious, but most have been well documented, and we describe many in great detail in the following chapters. Failure, though, is not the entire story, nor does a focus on failure address our question of what a new social contract might look like. Hurricane Katrina victimized the low-income and largely African American inhabitants of a highly vulnerable area who had no place else to live because of their limited incomes and restricted mobility chances. The economic tsunami victimized the far more affluent, and both disasters clearly show that no one is invulnerable or truly self-sufficient. Cancer, heart disease, old age, and bankruptcy reveal everyone's ultimate dependency.

The question that we are particularly interested in addressing and the one that is central to our analysis is how civil society and the state might complement one another to further the political, economic, and social incorporation of those who currently have little power. The economic crisis makes the ongoing role of the state in economic life clear. But states are made up of people, and people live their lives in groups. Even if they consist of many individuals, if those groups remain isolated from the sources of political and economic power, none of their members has significant control over important aspects of life. Today a greater hope for the potential of civil society has resulted in higher levels of volunteerism and a new interest in politics, if not necessarily formal political parties. The environmental movement, the women's movement, the human rights movement, and many other movements both local and international involve people in activities and processes that go well beyond voting or anything they might do alone.

As we have noted, critics of the new approaches see the Third Way and the New Democratic approach as little more than capitulations to neoliberal market maximization. What the morally superior or politically viable alternatives might be are as yet unclear. There can be no doubt that the old Keynesian paternalistic state-based approaches created dependency for some program participants, but the state provides the ultimate safety net for individuals who become ill, lose their jobs in economic downturns, or, because of diminished capacity, simply cannot provide for themselves. Civil society can complement those efforts, but its organizations cannot replace the state in assuring the welfare of populations.

A major problem with traditional welfare was that it required that one adopt the identity of pauper to receive assistance, especially cash assistance not tied to illness (O'Connor, 2001). Although increasing human capital through education and training has been part of welfare rhetoric, in reality most programs have been "work first" programs with very minimal educational components. Our purpose is to reaffirm the need for a functioning welfare state and social rights. We also affirm the principle of "no duties without rights" (Havemann, 2001). One incurs the duties of citizenship only to the extent that one is a true citizen. Our exploration of these issues is based on a study of a physical and social disaster that illustrates the precariousness of our basic physical and economic security and our collective dependence on one another. The study also illustrates the special vulnerabilities of minority Americans, whose sources of economic and physical security are particularly precarious because of long-term historical marginalization. The concept of exclusion relates well to their plight.

The problem with the "no benefits without responsibilities" approach arises, as we have noted, when the expectation that one should make a reasonable effort at self-sufficiency does not consider the very real structurally based differences in human capital, employability, and labor market capacity. The expectation that someone with little education or human capital should compete in a labor market in which some employers may still be racist, and in which wage rates are too low to allow one to move out of poverty, runs the risk of blaming the victims for their situations. At the very least, such a system is inefficient and self-defeating. We argue that a real attempt to improve the productivity of those on welfare has never really been made. Education and training programs are, of course, very expensive, and real increases in educational levels or human capital take years. The Red Cross and other organizations have a long history and much experience in responding to crises. They provide the victims of natural and manmade crises with immediate relief that allows those with sufficient human, material, and social capital to return to normal rather quickly. Those without sufficient human, material, or social capital often find that when the emergency aid ends, their situations remain precarious. In what follows, we illustrate the differences in the experiences of those who recovered in significant ways from the devastation of the storm and those whose lives remained precarious; we then relate those differences to important institutional forces.

2

An Emerging Methodology for a Crisis Situation

CASE STUDIES: TWO FAMILIES

Ted Johnson, an African American male, and his wife are both physical therapists who left New Orleans in their own car before Hurricane Katrina struck. The couple has two boys, and eventually the family relocated permanently in Austin. The decision to relocate was not a spur-of-the-moment one, nor was it made without qualms. The couple's disillusionment with New Orleans had been growing for some time. The storm was the catalyst that forced the choice because it made evacuation necessary and it began a series of events that ultimately resulted in their decision not to return.

The Johnsons' story is not typical of survivors in our sample and illustrates the importance of high levels of social and human capital in determining a successful relocation. As we will see, those families that were able to evacuate themselves had in general more material and social resources and were more successful in reestablishing their lives in Austin or in resuming their lives in New Orleans. The second case we present is of a family with far fewer resources and less human, material, or social capital that could not evacuate on their own. The capacity of individuals and families in similar situations to reestablish their lives, which were often precarious to begin with, was very limited and the outcome much less favorable.

We interviewed the Johnsons in their large new home in a middle-class subdivision of Austin some months after they had arrived. The home was well furnished and included a media room with movie screen and bar. As we have mentioned, Ted Johnson and his wife had been physical therapists in New Orleans, and had been stably employed for years. They owned a home with a pool, which they had built in a relatively affluent neighborhood in Orleans Parish. Ted's mother and father lived in the same neighborhood. The couple's older son was attending college and the younger was in middle school. Ted had been planning to return to school for additional education when the hurricane struck. Even though the family's life in New Orleans was comfortable, Ted reported that he and his wife had considered moving out of New Orleans because of the failing educational system, crime, and corruption. He told us that

...prior to the storm, we were talking about, my wife and I were discussing moving to Texas. In fact, we were [discussing] moving to Houston, Texas, but she said, "Honey, what I would like to do is have our youngest son,...finish up high school and then we can discuss that." So I thought about that. Well, okay, no rush, no big deal. Because I've heard of so many other states, other cities outside of New Orleans that had better education systems. And New Orleans was struggling for such a long time with their school system. They didn't have any solid infrastructure. We've had three or four [superintendents] in maybe the last two years. And also, some of the other political things that were really going on in the city, a lot of corruption. So those were some things that I prayed about and that God would turn around. So Katrina was more than just devastation to New Orleans, but it was also a cleansing for New Orleans. It was also an opportunity for people to move to better communities....

The family was very involved with the community in New Orleans, particularly with their church and local sports. Johnson viewed the hurricane almost as an act of God, and said that he had previously decided that if a major hurricane struck, the family might not return to New Orleans. As he put it,

You can take what has happened in two ways, of course, negative and positive. And I look at the positive because of my spiritual background with my belief and where I've been and where I've come up. So it was a blessing....I think I was ready...to move on to another level in my life. So, that was another prayer. I was asking God to use me wherever He needed me. And so when Katrina came, I never thought about it at that point, because I really thought that we would be able to go back and everything would be okay because for so many years, New Orleans always recovered and got going again. But, you know, as I thought about this [person], a mother [in our church] told me [about] some of the past hurricanes, Hurricane Betsy, Hurricane Camille, and I thought in the back of my mind, I said to myself, if a storm ever comes through here again of that magnitude, I don't think I would want to come back.

When the family heard that a major storm was approaching and might strike New Orleans, they realized that they would have to evacuate. Ted's

wife's work schedule presented a bit of a problem since she was expected
to report for work even as the storm approached. As they were deciding
what to do, a cousin from Austin called to suggest that the family come
there. Despite the fact that Ted's wife was supposed to report for work,
the family decided to leave.

The family evacuated by car and headed north, the direction in which
all traffic was directed. Ted described the trip:

…We got on highway LA 1 and we arrived in Baton Rouge about, I think it was
maybe about 6:00 in the evening.…We were on the road for a while, for about
twelve hours. Then we stopped there and finally found a restaurant that had
some food.…We just got as much as we could, we filled up our tank again. But
again, along the way, you saw families, cars broken down…and I tell you it was
a challenge because we had to get back on that road again. Got back on LA 1 and
you could just see for miles red lights along the way.…I was very familiar with
some of the highways going up through Louisiana. So we took some back roads
and got up to Shreveport, Louisiana. That's more northern Louisiana. They were
out of rooms. So I had to make reservations at a Motel 6…[that] was 30 miles
outside. So, it was still just bumper to bumper and then finally once we got to
Shreveport we stopped. I saw some relatives of mine and I was so happy to just
see them. I hadn't seen them in such a long time. And it was so funny to run into
them at that time.

The family stayed in several places during the trip. When it became
clear that returning immediately would not be possible, they decided
to go to Austin to stay with Mrs. Johnson's cousin. At this point, the
Johnsons still planned to return to New Orleans at least temporarily, but
they wanted to get their son registered in school because they were concerned that he would fall behind. The fact that the schools in Austin were
so much better than what they had experienced in New Orleans turned
out to be an important factor in their decision to relocate permanently.
As Mr. Johnson explained,

…we stayed with her cousin for about a week. And as school had just started
here, we spoke to her cousin and asked if [my son] could stay here for a week
and get him registered for school, and then we were going to head back to New
Orleans because a week later, we would be able to go back to New Orleans and
retrieve some of our items and to see the damage that had occurred. So we got
him registered in a school here…and they were glad to have him here. You know
the great thing about this…, he wasn't doing too good in school in New Orleans.
But when he got here, I mean, to say that we had this transition, he excelled in
school.…It was such a great change and it made me feel good and also it made
me think, now, wait a minute, if he is doing well here, why should I rush back to
New Orleans?

The Johnsons had a large and close-knit family in New Orleans. The storm, though, dispersed them and they were able to remain in contact only by telephone. As Ted explained,

…before the storm my mom was living in [another state] along with my [father]. My grandmother's home [in New Orleans] was just completely destroyed so she moved over to Alabama with her daughter. And she was there with my mother and my father. I had some aunts that flew to California. They are just scattered all over now.

By the time of our initial interview, Ted seemed to feel that he had been able to reconstruct the meaningful portions of his life in Austin. They were again involved in church and sports activities. The family received help from FEMA, but in the end it was their relatives and their own resources that enabled them to restart their lives in a new city. One old friend was instrumental in helping the Johnsons find work. As Ted explained,

…a friend [who] moved here thirty days before the storm came. His job…transferred him up here…so we had another place to send our son to because his son and my son grew up together.…I asked him where I would need to go to as far as human resources and he told me the people to ask for and so I did that and they were so welcoming. All we needed to do was to actually go there.

Since Ted and his wife were Hurricane Katrina survivors, their applications were given priority treatment and they were both hired. The family still owned their house in New Orleans, but at the time we spoke with them, they were planning to repair and sell it. They purchased a home in Austin because they decided that purchasing made better financial sense. As Ted explained,

Yeah, when I moved to the second apartment…we started house hunting. Because we knew that, well, FEMA told us that they were only going to pay for three months. So, I was thinking, after three months, then what? And the rent for a two bedroom, three bedroom apartment was like $1,600. Well, wait a minute.…I might as well buy a house. So we started house hunting and we got a lot of tips through FEMA to look under HUD [the Department of Housing and Urban Development] and also to try to find some houses that were under foreclosure. So we knew someone who had a business in renovating homes. He did a lot of flipping of houses. Flipped houses, in other words, he would buy a house and fix them up and sell them. And so, he started taking me through some of these communities and looking at some properties that were [in] foreclosure. We ran across this wonderful house. And we came through here and this is one of the last houses that the real estate agent showed us. She said, "Well, it needs some work." And she was telling us things that needed repair. Comparing this house to the house back home, I said this is a castle compared to our house back at home. So I said, "Yeah, I can do some of the repairs myself…," which we've done.…The neighbors have been really friendly. They welcome us here.

You know, there are so many blessings that have come out of Katrina. And so, my only burden that I have now is cutting the ties with the house back home so I can go on with my life and use whatever I get from those funds because my objective is to retire early. I want to be able to secure the future for my kids, secure their college future. And just enjoy the rest of my life right here in Austin.

A DIFFERENT EXPERIENCE

The Johnsons were rather unique in their ability to reestablish themselves in Austin and to replace what they had left behind in New Orleans. The couple had high levels of human capital in the form of occupational skills, and they had major social capital in the form of family and friends in Austin. Another participant's story was more common among the survivors we interviewed and reveals the major barriers to recovery that result from low levels of human and social capital. Louise Wilkins, an unmarried forty-one-year-old African American female, lived with three daughters and a son in a housing project in New Orleans. Three of the children were school-age, and the eldest, Tiffany, a young adult, worked as a waitress. Louise had worked previously, but had developed medical problems that made it impossible for her to work any longer, so she depended on social security.

Louise and her children stayed in their apartment during the storm. Although they had an opportunity to be evacuated by helicopter, they did not do so because Louise was afraid. As the water rose, though, the family realized that they would have to leave and waded to higher ground. They were able to take almost nothing with them. As Louise described the ordeal, "I got tired....I left with just the clothes on my back, I didn't bring no ID, I didn't bring nothing. When they told us we had to leave, I just put on clothes, my children put on clothes." The family walked to the Superdome, a trip that Louise estimated took six hours. According to her, there was a great deal of violence at the Superdome and members of the National Guard were hostile. She told us that

...they had their finger on the trigger. The whole time they [were] treating us like dogs, they [were] feeding this food that you have to heat up with water and we had to get in line for it...then they started throwing us water, throwing us water like we was dogs, throwing us food to us, riding around on the truck on top, in the dome, on the outside of the dome, beating little children.

Tiffany, Louise's adult daughter, added to this story:

...me and my mom didn't go to sleep. We let the girls and my brother go to sleep and we just watched our surroundings 'cause they was raping young kids. They raped two little girls and a little boy. So, me and my mom stayed up to watch the girls and my brother so they wouldn't be hurt. So, we just stayed up. That was Thursday night. Friday night, well Friday morning, the girls [were] used to taking a bath. Then, they couldn't take no bath; we didn't have no change in clothes. So the only thing we could do was just take the bottle of water they gave us and wipe off.

The family's situation during the evacuation was complicated by Louise's health problems. When they were evacuated from the Superdome, they did not know where they were going. As Louise recounted,

When they put us on a plane we didn't know where we [were going]. We asked them where we were going. They [told us they] didn't know. They even asked us if we wanted to go to Florida. [I said] no, you are not sending me to Florida 'cause I don't know [anything] nothing about no Florida.

The family lost contact with their extended family members after the storm. Louise also lost touch with a romantic partner. As she told us, "...I had a friend, a man friend. I don't know where he is. I would talk to him. He was an older person, stayed by [himself]. He used to come by [to see] me two or three days out of the week...[and] I talked to him." Louise told us that this friend helped her take care of the children. Louise did not know what had become of him. She had also lost touch with a sibling. She seemed resigned to these losses, though, and told us that "I don't care...as long as these [my] children here are safe, I don't care about nobody else over there. I am sorry, I am not going back to New Orleans."

When the family arrived at the Convention Center in Austin, they received help. Louise told us that when they were at the Convention Center,

...things [were] okay, things had got better. We left everything so the Convention Center was good because everything we lost was right in the Convention Center. It was not like we had to go across town. Go over here for social security cards; go over here for birth certificate. They had put everything right in the Convention Center, so that was nice. It was good. They even gave us food stamps, I mean; they help [helped] us get a house...strangers helped us. People we didn't know helped us out before people we did know. So, that was nice.

Louise admitted, though, that

...the hard thing was starting over. I never thought we'd have to start over. It was times we had to buy new things. If the TV conked out, we had to buy another one. If the radio stopped playing, you buy another one. But I mean starting over from nothing when you got to buy everything over, that was hard. We didn't know where to start. We didn't have no house and nothing. Then, it got harder at the Convention Center because we knew we had to leave at one point but we didn't think it was going to be that soon. So, we had to leave the Convention Center....

The family stayed at the Convention Center for approximately three weeks. During those three weeks, the family made new acquaintances and friends. As Louise told us,

...during the three weeks, I found friends. We've met a lot of people [including the interviewer]. [There was] a lady [who] help[ed] us out a lot. That's the lady who gave me the kitten. We met a reverend at the church that we go to. She's very nice. It just a lot of people that reached out to us that we thought wouldn't reach out to us because we were total strangers but they reached out to us and that was nice.

In contrast to the Johnsons, Louise and her children found dealing with the educational system in Austin to be problematic, and this was a source of dissatisfaction with the city. Louise's opinion of New Orleans and Austin was very different from that of the Johnsons. As she said, "[In New Orleans] I was scared, but not as much as I am scared in Austin, because my children [have so many] problems in school. They are getting picked on because...we come from the storm...they're stereotyping children by children calling them 'Katrina storm victims.'" Her two younger daughters had been beaten up at school and the police were called. Louise told us that, "my children...get jumped on, beat, scratched on the face. I never had no kind of complications with the police [in New Orleans]."

Again in contrast to the Johnsons, who were a nuclear family, Louise's family became extended when Mary Powers, a friend from New Orleans, and her children moved in. Mary and her children had lived near Louise in the projects in New Orleans. During the storm, Mary and her children were evacuated to Houston. She came to Austin because Louise had found out where she was and suggested that she come to Austin. At the time, Mary was about to be evicted from her hotel in Houston. She had been pregnant during the evacuation and had just given birth in Houston. After leaving the Convention Center in New Orleans, Mary and her family spent four or five months in a hotel in the city. She claimed that no social worker ever visited the family. During that time, she did not apply for any assistance, so the family survived on the original $2,000 they had received from FEMA and three months' worth of food stamps. The hotel in which they were staying served a complimentary breakfast, and Mary said she spent a lot of time going down to the kitchen to get snacks for the kids throughout the day. Her school-age children were not enrolled in school. A social worker finally became involved with the family when Mary went to the hospital to give birth to her daughter, Kenya.

Mary's story had a far-from-happy ending. During our interviews, it became evident that she had begun using drugs. Mary eventually lost custody of her baby to Child Protective Services, which eventually placed the child with Tiffany, Louise's daughter. We did not find out about the status of the other children. Tiffany had begun adoption proceedings despite having discovered that she was HIV positive. Louise had become very depressed. The depression was compounded by the fact that her teenage son had dropped out of school and had not found a job. Both she and Tiffany worked intermittently. They found it hard to maintain employment because of a lack of transportation, a lack of identification, as well as family and health problems. At the time of our final interview in April 2008, Louise had been diagnosed with cancer and she died later that year.

THE SAMPLE

These two stories present two extreme cases of disaster and recovery. For the Johnsons, social and human capital smoothed the transition to Austin and a new life. They would probably have recovered even if they had returned to New Orleans. For Louise and her family, the lack of such resources gave them little ability to create a new life or to return to New Orleans. In our sample, which consisted overwhelmingly of survivors who did not evacuate before the storm and who did not leave on their own, there were few cases like the Johnsons. In what follows, we tell the story of individuals and families that lacked the personal and social resources to recover from tragedy. We also show that the social safety net that is intended to assist individuals in distress is far from adequate. The data on which the analyses are based were gathered from several sources, including semistructured in-depth interviews with survivors of Hurricane Katrina who were evacuated to Austin, Texas, after the storm; interviews with service providers who attempted to assist them; and participant observation at meetings of representatives of governmental and nongovernmental organizations that attempted to share information and coordinate their activities. In addition, we drew on articles from Austin newspapers, agency reports, and other archival documents.

Our primary source of information was the set of semistructured interviews with survivors. Before proceeding, we describe the panel of survivors, whose basic demographic characteristics are presented in Table 2.1. The sample consisted of seventy-three participants, the majority of whom were women and African American. Only three of the interviewees were

TABLE 2.1. *Demographic Characteristics of the Sample*

Characteristic	Participants (n = 73)	Percent of total	Percent of New Orleans population pre-Katrina
Gender			
Women	44	60.27	53.1
Men	29	39.73	46.9
Race/ethnicity			
African American	52	71.23	66.6
White	15	20.55	26.6
Hispanic[a]	4	5.48	3.1
Asian	2	2.74	2.3
Age[b]			
18–35	21	28.77	25.9
36–65	49	67.12	35.7
66 and over	3	4.11	11.7
Pre-Katrina Occupation[c]			
In the labor force	45	61.64	57.8
Manual labor	10	22.22	10.1
Service/sales/clerical	26	57.78	36.4
Professional	7	15.56	29.6
Other	1	2.22	
Unemployed	1	2.22	5.5
Not in the labor force	28	38.36	42.2
Student	5	6.85	
Homemaker	4	5.48	
Disabled	9	12.33	23.2
Retired	8	10.96	
Other	2	2.74	
Displacement			
Timing			
Evacuated before Katrina	19	26.03	
Evacuated after Katrina	52	71.23	
Unclear	2	2.74	
Social ties			
Evacuated with family and or friends	58	79.45	
Evacuated alone	14	19.18	
Unclear	1	1.37	

[a] Survivors categorized as Hispanic identified themselves as such.

[b] Ages are estimates in some cases.

[c] Occupational data are based on survivors' descriptions of their past employment. Manual labor includes construction and manufacturing occupations; services/sales and clerical includes retail trade, accommodation and food services, arts, entertainment and recreation, administrative and support services, and "other services – except public administration"; professional includes professional, scientific and technical, management of companies and enterprises, finance, insurance and real estate, public administration, and educational services. The percentages of survivors in various occupational categories are based on their share of those in the labor force, whereas data on those not in the labor force are presented as a share of all survivors interviewed. The figure for disability for New Orleans does not specify labor force status.

Source: Survivor interview data and 2000 Census data compiled by the Greater New Orleans Data Center.

over sixty-five. Of the forty-five who were in the labor force in New Orleans, the vast majority were manual laborers or service workers. Of those who were not in the labor force, the majority were disabled or retired. The final column of the table presents comparable data for the City of New Orleans prior to the storm.

As the introductory examples suggest and as we will discuss later in the book, the circumstances of the move from New Orleans to Austin were related to the success and speed with which survivors reestablished themselves. Those with the material and social resources to evacuate themselves in their own cars before the storm struck fared better than those who remained through the storm and who were evacuated by others after the storm had passed and the city had flooded. In addition, the sample differed in terms of the size of the group with which survivors evacuated. Among the seventy-three research participants, fourteen evacuated alone, fifty-three evacuated with friends or family, sixteen were separated from their families, five were reunited with family members in Austin, and for one person the information was unclear. In what follows, we employ our data in many ways to characterize the evacuation from New Orleans and resettlement in Austin. We begin with the survivors' accounts of life in New Orleans before the storm, and then present their accounts of the evacuation and their experiences in Austin.

Since the data are not quantitative or the result of a systematic survey, the story is often based on information from different sources, including the survivors themselves, service providers, and other officials. While the interviews followed a general protocol and began with a specific topic, the interviewers allowed the survivors to direct the interview on the basis of what concerned them most. The interviews with survivors were transcribed and our accounts are based on the transcriptions. The interviews often move among a number of related topics, are occasionally inaudible to the transcriber, and often contained highly repetitious speech and accounts. To present the data in as concise and understandable a manner as possible, we edited the narrative information and note with ellipses where material has been omitted. When we change a word in order to make the sense clearer, we place the material in brackets. We also occasionally changed some descriptors of research participants to protect their confidentiality. In all cases, though, we stay as close to the original meaning of the communication as possible.

Our general approach might most usefully be described as a case study (Burawoy, 1998; Stake, 1995; Yin, 2009). The leaders of the research team had extensive experience in the collection of qualitative data from families and individuals in stressful situations (Angel, Lein, & Henrici, 2006; Bell, 2008; Edin & Lein, 1997). However, not all of the interviewers were experienced in field research, and the situation surrounding the evacuation and the speed with which events unfolded greatly influenced the nature and quality of the data collection. Ideally, any data collection effort is preceded by a lengthy period of planning and preparation focused on considerations related to protocol design, sample selection, interviewer preparation, and eventual analysis (Marshall & Rossmann, 2011; Padgett, 2008; Small, 2009; Wolcott, 2008). Even case studies ideally require extensive preparation and consideration of which cases are to be included in the study (Angel, Lein, & Henrici, 2006; Luft, 2009). Such planning is possible in the study of social phenomena that are relatively stable or change slowly over time. In the case of unanticipated crisis, events unfold extremely rapidly and the fluidity of the situation requires an immediate response, one that must be carried out without the luxury of extensive planning.

The unique and rapidly evolving events following the storm required adaptations of traditional research methods to deal with, among other things, the initial lack of research funding and dedicated paid personnel. In addition, understanding a unique experience such as the Katrina displacement meant proceeding without well-developed hypotheses. The collection of data in such a situation is inherently inductive and the process, in principle, is theory generating. The research design evolved as part of an emerging understanding of ongoing events that were unique to the circumstances and setting. Analysis was ongoing and proceeded alongside data collection. The question of who and how many individuals to interview or observe depended on the availability of both participants and interviewers, but was also based on the researchers' sense of "saturation," which occurs when the themes and issues that emerge from new interviews increasingly reflect what has already been discovered (Small, 2009).

Such research is clearly not generalizable in any statistical sense. Nor can the findings confidently be generalized to the situation of survivors in other cities, or even across Austin, which housed at its peak nearly ten thousand evacuees. The goal in qualitative research, and certainly for this sort of case study, is to make logical rather than statistical inferences from a relatively small pool of participants and observations presented in depth so that the reader may decide whether the findings are transferable to his or her own experience or research question (Small, 2009). One case of human suffering can reveal highly generalizable insights into how individuals and groups respond to adversity in other circumstances. Our core objective was to relate to larger social processes the experiences of a group of Katrina survivors who relocated in Austin and the community of service providers who received the survivors. We were interested in what the experiences of the victims of this particular crisis revealed about the complex nexus of social class, race, government, and civil society. Although Hurricane Katrina was in most respects a unique event, the sources of vulnerability of the primarily low-income African American victims and the inadequate and heavily bureaucratic governmental response revealed more general aspects of the historically determined system of social stratification in the United States. In what follows, we present the sequence of events that defined the research project and provide an overview of the research process as it evolved during the confusing weeks and months after the arrival of the first survivors of the hurricane.

THE BEGINNING: WHAT IS IN A NAME?

Perhaps the ideal of disinterestedness and objectivity is a myth in most social research given the inevitable reflexivity of even the most supposedly neutral observation. In the case of a major crisis in which one is dealing with potentially traumatized individuals, issues of sensitivity and ethics are paramount and objectivity is difficult if not impossible to achieve. As researchers and practitioners familiar with the causes and consequences of hardship in the daily lives of low-income families, members of the research team felt strongly that potential research participants should be treated with heightened sensitivity. They felt that individuals who had possibly been traumatized and who were in immediate need should not be accosted with requests for research interviews since the team was aware that the survivors were being constantly interviewed by any number of federal, state, and municipal agencies to determine their eligibility for assistance. Rather than being selected systematically, participants were recruited through the agencies that provided services to them and through family members and friends. Given that the survivors were required to fill out innumerable forms for FEMA and city services, research requests for demographic information and signatures on consent forms raised the risk that the survivors would equate the researchers with bureaucrats. Demographic information was, therefore, collected indirectly as part of the interview process, resulting at times in incomplete data on key demographic variables. The team also requested and received permission from the Institutional Review Board (IRB) to obtain verbal, rather than written, consent from the participants.

The emotional content of the evacuation experience and the precarious social situation of the victims of the storm are illustrated by what would appear to be an incidental process of finding a general label for the individuals who were evacuated to Austin. During the period following the evacuation, several labels were used by the media and others involved in dealing with the survivors. As it turned out, many of these labels carried strong emotional, social, and political loadings that rendered them potentially offensive or derogatory. Immediately after the storm, for instance, the term "refugee" was used in the media, but it was quickly rejected. For some survivors and their supporters, the term seemed to treat displaced individuals as if they were not citizens. As one research participant explained, "the difference between an evacuee and a refugee is, a refugee comes from another country; I'm a United States citizen, I was paying taxes in New Orleans, I'm still paying taxes over here." In response to the uproar, the term "refugee" was replaced with the term "evacuee" in many discussions. Even this label, however, conveyed excessive dependency and, shortly before the first anniversary of Katrina, the accepted name became "survivors," a label that emphasizes strength and resilience. That is the general term we use to refer to our participants in the following chapters.

PROJECT TIMELINE: SIGNIFICANT EVENTS
AND DECISION-MAKING POINTS

To present the stages through which the research project evolved and to identify key decision-making points, we divide the time from the day that Katrina struck New Orleans in August 2005 until the time of the writing of this book into four periods. We begin with a brief characterization of each period in terms of the major events that affected the survivors' situations, the key organizational and individual players involved, and the activities of the research team. A major objective of this presentation is to be candid about the challenges that the research team faced in attempting to understand what was going on. Although it would be possible to present our findings as if they were the result of a clearly planned and smoothly executed process, that was not the case, and we believe there are important methodological and practical lessons to be learned from our experiences.

Period one: The project begins

Period one began on August 29, 2005, the day the hurricane struck New Orleans, and lasted through the end of September 2005. During this period, survivors arrived in Austin, the research team came together, and preliminary work began, carried out primarily by volunteers. The events of the storm that begin this period were described in the first chapter. As we noted there, some survivors left New Orleans before the storm struck. Those who could not or did not evacuate sought shelter in various places, including the Superdome and the New Orleans Convention Center, and were finally evacuated to Austin and other cities. For us, this is where the story actually begins, since it is at this point that the research team began to envision the project and make contact with survivors. At the beginning of September, survivors who were evacuated to Austin were temporarily housed at the Austin Convention Center and other locations throughout the city. It was there that we made our initial contacts.

The research team comes together
It was in the context of the chaotic events of the evacuation that the research team came together to attempt to understand the needs of the survivors who were arriving in Austin, as well as to understand the nature of the response by federal, state, and civil society organizations. The team included anthropologists, social workers, sociologists, and individuals from other professional backgrounds, some of whom had worked together before on other projects. The researchers had specific interests motivated by their particular disciplinary backgrounds. What they shared in common, though, was a desire to understand the individual and collective response to the loss of community and whether governmental and civil society organizations could compensate in the short run and assist with reestablishing networks and communities in a new environment. A long history of research with minority and low-income populations by key members of the research team made them aware of the fact that historically determined social structures place certain individuals, families, and communities at serious risk in the event of crises. The fact that the majority of the hurricane's victims were low-income African Americans was no coincidence.

Almost immediately after the initial survivors' arrival, some team members volunteered to work with the American Red Cross and other agencies that were involved with the survivors at the Austin Convention Center and other locations. At this point, those collecting the data were little more than volunteers motivated by the desire to be of assistance. Other than general theoretical interests and the desire to help, the team had few explicit research goals. Yet initial contacts made in these capacities proved very useful. In one case, they led to the start of a relationship with a future research participant, and they resulted in contacts with agencies that placed us in contact with survivors who we eventually interviewed. These initial experiences helped us to identify some of the major issues faced both by survivors and those attempting to assist them.

During the early days, volunteer researchers began working with two local NGOs and made contacts with other organizations that resulted in further contacts and new participants. During this period, a group of students, faculty, and staff began meeting at the School of Social Work to develop a clearer sense of their shared research objectives and decide how to proceed. During these initial discussions, a common goal was to document the arrival of survivors in Austin and to understand the factors that aided or impeded that process. All the while, the crisis was unfolding and this newly formed research team was aware of the urgency of the situation. Despite the urgency, though, time was required to get organized and attempt to find funding for the project.

Despite the speed of unfolding events, the lack of funding and the absence of planning meant that there was no intensive data collection effort during September 2005. By the end of September, five initial interviews with survivors and three initial interviews with providers had been completed. On September 9, the National Science Foundation (NSF) announced a Small Grants for Exploratory Research (SGER) grant competition for research to investigate the social impact of Hurricane Katrina. Within days, the research team made plans to prepare an application that was submitted on September 23. At the same time, Hurricane Rita struck in eastern Louisiana and Texas, much closer to Austin, forcing the evacuation of portions of Houston. Many Austinites had family who were affected, and the Red Cross, FEMA, and local disaster agencies had to divert resources to a new group of displaced hurricane survivors.

Period two: Funding and consolidation

Period two began in October 2005, with the closing of the Convention Center, and ended mid-January 2006, when the team learned that its NSF proposal had been funded. During this period, the City of Austin Neighborhood Housing and Community Development Department entered into a contract with FEMA to provide public assistance to approximately 1,800 survivor families under section 403 of the Stafford Act. As part of this program, the City of Austin paid approximately four hundred local landlords with FEMA funding to provide housing for survivors.

Local agencies then began to organize to help survivors acquire basic necessities such as furniture, bedding, clothing, and household goods. Local service providers quickly realized that many survivors would likely be in Austin for quite some time and that they had multiple and urgent needs. In response, these providers began organizing to assess and meet those needs. Before the end of October, there was an initial meeting of case managers at a local NGO that took major responsibility for coordination among service providers.

In November, a low-income housing organization established resource centers with case managers at an apartment complex in East Austin quite far from the center of town, where many families were placed after the Convention Center was closed. Case managers were also assigned to other housing complexes with large numbers of survivors. These were the first funded Katrina case managers. During the fall, Texas Interfaith/ Interagency Disaster Relief (TIDR), a new interfaith disaster relief agency, emerged to fill a vacuum in the coordination efforts and began holding meetings primarily with faith-based organizations. Both the United Methodist Committee on Relief and the United Way of America announced funding for local case management. The City of Austin hired a group of assessors to follow up with all those who were receiving FEMA 403 assistance to assess their other needs and refer them to local agencies. However, these assessors were pulled off this task when FEMA announced that on December 15 it would evict six hundred survivors who had been housed in local hotels and asked the city's assistance in relocating these survivors. The assessors were then given the task of locating and assisting these hotel residents. After protest from Austin and other host cities and a class action suit, however, FEMA extended the deadline for relocation until after the holidays.

The research project gears up

During phase two, more initial interviews were conducted as the larger study was gearing up. These interviews were based on a list of topics that focused on survivors' lives before the storm, the evacuation, how they arrived in Austin, what kind of services they received since they arrived, and how they were thinking about their lives at the time (for example, whether they were planning to stay in Austin or return to New Orleans). The interviews were loosely structured, largely because it was not clear exactly what topics might be of greatest salience to the survivors. The interviews were theory generating and inductive. They were not based on a particular protocol since we wanted to let the survivors tell their stories.

Given the extreme trauma of the events, it was unclear how best to probe, so we let the survivors decide what to relate. For some participants, talking about the evacuation seemed to be cathartic and they returned to it multiple times. For other participants, the experience was too traumatic to recount or they were simply not ready to open up to the interviewer on the topic, and so they focused more on the present. These unstructured interviews provided useful insights into the survivors' experiences. They revealed several central themes, including the highly militarized nature of the evacuation, the sudden and forced disruption of social networks, and the sources of the survivors' distrust of government. However, the interviews were hardly uniform in the data that were obtained. In addition to the task of locating and interviewing survivors, during this period the team developed and implemented the data management system for the project.

Once the Austin Convention Center closed, survivors who did not have other local connections or resources were dispersed throughout the city, often to apartment complexes in outlying areas, making it challenging to locate our research participants. There was no longer a central location at which survivors congregated. A list of apartment complexes in which there were large numbers of survivors was obtained, but "hanging out" at these complexes to try to meet survivors did not work, largely because the research team did not feel comfortable with this approach. In an attempt to recruit participants, invitations to participate in the study were placed on the doors of survivors' apartments in some complexes, but these also proved to be ineffective. The researchers later learned that many other groups were attempting to contact survivors this way and that low literacy and the fact that they were emotionally overwhelmed kept survivors from responding. Finally the team distributed fliers explaining the project in resource packets distributed by the group that the city had appointed to assess survivors' needs. Survivors were much more comfortable when the research was introduced by a trusted intermediary.

Ultimately, through contacts made at the Convention Center, at local agencies, through fliers, and by word of mouth, survivors willing to participate in the research were located. During this entire period, ten interviewers conducted thirty-three initial interviews with survivors. December 2005 was a particularly busy period as thirteen interviews were conducted. Once the semester was over, potential interviewers had more time and the offer of a gift card increased the number of survivors interested in participating. During this period, two interviews with service providers were conducted.

Period three: The reality of a long stay

Period three lasted from mid-January 2006 to the end of the summer of 2006, the first anniversary of Hurricane Katrina. This was a period of continued instability for the survivors, as FEMA continually changed its timelines. At the same time, federal programs such as food stamps, Temporary Assistance for Needy Families (TANF), and Medicaid, which had relaxed their rules for survivors immediately after the crisis, reinstated their usual eligibility requirements, resulting in many survivors losing benefits. The local case management system was becoming more organized, as agencies received funding for Katrina-specific programs, although there was ongoing tension about who was in charge of this process.

By this point, any initial euphoria that the survivors might have felt disappeared as they realized that they could not return to New Orleans and would be in Austin for some time. They faced housing and food insecurity and encountered serious problems finding work. Many had difficulty obtaining documentation of identity, including driver's licenses and birth certificates; they encountered problems obtaining health care; and confronted many more barriers to establishing normal lives. During this period, the agencies charged with addressing survivors' needs faced new challenges and experienced fatigue. Eventually, they consolidated their efforts and developed a stable, ongoing collaboration. However, case managers continued to find it difficult to engage survivors in case management. A local African American faith-based organization developed some culturally specific programs to address this problem. As they commemorated the first anniversary of the storm in August 2006, many survivors were facing eviction as they lost FEMA assistance.

THE RESEARCH TEAM TRIES TO STAY
IN TOUCH WITH SURVIVORS

Survivor contacts through agencies and referrals to friends and family by those already in the study resulted in sixty-one interviews with survivors during this period. These included twenty-eight initial interviews, twenty-seven second interviews, and eight third interviews. Because of their housing instability, keeping in touch with survivors for ongoing interviews was exceptionally challenging. It became clear that in order to really understand the complementary roles of government and civil society in dealing with the needs of survivors, interviews with service providers would be necessary. Interviews with providers and observation of participants at their public meetings began in earnest in February of 2006. Through a snowball process of making new contacts through recommendations of previous contacts, sixty-five interviews with providers were completed during this period. These interviews provided useful insights into the reasons for the successes and failures of various programs. They also provided additional survivor contacts and furnished secondary data on the experiences of a broader group of survivors than we could contact on our own. During the summer of 2006, a social work graduate student intern helped develop a census of NGOs and followed the institutional distribution of new funding that became available during this period (see Gajewski, Bell, Lein, & Angel, 2011).

As the efforts of the research team became known, we were asked to participate in three additional projects in the spring and summer of 2006. The City of Austin requested assistance in analyzing data on survivors collected by the city's assessment team (see Lein et al., 2009). Two large faith-based service networks that were providing services to Katrina survivors approached the team to conduct midterm evaluations of their case management projects (see Bell et al., 2010). These projects provided an opportunity to compare what was happening in Austin to what was happening in other cities to which survivors were sent.

PERIOD FOUR: THE PROJECT WINDS UP

During the period between the first and second anniversaries of the storm (August 2006 to August 2007), the data collection portion of the project was effectively concluded and all but the last several interviews with survivors were carried out. During this period, some of the core support for survivors, especially that provided by FEMA, ended. Without FEMA assistance, many survivors had no way to pay their rent and faced eviction. Although they continued to attempt to provide supportive services to survivors, local agencies ran up against the shortage of affordable housing in Austin, which eventually proved to be an insurmountable problem. By August 2007, many Katrina-specific NGO programs began to lose funding and survivors were transferred to the more limited local programs for low-income families. FEMA announced in August of 2007 that the very few families still receiving assistance would be transferred to HUD in October 2008.

DATA COLLECTION WINDS DOWN AND ANALYSIS BEGINS

During this period, the team conducted a few more initial interviews, but focused primarily on trying to contact survivors for additional interviews. Team members also turned their attention to the detailed coding, interpretation, and analysis of the data. The interviews had been digitally recorded and transcribed. One of the challenges of conducting this sort of research is accurately transcribing unfamiliar speech. Given the often confused interview environments, part of the interview material was hard for those listening to the recordings to understand and successive iterations of cleaning and correcting transcripts were necessary as the researchers learned more about the experiences of survivors. Another challenge for the transcribers was managing their reactions to the traumatic stories. Even heard thirdhand, survivors' stories of their experiences during the evacuation was upsetting to some transcribers.

A team of research assistants and senior researchers coded the interview transcripts as well as observational and archival data. Multiple interviews from both survivors and service providers were read by a team of coders and a master list of codes was developed that reflected major topics and themes. The code development process went through multiple iterations. Once a relatively stable list of codes was developed, a team of researchers coded the individual documents. The data were organized using N6, a qualitative data analysis software program (www.qsrinternational.com). The coded and cataloged data allowed researchers to locate more easily material that was relevant to their topics of interest. However, this was just the first stage of the analysis. Researchers then used a variety of techniques, depending on the topic, to conduct further analysis. For example, in an analysis of changes in survivors' housing, researchers generated Excel spreadsheets that documented changes in housing over time. Similar techniques were employed to generate timelines of federal, state, and local policy changes that affected survivors after their arrival in Austin.

Throughout the project, the team disseminated emerging findings. In December 2006, we presented some preliminary findings at a research seminar. A group also submitted papers to the Society of Anthropology, held in New Orleans in April 2007. At this time, researchers were able to see firsthand the dramatic destruction and lack of rebuilding in New Orleans and connect with some survivors who had been able to return. They also learned, to their surprise, that there was very little research being conducted on the long-term recovery of displaced individuals and families. Throughout the study, we also sought feedback from service providers concerning our findings.

A METHODOLOGY THAT FITS THE TOPIC OF STUDY

A major strength of the sort of qualitative research on which this study is based is its allowance for necessary reflexivity in the data collection process. Unlike quantitative research, which proceeds from a positivist perspective that focuses on eliminating bias in data collection, qualitative research considers the perspectives of researchers and the processes of data collection to be data themselves. From this perspective, aspects of data collection that might be seen as sources of potential bias can represent important data in their own right. In this sort of study, interpretation is necessary and inevitable. In many ways, the experiences of the research team mirrored the experience of service providers in Austin and, to a much lesser extent, the survivors, who had to process and interpret a huge amount of information in a short period of time, all on top of their other activities. Reflecting on our methods and the limitations of our data provides insights into what have come to be considered failures in the recovery effort overall: some gaps in data, an incomplete understanding of survivors and the city and culture from which they came, the lack of planning, and the need to develop systems of coordination after the fact. Understanding the venue and the organizational actors, both governmental and nongovernmental, was absolutely necessary, but the effort took time that might have been used for locating and interviewing additional survivors. Given the nature of major crises, a rigid methodology that brackets the human aspects of the data collection for the sake of supposed objectivity would, in our opinion, limit the possibilities for discovery. As a result, we have a modest, nonrandom sample of interviews with survivors, a large number of interviews with service providers, and our own experiences of the volunteer efforts that we think provide a lens into the complex process of survivors' recovery and the complementary roles of the state and civil society actors.

3

Life before the Storm

The Old Community

Before the storm most Americans knew New Orleans for Mardi Gras, the French Quarter, Bourbon Street, and the Jazz Festival. For tourists, the Big Easy offered a unique atmosphere of escape; it was a party town where visitors ate, drank, and listened to sultry music into the wee hours. The city was famous for its unique mix of French and African cultures, its gumbo and beignets, and its art and southern culture. For visitors, New Orleans offered diversions that they could enjoy for a limited time before returning home, but for those who called the city's low-income neighborhoods home, New Orleans was a very different place. It evoked little of the mystery and charm that attracted outsiders. For the victims of Hurricane Katrina, the neighborhoods in which they lived consisted of familiar communities in which the residents had often lived for generations, but it would be a mistake to romanticize these communities. As our participants recounted to us, these neighborhoods were beset by problems of poverty, crime, poor housing, and inferior schools. Yet these areas were the familiar physical and social locations in which people were born, lived their lives, and died. The poverty and disorganization that characterized the poorest wards of the city required strong bonds of family, friends, and neighbors for basic survival. The loss of these communities and the strong social and family ties that characterized them represented a major loss. Rebuilding those communities and social ties, or even approximating them, in a new and unfamiliar city proved to be an extremely challenging task. As we show in this and later chapters, the attempt was frequently unsuccessful. Despite the assistance of many governmental and nongovernmental agencies and organizations, many individuals and families remained marginalized.

First, though, we must begin the story with what the survivors recalled of life in New Orleans before the evacuation and their general views of the communities that they left behind, as well as some sense of what they felt that they had lost. We should reiterate that what we recount of New Orleans is based on what survivors told us about their lives in their old neighborhoods. Although members of the research team visited New Orleans after the storm, we did not do any direct fieldwork in New Orleans, so our impressions are secondhand. One of the most important aspects of residential community, of course, is the institutional environment that defines it. This institutional environment consists of the police and other governmental agencies with which low-income people engage, but even more important it consists of the businesses, community centers, schools, churches, fraternal organizations, and other voluntary and charitable organizations that are not only sources of material support, but places where people can interact and potentially even engage in political action. Robert Putnam and others see the interactions of individuals in such institutions as forming the basis of civil society (Putnam, 1993, 1995, 2000). While Putnam laments what he sees as a decline in such voluntary civic engagement, others have documented the rapid rise of citizen groups with effective political voices (Berry, 1999; Schlozman, Verba, & Brady, 1999).

For the most part, though, the citizen groups described in the literature are made up primarily of middle-class individuals who, unlike the subjects of our story, have material and social resources that can be leveraged into serious political power. Yet citizen action does take place in low-income communities and mutual support is common, perhaps even more than in more affluent groups. Because of a lack of resources, collective action in low-income communities may be less organized and consequently less politically effective than is the case in more affluent communities, but mutual assistance and community involvement clearly take place (Agnitsch, Flora, & Ryan, 2006; Burcher, 2008; Edin & Lein, 1997; Silverman, 2004; Stack, 1974). Our participants provided descriptions of New Orleans before the storm that portrayed a rich network of strong bonds of family and neighbors, but which was far poorer in terms of the information-rich weak ties that characterize middle- and upper-class social networks. Understanding the institutional environment in our participants' communities of origin provides insights into the social and material resources that the survivors were able to bring with them to use in the attempt to reestablish themselves in a new city.

SOCIAL CAPITAL

Almost by definition, the majority of our sample of survivors had little wealth or human capital in terms of education and job skills. As we have noted before, most of those who were forced from their homes and who remained in Austin for protracted periods had little to which to return. In this sample, the number of survivors with higher levels of human capital and more resources was small, but as we will see, those with higher levels of human capital and more economic resources were able to return to New Orleans or to reestablish themselves in Austin far more easily than those with fewer resources. In many cases, higher levels of human capital were associated with more social capital in the form of contacts with other acquaintances and relatives who lived outside of New Orleans. Although we have only a few cases of individuals who voluntarily evacuated before the storm, our interviews strongly suggest that those families had in general far greater success in rebuilding new lives than those who were evacuated by FEMA after the storm. Many of those had the capacity to leave on their own. They owned cars, had other resources, and often had relatives in other places on whom they could rely for help.

Accounting for the differential levels of success among the survivors in reestablishing themselves in Austin requires that we identify those factors that account for differential levels of power among different communities, social classes, and racial and ethnic groups more generally. One need perhaps look no further than historically determined class and race-based differences in education, employment opportunities, and income, but how exactly those disadvantages were structured and institutionalized in New Orleans requires explanation. A frequently employed concept in discussions of differences in group power has been labeled "social capital," which like material capital represents a resource that can be used to further individual and group interests. Most generally, the term refers to the potential power inherent in social networks and the collective capacity of members of groups to act instrumentally to further collective and individual ends (Coleman, 1988, 1990; Portes, 1998; Putnam, 1993, 1995, 2000; Warren, Thompson, & Saegert, 2001).

Clearly groups differ in the amount and nature of social capital that they possess. Middle-class neighborhoods have more banks, country clubs, and high-end restaurants where the well-heeled can meet and do business than do low-income communities. The residents of affluent communities have greater access to loans and other resources that they can use to buy houses, start businesses, or send children to college. Middle-class families have their own resources, but collectively those resources represent a source of group power that low-income communities lack. This greater material capital translates into greater political power since affluent communities can support political parties and candidates who represent their interests. The appeal and potential utility of the concept of social capital for understanding the situation of low-income communities and for framing the situation of the survivors of Hurricane Katrina derive directly from the fact that social capital represents a collective asset and not just an individual characteristic or attribute (Coleman, 1990; Warren, Thompson, & Saegert, 2001). Individuals may benefit from social capital, but they do not possess it as individuals. The use of the term "capital" emphasizes the instrumental nature of this particular resource and source of power.

Social capital is important in providing what individuals alone cannot acquire, including public safety and a healthy environment, political influence, and collective material capital (Fukuyama, 2001; Guiso, Sapienza, & Zingales, 2004; Sampson, 1999; Sampson & Groves, 1989; Vieno et al., 2010; Zak & Knack, 2001). Social capital has both individual and collective benefits. At the individual level, the social support that reflects high levels of social capital protects one's health (Berkman et al., 2000; Fujiwara & Kawachi, 2008; James, Schulz, & van Olphen, 2001). It reduces the risk that students will drop out of high school (Coleman, 1988), and it fosters individual occupational and social mobility (Burt, 1992; Lin, 1999). At the community level, it results in greater neighborhood stability and more effective rural community action (Agnitsch, Flora, & Ryan, 2006; Portney & Berry, 1997; Saegert, Thompson, & Warren, 2001; Silverman, 2004; Temkin & Rohe, 1998). At the national and international levels, social capital translates into higher levels of economic development (Knack & Keefer, 1997; Portes & Landolt, 2000; Woolcock, 2002).

Despite its immediate intuitive appeal, the concept of social capital has been criticized as being empty of substance or even representing little more than a variation of "blaming the victim" explanations of poverty (Somers, 2008; Van Deth, 2003). The term can obviously be tautological in that we can attribute individual success or community cohesion to a high degree of social capital, which is itself measured in terms of factors related to individual success or community cohesion (Portes, 1998). Unlike human capital, which can be operationalized in terms of education and job skills, social capital is more elusive. Without a clear definition or an understanding of the mechanisms that make social capital an asset for individuals or groups, the statement that a group lacks social capital is just another way of saying that it is disadvantaged, in which case little of intellectual or practical value has been gained. It is necessary, therefore, to specify the major dimensions of social capital in specific contexts and specify the mechanisms whereby various forms of social capital benefit individuals and groups. It is also necessary to identify those factors that foster or impede its development and effectiveness.

Theorists and researchers who deal with social capital for the most part clearly recognize the fact that social capital's value inheres in its potential to be leveraged into material and political power (Bourdieu, 1986; Wacquant, 1998). Ivan Light, like Pierre Bourdieu and others, argues that social capital can be understood only in terms of its association with cultural capital, financial capital, and human capital (Light, 2004). Cultural capital refers to a high level of cultural knowledge that increases the effectiveness of social interactions and can result in economic and social advantages; financial capital refers to money; and human capital refers to education, training, and labor force–relevant skills that increase income and wealth. Social capital does not exist in an economic or political vacuum, and a highly developed welfare state with specific programs for fostering the development of and sustaining the activities of community organizations is necessary (Silverman & Patterson, 2004). Numerous studies show that the lack of effective social capital in low-income communities is to a large extent due to hostile actions by those in power (Lopez & Stack, 2001; Wacquant, 1998). Studies focused on development also find that institutional and structural factors account for much of the difficulty that low-income communities have in institutionalizing grassroots efforts in order to bring about radical change (Peruzzotti & Smulovits, 2002; Portes & Landolt, 2000; Stahler-Sholk, Vanden, & Kuecke, 2008). In the United States, a lack of institutional support for social capital has been shown to have negative consequences for collective action (Cohen, 2001).

We begin, then, by framing life in New Orleans through what the narratives of those who evacuated to Austin revealed about the social capital of their old neighborhoods. We relate the concept to individual resilience and potentially effective civil society action to enhance social capital (Cohen, 2001). The appeal of a social capital analysis for our purposes resides in its emphasis on collective attributes that are historically and structurally determined and that go beyond labor market phenomena. Our objective is not only to document the plight of the survivors, but to understand it theoretically in terms of the institutional and community context in which the evacuation occurred.

Social capital has been conceptualized and operationalized in many ways. We focus on the nature of the interconnections inherent in social networks as well as the material, social, and political resources that they make available. Our interviews revealed that social capital, characterized by the strong bonds among family members and neighbors who defined community in New Orleans, was not readily transferrable to Austin and that in the absence of other resources, families had a difficult time establishing new connections. We have no truly objective measures of social capital and rely on narrative material to infer its presence and assess how it operated for individuals and groups in specific settings. Clearly such an approach involves judgment and interpretation and the possibility that what we see as social capital someone else might interpret as something else. Narrative, though, provides insights that are impossible to obtain with purely quantitative approaches, and as we explained in the methodological discussion, data collection in emergency situations cannot be structured in accordance with textbook prescriptions.

Our approach also allows us to explore how racism undermines the effectiveness of social capital for a large group of Americans, particularly in the context of displacement. A number of theoretical concepts are useful in conceptualizing and understanding social capital and a group's ability or inability to translate it into political power. Mark Granovetter has offered a useful characterization of the nature of connections among people in different networks that reflects what we might describe as their degree of supportive intimacy and informational access (Granovetter, 1973). He refers to relationships among people as ties, and characterizes them as strong or weak. Strong ties are the emotionally and materially supportive relationships that one has with intimates, such as family members and close friends. These are the sorts of relationships that one relies upon on a daily basis and that provide essential social and material support. Weak ties refer to less intimate and intense relationships with acquaintances, members of professional organizations, business contacts, or the friends of friends. Such ties are useful in making contacts with other individuals and organizations at a distance.

Clearly, any one tie might have aspects of each, but the conceptual distinction is useful in framing the situation of low-income communities. Another way of characterizing the nature of interactions and ties among group members and the members of other groups or society at large is in terms of their bonding or bridging characteristics (Agnitsch, Flora, &

Ryan, 2006; Putnam, 2000). Bonding social ties are exclusive; that is, they define the in-group. To use Robert Putnam's characterization, these are inward looking and tend to reinforce exclusivity and homogeneity (Fiorina, 1999). Examples include ethnic fraternal organizations, church-based women's groups, and exclusive country clubs. Groups such as the Ku Klux Klan and the American Nazi Party are examples of the most extreme negative manifestations. Closely knit communities, to the extent that they provide material and emotional support to low-income families, are clear examples of bonding (Agnitsch, Flora, & Ryan, 2006; Stack, 1974). Among low-income families, such bonding ties are necessary for survival and, among other benefits, they provide rich information about dealing with governmental and nongovernmental organizations.

Bridging ties, on the other hand, look outward toward other individuals and groups and bring together people from different social locations. Examples include the civil rights movement, ecumenical religious organizations, Internet chat rooms, among others. As with Granovetter's weak ties, bridging relationships potentially put individuals and groups in contact with a far wider range of individuals and organizations. These ideally include ties to influential individuals with economic and political power of the sort that is necessary to allow social capital to be translated into the human, financial, and cultural capital that we mentioned earlier. Organizations or groups can have aspects of both bonding and bridging ties. African American religious congregations, for example, can bring together people of the same race but of different social classes. It is perhaps this characteristic that has made the black church so important in increasing the social capital of African American communities (Foley, McCarthy, & Chaves, 2001).

THE TRANSPORTABILITY OF SOCIAL CAPITAL

In the context of the post-Katrina evacuation, a major theoretical consideration is the transportability of social capital, that is, the extent to which it can it be taken with one when one moves to a new place, as the survivors in our study were forced to do. Granovetter's conceptualization of strong and weak ties takes us a good way toward framing the question theoretically and operationally. Strong ties – those based on kinship, residential propinquity, and close interaction – are almost by definition tied to place. For individuals without the resources to travel often and far, networks of strong ties are local and could be transplanted only by moving the entire group of network members. It might also require moving aspects of the physical and cultural environment in which those strong ties operated in the original location. An individual or family that is removed physically from a familiar location with its familiar institutional and cultural ecology and moved without family or neighbors to a new location is truly deracinated and may not be able to grow new roots and thrive in new soil.

Networks of weak ties are by definition more diffuse and not confined to a particular location. Networks of professional contacts and business associates can be national and even international in their reach, and cell phones, the Internet, and other media make contact among members easier. A move by any network member has little impact on his or her ability to contact associates. In addition to having a greater number of weak ties, individuals with high levels of human capital – as in the case of the couple we mentioned at the beginning of the last chapter, both of whom were physical therapists – find it easier to rebuild social capital in the new location. Rather than transporting the social capital that was defined by the old location, successful relocation requires finding or constructing new sources of social capital. As the cases that we present in the following chapters show, social capital for individuals with low levels of education, limited job skills, and little cultural knowledge cannot be transported, and what these cases clearly illustrate is that those same individuals face major obstacles to developing new sources of social capital.

The nature of the migration experience itself presents a related and highly salient theoretical and practical issue. The more disadvantaged survivors in our study were mostly involuntary migrants. We might categorize them as internally displaced persons, a term employed by the United Nations and others to distinguish individuals who are forced from their homes but who do not cross international borders from international refugees (OCHA, 2010). Internally displaced persons, like refugees, differ significantly from voluntary migrants (Hathaway, 2007; Larrance, Anastario, & Lawry, 2007; Porter & Haslam, 2005; Weiss, 2003). Even the citizens of poor countries who migrate seeking a better life in a richer country usually have some control over the process and, as in the case of illegal immigrants from Mexico, they often have contacts in the host country (Aguilera & Massey, 2003; Munshi, 2003; Portes & Bach, 1985). Such networks represent a very useful form of social capital. Many, if not most, of the involuntary migrants in our study had little control over the migration experience and arrived in a situation in which there was no one who had come before them to test the waters or establish a home base for themselves and others. Again, the few cases of survivors with contacts outside Louisiana who were able to evacuate themselves were the exception. Given their greater resources, these individuals displayed many of the characteristics of voluntary migrants.

AGENCY AND STRUCTURE

In attempting to understand the sources of social capital and why certain groups lack the capacity to improve their lot, we relate the concept of social capital to the parallel concepts of "agency" and "structure" again to better understand the institutional forces that placed the low-income residents of New Orleans in such a vulnerable situation. In social theory, agency refers to humans' ability to exercise their free will and engage in instrumental action, both individually and collectively, to control their lives and influence institutional arrangements in their own interest (Ritzer, 2008; Ritzer & Gindoff, 1994). Effective agents are individuals and groups who have the power and freedom to control their lives and to engage in advocacy for political objectives, to advance basic human rights, to change laws, and more.

Structure, on the other hand, refers to the wide range of factors, such as social class, income, wealth, education, religion, gender, ethnicity, and norms, that limit the ability of individuals or groups to act as autonomous agents. In the case of New Orleans, the multiple race-based handicaps faced by low-income African Americans represented structural barriers that have historically undermined their ability to control their lives or change the fundamental economic and political rules of the game. This structural social vulnerability, and not just the structural vulnerability of the levees, was the core reason that low-income neighborhoods faced an elevated risk of disaster as the result of the storm, and it helps to explain why the residents of these neighborhoods had fewer resources for recovery than more affluent residents of white neighborhoods. Modern social theorists have pointed out that agency and structure are conceptually or practically intertwined and that it is pointless to attempt to isolate either (Berger & Luckman, 1966; Bourdieu, 1977; Giddens, 1986). From this perspective, agents can act only in relation to structures and in doing so reaffirm or redefine them. Racism is institutionalized at multiple levels and it undermines individuals' and groups' capacity to act to end it, creating what some have described as a culture of poverty or an underclass mentality.

We bring up the issue of agency and structure to emphasize the fact that humans' ability to affect their worlds is constrained by historically determined factors outside of their control. This is a vitally important point, especially with reference to socially marginalized groups. Much public policy focused on low-income people, including the War on Poverty, is aimed at changing individual behavior and ignores the structures that undermine individual or group efforts. Programs such as Head Start, Upward Bound, and the Job Corps were based on laudable desires to improve the situations of low-income people, but they did not address the fundamental educational, labor force, and residential problems that undermine individual efforts to get ahead and make such efforts appear useless to those they are intended to help in the first place (Germany, 2007; O'Connor, 2002). Conceptions such as the underclass and the culture of poverty are based on observations of the extensive damage that poverty does to its victims, but such concepts are limited if they focus primarily on those victims and not the structures that account for their allegedly pathological and self-destructive behaviors.

STRUCTURAL VULNERABILITIES IN NEW ORLEANS

In the wake of its tremendous destruction, Hurricane Katrina exposed the multilayered structural disadvantages that low-income African Americans faced in New Orleans, as they do in all major American cities. Our basic question has to do with whether and to what extent local collective action by individuals themselves or more formal nongovernmental organizations compensated at least to some degree for the structural disadvantages this population faced in the period before the storm and how it operated during the immediate crisis. We are also interested in the importance of formal governmental supports and social policy for fostering and sustaining social capital. To do so, we examine accounts of the support systems that our survivors who arrived in Austin drew upon in New Orleans. These narrative data, provided by survivors who we interviewed in Austin after they had evacuated, reflect their memories and subjective assessments and are not based on a detailed examination of the city by outside observers. In later chapters, we will investigate the extent to which civil society organizations facilitated survivors' ability to rebuild aspects of community and to get back on their feet in a new and very unfamiliar city.

Pre-Katrina New Orleans was the product of a history of slavery and a post-Reconstruction Jim Crow social and legal order (Campanella, 2007; Fussell, 2007; Germany, 2007). The neighborhoods that many of the survivors were forced to evacuate reflected the economic and social marginality of one of the most segregated cities in the country. The exclusion of this population from the economic mainstream resulted from a long history of institutionalized racism that reached from the local level to the highest levels of government (Berube & Katz, 2005; Colten, 2006; Dyson, 2006; Fussell, 2007; Henkel, Dovidio, & Gaertner, 2006; Lavelle & Feagin, 2006; Lipsitz, 2006). After Reconstruction, the committee structures of the U.S. Senate gave southern states disproportionate power. Southern senators dominated key committees and blocked socially progressive legislation, including antilynching legislation, that would have benefited southern rural African Americans, who remained little more than indentured servants (Alston & Ferrie, 1993; Finley, 2008; Orloff, 1988).

This power along with local Jim Crow laws and the principle of state's rights denied African American residents basic civil rights, educational opportunities, and equal pay and left them ghettoized in low-income, racially segregated neighborhoods. In the case of New Orleans, those neighborhoods were the most vulnerable to the storm's ravages (Germany, 2007; Quadagno, 1994; Weir, Orloff, & Skocpol, 1988; Wilson, 1987). A concentration of victims of Katrina were low-income African Americans and most lived in the impoverished Lower Ninth Ward (Henkel, Dovidio, & Gaertner, 2006; Lavelle & Feagin, 2006). Among the victims, those who suffered most were single women with children, renters and those living in older housing, and those with no vehicles with which to flee the storm (Frey & Singer, 2006).

Like many other American cities, New Orleans was characterized by concentrated urban poverty largely reflecting its racial ecology (Germany, 2007; Landphair, 2007). Although all major cities experience serious urban problems, New Orleans stands out among major urban areas. In 2005, on the eve of the storm, nearly a quarter of the city's residents lived below the poverty line, compared to only 13 percent of the country as a whole. Nearly 18 percent of residents had not completed high school, a figure higher than the nearly 16 percent for the country as a whole, and while the median household income for the nation was $46,242, in New Orleans it was only $30,711 (Fussell, 2007). These figures were even worse for the city's African American population and clearly accounted for their elevated risk (Berube & Katz, 2005). Nearly 80 percent of New Orleans' minority population lived in the flooded areas. Only half of the white population lived in vulnerable areas. The average household income of those living in the flooded areas was $17,000 less than that of those who lived on higher ground, a huge difference given the city's low median household income (Berube & Katz, 2005). Despite these high levels of poverty and need, Louisiana has very restrictive eligibility and benefit policies for social services. Prior to Katrina, approximately 85 percent of low-income Louisiana families that were income eligible for TANF did not receive benefits (Winston et al., 2006).

It is clear from the statistics, then, that New Orleans had more than its fair share of social problems and that these problems disproportionately affected the African American population. Yet as ethnographers have documented, poverty and adversity give rise to community and group strategies for survival (Edin & Lein, 1997; Stack, 1974). This appears to have been true in New Orleans as well. Juliette Landphair notes that the historical geographic isolation and social marginalization of the Lower Ninth Ward fostered the development of close-knit and connected communities (Landphair, 2007). Many of those residents had never left the city before they were boarded on buses and airplanes bound for Texas and beyond. Although we heard of many problems from the survivors, it was clear that New Orleans had been their home and most, although not all, longed for the deep familiarity of place.

SURVIVORS' STORIES OF NEW ORLEANS

For better or worse, the place in which one lives represents more than a mere geographical or physical location. One's sense of "place" reflects social relations that make up an integral part of one's sense of self (Chamlee-Wright & Storr, 2009; Falk, Hunt, & Hunt, 2006). Classical social theorists such as Charles H. Cooley and George H. Mead pointed out that the self is created reflexively in interactions with others in the social environment (Cooley, 1922; Mead, 1934). The survivors' accounts of life in New Orleans before the storm revealed the depth and complexity of the meaning that the city and their old neighborhoods held for them. Some memories were positive and others were more negative. The extent and nature of individuals' sense of "home" in New Orleans and their positive or negative feelings played an important role in their decision to return or not, and it also influenced how they reacted to their enforced stay in Austin.

The survivors' accounts of New Orleans also revealed very different senses of the institutional environment and the nature of the social capital that characterized their old neighborhoods. Many clearly longed for their old homes and the lives they had left behind. For these individuals, the loss of the familiar place and life contributed to ongoing depression and post-traumatic stress. For others who were less tied to their old environments, and perhaps even felt negatively toward them, the move came to be seen as an opportunity for a new start. As part of our interviews, we asked the survivors to describe their lives in New Orleans before Katrina and to tell us about their old neighborhoods. For most of them, these were the places in which they had lived their entire lives. From these interviews, we developed a picture of the organizational environment and social capital that characterized the old neighborhoods and some sense of the role of those organizations in daily life.

The survivors we interviewed reflected the different cultures and some of the different social strata of New Orleans. Most were African American, but we also interviewed four transplanted white artists and writers who had migrated to New Orleans because of its cultural appeal. We also interviewed fourteen Hispanics and two members of the Vietnamese community. The New Orleans that these survivors described was racially, culturally, and socially very different from what they encountered in Austin. One common theme that emerged in the interviews was a longing for the familiarity of the old communities, but nostalgia was also tempered by a realistic sense that crime and other problems were serious and had compromised the quality of life in those communities. The role of religion was another important theme. Church and congregations played important roles in the lives of many of our participants, and the church was clearly a central community organization. Two other major common themes related to the inadequate social service environment and the seriously inferior schools in New Orleans. Overall, the interviews revealed a complex set of organizational contacts and use among the former residents of the city.

A FAMILIAR AND UNIQUE ENVIRONMENT

The survivors' accounts of their lives before the storm focused heavily on themes of familiarity and the unique culture of New Orleans, as well as some negative aspects of life in their old communities. Jeri Anderson, a fifty-six-year-old African American woman, talked about the importance of family and friends. She told us that

…being in New Orleans…was great. Being around family and people because the neighborhood I lived in…I was living there for eighteen years and I knew everyone. Just, I mean, I might not have known their names but I knew faces.

Chantal Anderson, an African American woman in her late twenties who lived in the midcity area, also talked about the culture of mutual aid that was an important part of many people's lives in New Orleans. As she said,

I grew up in the projects. I went from the projects to my own house that I lived in for almost five years before the hurricane...it was a real nice area where everybody was a neighbor, like if somebody was sick, somebody else would come over and help you out...even when I had my second baby there, everybody used to come over there [and say,] "let me wash the clothes, wash the dishes," and stuff like that...everybody stayed together...I had a mechanic stay right next door. Anything I needed help with, I had my neighbors around.

Another survivor, Bret Carmelo, a twenty-seven-year-old white male, said of the city that it

...has...its own culture and its own ways. You get so settled in it, which is very unique and there is no other city really like it....Once you leave the city, it's like going to a different country....It's like everything is different outside, it's its own little world.

The city's unique cuisine was vivid in many participants' accounts, and almost all expressed a longing for the food. Whitney Morris, a forty-one-year-old African American female, said, "I'm telling you, I miss my bowl of crabs and crawfish." Mary Ann Hoskins, a white female in her midforties, had this to say:

New Orleans was magical, I can't believe I was so privileged to be there right before this happened. You'd walk down the street into the art galleries and there'd be Chagalls and Picassos in the art galleries....It's the best architecture in America....It was less segregated than I find Austin or almost any other city.

Whitney described her life in New Orleans as "beautiful," commenting on the spirit of the people there. She noted that,

...they have some real characters, they have spirit in New Orleans, good spirit, you know, people are together there, they have original people, I mean musicians are...phenomenal, and the food is good. The restaurants when you come, the people treat you with open arms like, as if you're family, you know....

Another survivor, Jeffery Adams, an African American parking lot supervisor in his thirties, vividly described the following scene:

In the French Quarter, it was just so...how would I say it, how would, it was just ...alive...but we had a lot of characters....You always had musicians playing down by the riverside, get nice pictures...sun setting behind a musician. There [were] always children tap dancing with Coke bottles under their tennis shoes. It was just so much of the culture side of it,...all the neon lights in the French Quarter areas,...the little stores and shops and the street cars. It was a, just a lot, you know. I kind of miss that at times.

CRIME

Yet beneath the familiar surface, the quality of life in low-income neighborhoods was compromised by crime. Many survivors mentioned crime as a serious problem. The facts justify their assessments. In 1994, New Orleans was identified as the murder capital of the world, and the high crime rate was clearly fueled by the city's lagging economy (Frailing & Harper, 2007). In 1994, the city had an overall unemployment rate of 9.5 percent, but for African Americans it was 15 percent (Fiorina, 1999). Some survivors we interviewed were aware of the crime, but for some reason they did not feel threatened by it. As one female survivor, Danika Knight, an eighteen-year-old African American woman, told us, "I miss where I stayed...because it was worry free, even though there was shooting and everything, but I never was in a gang or nothing, so I never had anything to worry about....So it was like worry free."

For most survivors, though, crime was a pervasive and negative part of life in the city. Antoinette Theroux, a twenty-four-year-old African American female, told us that in the ninth grade someone tried to kill her, so she didn't go back to school and never finished. She said, "It's just a rough life, you know, living in New Orleans like in the ghetto growing up, growing up watching your uncle getting killed, shit like that in front of you." Jewel Banks, a sixty-three-year-old African American female, described the atmosphere of crime in the projects where she raised her children:

...we knew the crime was high, because you could hear the police. You knew that there was a killing; there was gunshot because we would walk from one side of the project to another project to get to church. We would have to walk, many people that I knew, we would all get together and we would walk.

Some lucky residents were shielded from the crime. Bill Smith, a white professor in his late fifties, felt protected in the college's gated community, which had its own police force. He was an exception.

Some survivors told us about their own criminal behavior. Antoinette Theroux told us that she had become a prostitute at age thirteen and began smoking and dealing crack at fifteen. She told us that,

Before I steal from a person, if I need money...so bad, I [would] go in the streets, ...[I would] dance and if I don't make no money dancing, I prostitute....I had to prostitute to keep a, to keep a roof over my head. I had to prostitute for clothes and everything, you know. I [didn't] have no regular childhood....I took care of myself since I was twelve years old....

Antoinette spent three years in prison. Several other of our interviewees also admitted to criminal activities that often resulted in jail or prison. Needless to say, a serious criminal record made reestablishing oneself even more difficult.

Given the high levels of crime in the low-income neighborhoods of New Orleans, relations with the police were often strained. Linda Tompkins, a middle-aged African American woman, told this story about police harassment:

...One time, the police stopped me. Let me tell you what happened. When I was walking in the projects and the police stopped me and asked me if I had my ID with me. And I told him no. I was two and a half weeks from delivering my baby and I told him I didn't have my ID and he told me to get against the car. I told him, "Please, mister, I'm fixing to have my baby any day." [Inaudible] and he tell me, "What's your name?" So I told him. And, he called it in and I had a little misdemeanor and I told him I was about to have my baby in two weeks. He didn't have to take me to jail for nothing like that. So he took me to jail. Yes, and when he took me, my [blood] pressure went [up] and when he took me there [to the police station], they told him he had to take me to the hospital. It was five o'clock in the morning. He was getting off at six, and but, by my pressure going up, he had to take me to the hospital. He didn't know how long he was going to because that's how long they kept me there.

Some participants identified crime as a reason that they did not wish to return to New Orleans. Lynn Hughes, a sixty-two-year-old white female, told us that she had had her fill of New Orleans as a result of the filth, crime, and vulgarity. Other participants expressed a longing for aspects of their old city, but hoped to resettle in Austin. When asked whether he wanted to go back to New Orleans, Reggie Vinton, an African American male in his late forties, said,

...no, I like Texas, cause Texas is my dream you know....I was born and raised in New Orleans...you know I got tired of hearing that shooting. So corrupt there, you know. People, you got a lot of good people, but it was just, it was just, you know, this environment. I [was] born and raised [there] and it was just too much, you know. I could have been killed a couple times [by being] at the wrong place at the wrong time.

Some survivors attributed the crime to the tourist atmosphere of the city. Xia Baker, a thirty-three-year-old African American female, characterized New Orleans as "sin city." She told us that it was as if there was a party taking place twenty-four hours a day, seven days a week, and that this atmosphere often caused people to behave in irresponsible ways. Several survivors told us that there were stores on every corner where one could buy alcohol any time. Small businesses that sold alcohol were clearly a major component of the institutional environment.

Of course, there was always some major activity on Bourbon Street. Again, though, some survivors recalled the party atmosphere as negative. Alisha Bell, a twenty-three-year-old African American woman, told us, "...you can't have no fun in New Orleans. Everybody says it's a good fun place down in Bourbon town, but you [are not 100 percent sure] you going to make it back." Thomas Lawson, a sixty-one-year-old African American man, agreed, noting that, "yeah, it was another Sodom and Gomorrah, you know, because New Orleans, you know, people come there talking about Mardi Gras and the French Quarter, you know, all that's good, you know, but it's just a mess in New Orleans, you know."

Despite the concentrated poverty, crime, and other social disorganization that the survivors experienced on a daily basis in New Orleans, the neighborhoods in which they lived reflected high levels of solidarity and community identity. The familiarity of their old neighborhoods and the loss of the community they felt as part of the evacuation were reflected in the fact that nearly all of the participants described Austin as less friendly than New Orleans. Many of the survivors we interviewed had lived within walking distance of other members of their families in New Orleans. Some lived in multigenerational households that included grandparents, parents, and grandchildren. Often these houses had been in the family for generations. Samantha Bell, a thirty-nine-year-old African American woman offered one example. She referred to herself as "the old lady in the shoe," because she, her nine daughters, and six grandchildren lived together in a rented house in the seventh ward. She said she wanted "everybody at home." In such situations, tight social networks and mutual support were critical to basic survival, and the close interconnectedness of life in the neighborhood was clear from the survivors' accounts.

One young mother's experience in terms of the locations of the services that she needed in order to care for her children illustrates an important aspect of community. Chantal Anderson, who was introduced earlier, told us that in the morning she dropped her baby off at a nursery around the corner, while her six-year-old son had just started attending a kindergarten that was across the street from her own mother's house. When her son got out of school, he would go to his grandmother's house. She characterized the situation by saying that "...everything is convenient in New Orleans." Survivors also talked about being able to manage daily life without a car. Because of the density of the inner city, many walked or rode the bus. In Austin, bus service is much less available and because the city is spread out, walking to work or to the store is rarely a realistic option, especially in the outlying neighborhoods where many of the survivors were located.

Nearly all the survivors noted that the cost of living was lower in New Orleans than in Austin. Because housing was much less expensive there, it was possible to support a stable life working in the tourist industry or food service. Justine Betts and her husband, the couple we met at the beginning of Chapter 1, both worked at the same restaurant. As she described,

> ...when we get paid every week, she [their boss] would give us our check in cash every week. But he [her husband] has tip money coming home so it wasn't hard for us. It was easy. Every day he's bringing fifty, sixty, seventy hours of tips home. So, ya know, we made it off that and all the check went on our bill. And [inaudible], ya know, played around with work, ya know. Do little things, went out, eat dinner out sometimes, ya know? Then go shopping and buy a little outfit to put on, ya know, [inaudible] we still had our bills paid. We still had everything needed in our home....

Despite the lower cost of living, though, not everyone we interviewed was residentially or financially secure before the storm. One of our participants, Gary Lee, a forty-four-year-old white male who was somewhat anomalous in our sample, was homeless, and several others described very irregular incomes.

After their initial euphoria at safely arriving in Austin, the dramatic differences between the two cities rapidly became apparent and frequent comparisons with the old city were inevitable. Lynn Hughes, the sixty-two-year-old white female we introduced earlier, reacted to the slogan "Keep Austin Weird," the slogan that expresses Austinites' sense of their own uniqueness that one sees on bumper stickers and elsewhere, by saying, "...I think it is amazing that they have all of this "Keep Austin Weird." You don't know what weird is....Coming from New Orleans, you just don't know and I haven't seen anything weird yet, you know."

WORK

Most of the survivors we interviewed were either not in the labor force or employed in a variety of low-wage occupations in New Orleans before the storm. Most of those who worked were employed in food service, health care, cleaning, clerical work, or manual labor. Will Charleston, a thirty-one-year-old African American, was a cook at a New Orleans café, and Reggie Vinton, a forty-seven-year-old African American, had been a dishwasher at a restaurant. Whitney Morris, whom we met earlier, described finding a job as a waitress at a restaurant in New Orleans:

...So, after that I went to the [restaurant]. And that was my favorite place to eat, you know....I was about twenty-four, but, it was my favorite place, 'cause I like Italian food. So I just went there one day because I just liked it, the way the building looked, when I got inside, just loved the uniforms, I was like, "This is me." And it looked relaxing, and so like you're having fun, and you're moving around, too. You know, it's not just, you know, like your job.

Ten survivors worked as manual laborers. They worked in jobs such as lawn trimming, house painting, and janitorial services. Not all of our participants worked in the low-wage service sector, though. Seven were professionals, such as Ted Johnson and his wife, whom we met in the last chapter, and Bill Smith, the professor we introduced earlier in this chapter. Twenty-eight survivors had been out of the labor force, either because they were full-time students, stay-at-home parents, disabled, or retired. For the most part, though, the survivors were generally members of the working class and had been employed in jobs offering low wages, few benefits, and frequent turnover.

Employment patterns in New Orleans before the storm mirrored more general changes in the U.S. economy. Since 1964, New Orleans had experienced a dramatic decrease in high-paying manufacturing jobs, due in part to changes in the shipping industry, and a 200 percent increase in low-paying service sector jobs (Frailing & Harper, 2007). The increase in low-wage employment only exacerbated the serious race-based inequality. White workers earned twice as much as African Americans. Census data from 2000 indicated that in some of the poor neighborhoods in New Orleans, nearly 80 percent of the residents were not only unemployed, they had ceased looking for work.

CHURCH

The church had clearly been an important part of the survivors' lives in New Orleans, although church was more central to some than others. Twelve survivors mentioned attending church regularly and four more talked about being raised in the church, even though they had not been attending regularly. Jeri Anderson, introduced earlier, told us about her church in New Orleans. As she said,

...it was very unconventional,...it's not about money – it's about helping people....We would have homeless people come up, you might have to fan a little bit, but they was welcome, and we would have meals once a month and they was all welcome, and nobody looked at your shoes or, [whispers] "that lady she had that dress on last Sunday," it wasn't about that....And it was just about being yourself and helping people who needed help....

Susan Doyle, an African American woman in her late forties, also talked about being happy with her church in New Orleans and having a hard time replacing that relationship in Austin. She told us,

Well, I haven't gone to church after I've attended church in the beginning, I haven't found a church like that would interest me, you know, it's one God that we worship, but we do have a preference. I'm Catholic, and, I want to, um, I want to attend a Catholic religious church, and that's just the way I am, in New Orleans, you know, quite satisfied with our church, our Catholic church, and we had a shrine that we would go to and there was a chapel we would go to where you could light candles and, you know, light your candle, and say your prayer. You know, it was just a contentment in a way that we worshiped in New Orleans, that I don't find here, because I haven't found a church, and that's important to me.

For Huynh Vahn, a Vietnamese senior citizen, the church was the center of his community. As his translator relayed to us, "…it [was] exactly like a Vietnamese village, all the neighborhood and everybody [attended] the big Catholic church right there."

In addition to providing community and spiritual support, survivors also told us about churches providing material assistance. Louise Wilkins, whom we met in Chapter 2, told us about the assistance she received from St. Mary's Church: "Monday through Friday, you come to get bags of groceries and clothes and whatever you want to come in for. Or they help you pay bills or they help you find a job. Oh, they'll help you do a lot." Jewel Banks, a sixty-three-year-old African American female whom we mentioned earlier, told us that her involvement with the church helped keep her five sons out of trouble while she was raising them in a housing project. As she said, the neighborhood was dangerous:

So it was more like you would hear…all sorts of news about our project, a man got killed but still my kids and my life and the life of a lot of my associate church members [went on normally], we just communicated [and shared] dinners…so we stayed involved with activities that kept you away from the things that [were] depressing….

It was clear that within the organizational ecology of the New Orleans neighborhoods from which the survivors came, churches and congregations were important for many and provided for the social, spiritual, and sometimes the material needs of their parishioners.

SCHOOLS AND SEGREGATION

New Orleans is notorious for having one of the worst public school systems in the country. Only 44 percent of fourth graders and 26 percent of eighth graders could read at grade level based on data from standardized tests. Nearly three-quarters of the schools in the city had been rated academically unacceptable in the 2004–5 school year (Hill & Hannaway, 2006). As a result of years of corruption and mismanagement, the district was facing a $25 to 30 million deficit for the 2005–6 school year (Hill & Hannaway, 2006). The student/teacher ratio was higher than the national average and white flight was both a cause and consequence of poor school performance. During the previous thirty-five years, district enrollment had gone from approximately 70 percent African American and 36 percent low-income to 93 percent African American and 80 percent low-income as more and more affluent families fled to private or charter schools (Casserly, 2006). At the time of the hurricane, 40 percent of New Orleans students were in parochial schools (Hill & Hannaway, 2006).

Although we do not have many first-person accounts of school experiences from young people in our data, one young African American woman, Danika Knight, whom we met earlier, was in the tenth grade in New Orleans at the time of the storm, and she told us about some of her school experiences. She said that she had failed the standardized tests in both the fourth and eighth grades. According to her account, she had both positive and negative experiences in the public schools, as the following exchange with the interviewer reveals:

Interviewer: What was school like in New Orleans?
Danika: My first two years at, I went to [inaudible] high school, it was fun, very fun, I liked it very much, as far as the teachers, I liked how they was working, how they was doing their work; my last two years it was boring.
Interviewer: Why boring?
Danika: Because [I] had switched to another school.
Interviewer: Was it boring socially or academically...?
Danika: Both, it was just boring, I was just bored, that's why I didn't want to go, but I said I was going.
Interviewer: Do you think you learned what you should have learned at school?
Danika: Yes, I did. Most people say...school wasn't teaching, but...mine was, I know that....They taught what they were supposed to teach.

However, she felt that the schools did not prepare students for the standardized Louisiana Educational Assessment Program (LEAP) tests. She explained that the schools did not teach the subjects that were on the test:

Danika: On that thing [the LEAP test], they might have geometry, algebra; they probably have all kinds of subjects that they didn't teach us, so you're gonna flunk if you [are not] learning.
Interviewer: It seems like a lot of people would flunk that test.
Danika: Yeah, everybody in our school, probably four people might make it, out of the whole school…[none of] the seniors would [ever] pass.
Interviewer: Did a lot of people not ever graduate?
Danika: No, I have a friend right now she just stopped, it's designed to make you drop out. A lot of my friends right now, they just dropped out.

Danika told us that there were no books in the classroom and it was only in the last two years that her school had gotten computers. She said that discipline was lax and students wandered in and out of the classrooms. The teachers did not feel that the students were serious and Danika felt that they lost interest in teaching. Danika also told us about the danger posed by other students:

Danika: Whatever come[s] to their [student's] mind, they're gonna say it, in the classroom, if it start[s] a conflict or what. So if you get in a fight, you're gonna be half-dead before they [teachers] come because they scared [themselves].
Interviewer: Were there a lot of guns…?
Danika: Yeah, we had metal detectors when we first walk in our school, they take your purse and search it, they make you run through a metal detector, they search us three times.

Antoinette Theroux, whom we met earlier, told us how her education was cut short by violence:

…I dropped out. Really, in the sixth grade, they skipped me, they skipped me to the seventh. I went there. I graduated seventh, seventh grade. Went there to eighth, I failed eighth grade. They skipped me again to ninth grade. Went to ninth grade, I had somebody try to kill me and I ain't been to school since, you know.

Another survivor, Will Charleston, a thirty-one-year-old African American, also recounted his experience of violence as a student. He dropped out of the ninth grade. He received his general equivalency diploma (GED) certificate while he was in the hospital after being shot in the leg. The potential for violence also forced Jewel Banks, a sixty-three-year-old African American female, to consider moving. She had raised her five sons in the projects and had kept them safe and away from bad influences with the help of her church. However, she told interviewers that when her sons became teenagers, she felt that she had to move in order to protect them.

A number of survivors commented on racial issues in New Orleans. A twenty-six-year-old African American female, Kita Godwin, claimed that there were not as many racial issues as people imagined in New Orleans. Mary Hoskins, whom we met earlier, said, "it was less segregated than I find Austin or almost any other city." A white couple, Louise Davidson and Nicholas Goldstein, noted that Austin was more segregated than New Orleans. Davidson noted of New Orleans that, "there is really no segregation in neighborhoods or anything. It's like, good block, bad block, rich block, poor block, and everybody's mixed in with everybody else. Not like here."

SOCIAL SERVICES AND HEALTH CARE

The survivors differed a great deal in their perceptions of the availability of various social services in New Orleans. Some felt that there were more services there than in Austin, while other felt the opposite. Mary Powers, an African American female in her forties whom we met in Chapter 3, told us that,

New Orleans was a party city, it was more fun, you can never say you're bored, even if you is bored, there's something, some type of action going on, some type of party, you know, somebody giving a party, going out to clubs, things like that, it was fun, as far as helping wise, you had to do that on your own, get a job on your own, had to, you know, you need food, you got to get it on your own, there was no place you could go to get food, you know, things like that run out, you had to do things on your own.

These perceptions are reflected in administrative and statistical evidence. In 2002, Louisiana ranked near the bottom among states in terms of its fiscal capacity and, consequently, on spending on safety-net programs (Yilmaz et al., 2006; Zedlewski, 2006). As a consequence, many single mothers, unemployed older individuals, and individuals with disabilities remained in poverty (Zedlewski, 2006). Although welfare caseloads dropped by two-thirds between 1996 and 2003 in response to welfare reform, because of a lack of work experience, low education, and other problems in addition to a lack of employment services, many of those who left the rolls remained unemployed and had to manage without a safety net (Zedlewski, 2006).

Prior to the storm, Louisiana had among the highest food stamp participation rates in the country, and over 80 percent of school-age children received free or subsidized school breakfasts and lunches. New Orleans' Housing Authority was one of the worst in the country. The residential facilities that it operated were plagued by high levels of crime and high vacancy rates. Many included abandoned units (Popkin, Turner, & Burt, 2006; Zedlewski, 2006). As a consequence of the lack of public housing, more than half of very low-income families paid more than half of their incomes for housing, a rate higher than in other cities (Popkin, Turner, & Burt, 2006). Even those who owned their homes, though, were unlikely to have flood insurance and many found it impossible to rebuild after Katrina.

Many of the survivors we interviewed reported receiving some sort of federally subsidized assistance, including food stamps, housing assistance, and Medicaid, before the storm. In most cases, we do not have a lot of information about survivors' experience of these programs.

Louisiana had one of the highest rates of persons without health insurance in the country due in part to low rates of employer-sponsored coverage by small businesses in the service and tourism industries, high rates of unemployment, and limited Medicaid coverage (Rudowitz, Rowland, & Shartzer, 2006). The city had a two-tiered health care system in which those with public or private health insurance had access to community hospitals while those without coverage received care in one of the state-run safety-net hospitals operated by Louisiana State University. Charity Hospital, the flagship hospital of that system, accounted for 83 percent of all uncompensated inpatient and 88 percent of all uncompensated outpatient care. It was also the only large trauma center on the Gulf Coast and provided most of the psychiatric, substance abuse, and HIV/AIDS care in the city. We asked Mary Powers when she first received Medicaid:

Powers: I was in the hospital when I got my Medicaid. That was when I had my children, after I had my children. I signed up right now.
Interviewer: And which was the hospital that you would go to?
Powers: Mother Charity. Charity Hospital, we call it Mother Charity because that where everybody go.
Interviewer: Alright, Charity Hospital. And would you go there, um, when you had your babies?
Powers: To have babies, cut wounds, shot wounds, Charity was the place.

With such limited options for uninsured persons, Gary Lee, a forty-four-year-old white male who was suffering from post-traumatic stress disorder (PTSD) and depression, talked about the challenges of getting medications:

I had to go once over there [Charity Hospital] to get medication. See, the thing was is that in November of 2003, I had lost my job. Things were real slow for them [his employer] and things like that, they ended laying people off, and like that. I was being treated then, but the company didn't know anything about it. I was going to see the doctor but I was masking it because I was afraid that if they knew that I was taking medication for depression and so forth like that, that they would just let me go. And so when I lost that job, I went looking for work. But...I had filled out application after application, I mean, for the longest time, just never could find any work. I ended up homeless and on the street. That was on the West Bank of the river, over in Jefferson Parrish. And I ended up, I had to go to New Orleans to live, as a homeless male, because there were no clinics or anything, there was no homeless shelters for men in Jefferson Parish, on the West Bank of the river. So there I am, downtown New Orleans, living in the French Quarter, living in the shelters, the homeless shelters, and like that. But my doctor is on the West Bank. Ten miles I had to go walk to go see my doctor. If I wanted to see my doctor, I had to walk ten miles. That went on for the longest time. So I was getting my medication then sporadically, and like that.

THE NEW CITY

As the survivors' narratives reveal, the neighborhoods in which they lived in New Orleans consisted of vibrant, supportive communities, although they were plagued by serious social problems, including crime, poor schools, and inadequate social services. The familiarity of the old neighborhoods and the city was a recurrent theme in the survivors' accounts. Their stories reflected the human tendency to endow a certain place with the special identity of home. That familiarity included social relationships and the local institutions, such as the church. When the survivors were forced to leave, often literally without the opportunity to pack their bags, they abruptly lost their ties to the old physical locations and the relationships that defined their communities. Regardless of their opinion about the old city, learning to navigate a new and unfamiliar environment proved to be a challenge. Although most survivors arrived in Austin with very little material or social capital, some had higher levels of education and more intact families than others. As we will see in later chapters, these resources resulted in a different incorporation experience in Austin than was experienced by those who arrived with fewer resources. Perhaps reflecting differences in material and social capital, some found the new environment very foreign and felt unwelcome in Austin. Others did not have the interpersonal skills required to forge new ties and adapt to a new environment. A few made new lives for themselves and their families and made a successful transition to Austin. In the next chapter, we will recount the survivors' experiences when they arrived in their new city.

4

Evacuation and Arrival in Austin

In October 1998, Hurricane Mitch, a category five storm, killed more than eleven thousand people and left millions homeless in Honduras, Nicaragua, Guatemala, and El Salvador. Twelve years later in January 2010, a magnitude seven earthquake struck Haiti ten miles west of Port-au-Prince, causing thousands of deaths and leaving millions more homeless. These were but two of numerous natural and man-made disasters that have cost the lives and livelihoods of millions of people all over the world in the recent past. Despite their differences, though, disasters share one common feature: they cause the greatest suffering among those who have the fewest possibilities of escape and the fewest resources with which to recover. It may not be surprising that this is the case in the developing world or in an impoverished nation such as Haiti, but as we showed in the last chapter, it was also true in New Orleans. In Louisiana, the suffering of those who were most affected cannot be attributed solely to nature's wrath; it was an almost inevitable result of governmental policies that placed the victims in harm's way, that left them with few avenues of escape, and that undermined an adequate governmental and civil society response to the longer-term crisis.

Economic crises, like disasters, also take their greatest toll on those with the fewest resources, whose vulnerability is largely determined by governmental policies. In the wake of the debt crises that racked Latin America in the 1980s, lending institutions, including the International Monetary Fund and governments in rich lending nations, forced drastic macroeconomic adjustment policies on the affected nations. In addition to market and currency reforms, these included sharp cuts in public spending and social services (Brown & Hunter, 1999; Thorp, 1998). The result was the loss of the minimal safety net upon which the most disadvantaged citizens relied. Although serious fiscal austerity and retrenchment may be unavoidable economic realities when dealing with major economic crises, as in the case of disasters, the pain is never borne equally by everyone; the rich never make the same proportionate sacrifice as the poor. As in Latin America, the serious underfunding of public programs that has occurred in the United States in recent years has inevitably had its greatest impact on those most dependent on public programs. As we showed in the last chapter, the race and class dimensions of the impact of the storm revealed the historical and structural sources of group vulnerability.

In this chapter, we review the survivors' experiences during and immediately following the storm and examine their arrival in Austin, Texas, one of the several cities to which they were sent. The stories reveal the collapse of social order and civil society in the flooded neighborhoods in New Orleans for days after the storm. Neither government nor civil society organizations were prepared for the magnitude of the crisis. In the immediate aftermath of the storm, the survivors found themselves struggling for survival in a situation with no rules or effective authority. They survived in groups in which they provided mutual assistance. Some were forced to step beyond the law to find food and supplies. In such a situation, one has only oneself and one's immediate network upon which to rely.

After they were evacuated to Austin, the difficulty that those who did not immediately return to New Orleans faced in reestablishing themselves in a new city further revealed the structural sources of their vulnerability. Their difficulties clearly exposed the local and nontransportable nature of the strong bonding ties they had in New Orleans. Those ties had defined their old neighborhoods and were vital in daily survival, but they were almost completely destroyed by the storm. As we will see, those few families with more extensive bridging ties and greater human capital fared much better. In this chapter, we examine the efforts of civil society organizations and individuals to help the survivors find shelter, work, medical care, schools for their children, and the other necessities of a stable life, and we explore the ways in which the efforts of these organizations were affected by the bureaucratic rules, regulations, and policies of federal and state agencies. As we show, those rules, regulations, and policies seriously limited the ability of nongovernmental actors to improve significantly the survivors' situations.

After the survivors arrived in Austin, FEMA continued to play a major role in their recovery since it had formal authority and the greatest financial resources. The agency was immediately and widely criticized for a slow and inadequate response in New Orleans and for an overly bureaucratic and uncoordinated response in the cities to which survivors evacuated. Few outside of the Bush administration defended the government's initial response, but the first week after the storm is not our primary interest here, except insofar as the initial response illustrates the inability of either the state or civil society to respond to disasters in the absence of adequate governmental preparedness. In the weeks, months, and years following the evacuation, the criticisms of FEMA's often cumbersome and bureaucratic procedures only increased. As we will see, those procedures were difficult for the survivors, governmental employees, and potential nongovernmental help providers to comprehend. The lesson learned was that volunteers or communities cannot effectively respond to a crisis or to the longer-term needs of vulnerable groups in an organizational and leadership vacuum. The responsibility for responding to large-scale crises cannot be devolved to local or civil authorities. The situations in New Orleans immediately after the storm and the survivors' experiences in Austin illustrate one of the basic lessons that we learned from this study: Civil society organizations cannot operate effectively except in conjunction with an effective state.

THE DAYS BEFORE THE EVACUATION

The accounts by survivors of the days prior to their evacuation reveal certain common themes related to the flood and the events immediately following it: the chaos and danger that accompanied the breakdown of civil order; feelings of abandonment; fear of their rescuers; and a profound sense of uncertainty about where they would finally end up. The story of Whitney Morris, an African American female we first met in Chapter 3, was typical. Like most of the others who were unable to evacuate before the storm, she and her family survived the hurricane only to face a larger disaster. Whitney's story begins after the hurricane had passed but before anyone had realized that the levees had failed. Her story, like many accounts that appeared in the media, is filled with graphic accounts of violent acts, including rapes and murders at the Superdome and the Convention Center, some supposedly committed by military rescuers. Many of those accounts were contested in later reports by the media (Barsky, Trainor, & Torres, 2006; Brasch, 2006), and it is impossible for us to know the extent to which what we heard from survivors was based on firsthand experience or reflected the sorts of rumors that are typical in confusing and fearful situations. What is clear, though, is that most survivors to whom we spoke told us of having witnessed such things and they had clearly been traumatized to varying degrees.

Whitney was one of those, and we present a summary of her account of conditions at the Convention Center immediately after the storm. In Whitney's words, immediately after the storm,

[There] was four feet of water in our area then, so we were thinking, well, the water's going to go down, it's just flooding, it's going to go down...but [I saw] it was rising more and more, so...I told my momma, you know, we got to get out of here, the water's getting higher. And [at] that point the radio...was saying if you can get to the Convention Center or whatever because the levees [have] broken and the waters are rising....Well my mom, being an elderly woman, [said], "I'm not going anywhere, I'm going to stay right here...." So [I said], "Mom, the water's getting really higher."...my other sisters and brothers and everybody [were] there....I had my daughter and my grandson, he was only...one year old then, and...I took a blow-up mattress and put him on it and my daughter...was holding on and we tried to tread the water to higher ground. About twelve hours later, we made it there [to the Convention Center], and it was no better there, because [there] was no light, no air, it was hot, no food, no water...some people [were] panicking, people [were] dying, they had dead bodies all around the Convention Center, elderly people dead in their wheelchairs because they didn't have medication and water – nothing, we had no help...it was just a disaster...[there were] people getting raped, killed, shooting, killings, people were panicking, breaking into buildings just to find food and water ... some people made it bad for everybody....So we sat there for four days...so then the military came and that's when they...killed a few people that was trying to jump on the helicopters...they were out of control and they had to do what they had to do to get order, so they got some kind of order and after that, they served us food, they were giving out food at different stations, the little military packets...and that was good...but, after the third day I was kind of panicking...because it was like, "Oh, God, not another day." Because at that time, people [were] making bowel movements everywhere, you couldn't wash...it was just getting hectic. It was like, you know, they're going to leave us here to die or something....So I'm just thinking how can they not see this happening, see us on camera? I see helicopters passing but no one's coming to rescue us. So I was just basically wondering why [it was] taking so long to rescue us. You know, it was just unbelievable they took four days to rescue us out of there...and then the fact that when they came they were only taking ten people at a time in the helicopter and they had millions of people there, you know, and [we] had to stand in line to be rescued. So, they took us to airports once we got to New Orleans Armstrong Airport, they had different airlines taking us different places, so you never knew where you were going.

Several other survivors provided accounts of having to wade through deep, fetid water for hours while caring for others, including older people and children. Almost all reported seeing dead bodies and being afraid of drowning or other dangers in the water. They experienced hunger, dehydration, and illness as a result of being out in the elements for days. They also recounted the horrific sights they were exposed to as they waded toward what they hoped was safety.

Many survivors told us about their own behavior in making a way for themselves and their families. When families exhausted their supplies of food and water, they had to find provisions wherever they could. For many individuals, this involved stealing and even robbery. Lamont Brown was one of several African American men who reported looting and committing acts of violence to feed his family. He had planned to evacuate with his fiancé, but her mother convinced them not to leave. They stayed in the fiancé's second-floor apartment for five days until they lost power and the roof collapsed as a result of the heavy rain. Other family members and friends came to the apartment seeking shelter, and at one point there were eighteen people who sought shelter there. When the food ran out, Brown stole food. He told us that he did not want to loot, but that he had no choice. In addition to food, he looted a Family Dollar store for a barbeque grill to cook on. He also tried to break into a pawn shop for a generator, but encountered men with guns. Brown told us that he shot a man while taking food from a grocery store with police officers present. He said that conditions got worse as time went on and the violence increased. He said that at one point he helped police pull twenty-five bodies out of the grocery store. He said that they had been shot.

Xia Baker, a thirty-three-year-old African American woman whom we first met in Chapter 3, also told us about looting to get food during the six days that she, her husband, and children were living on the I-10 bridge. As she recounted the experience,

> ...eating out the damn gutter in the trash is how we fed them for six days. If you passed a store, you might see something and [decide I'm] going to get it...too, my children [were] hungry. You know what I'm saying, if...the store...ain't got no windows or nothing and I see they got food...if there's a can good, I'm going in there and get it because I have a knife. I'm able to open it, eat it out the can, we [are] all soldiers now, you know what I'm saying, you have to do what you have to do to survive and make it.

Several survivors told us about feeling abandoned by those who were supposed to rescue them. John Washington, a fifty-five-year-old African American male who lived in a complex with about six hundred people, told us that they had burned mattresses to attract the attention of helicopters that seemed to be passing them by. Helicopters seemed to play a prominent role in nearly all the stories we heard, and survivors told of seeing helicopters pass over without making any attempt to rescue them. Thomas Lawson, a sixty-one-year-old African American man we met in an earlier chapter, suggested that the stories of shots fired at helicopters that were often reported in the mainstream media were actually attempts to draw their attention. In addition to feeling abandoned, survivors reported fearing those who came to save them. The immediate response to the storm included the National Guard and was highly militarized; one survivor, Katherine Smith, a seventy-eight-year-old white woman, characterized the military presence as "like Hitler and Mussolini." John Washington told us that when rescuers finally arrived, "they" (we assume that it was the National Guard) made everyone lie on the ground and then put a gun to their heads. He also said that he was threatened and beaten by police as he tried to get supplies at the store. Many survivors reported being split up during the evacuation, sometimes forcibly. Xia Baker told us that she was threatened at gunpoint but refused to split up her family.

All of the chaos and uncertainty fueled insecurity and undermined any trust that might have existed. Although it was clear to everyone that evacuation was inevitable, survivors reported great uncertainty and fear of being evacuated into the unknown. They had virtually no control over their situations or their futures. Survivors who had not evacuated on their own before the storm generally had no choice as to where they were going. Most who came to Austin knew nothing about the city, nor did they know anyone who lived there. Charlotte Hendricks, a fifty-one-year-old African American woman, described the situation as follows:

When they put you on the bus, they didn't tell you [where you were going], they didn't know...themselves, they were like, "Yeah well, some of you guys go that way, some buses go that way," there was no destination. It was just trying to evacuate everyone out of the city as fast as they could in any direction that was available, so that's how it [was].

ACTS OF KINDNESS

Although not as common as stories of horror, abandonment, and terror, survivors also told stories of kindness and generosity by others. For example, Katherine Smith, who was living in a senior citizen complex, said, "I really enjoyed every minute of my experience, even though we, you know, were filthy dirty in the Convention Center and I had my first plane ride and I'm here...." She told of many acts of kindness during the evacuation. Smith refused to leave when her oldest son offered to evacuate her before the storm. She stayed in her apartment and went to a "hurricane party" with her neighbors in the complex. When their building flooded, she walked to the Convention Center with one of her neighbors and stayed with him there for about a week. She described many acts of kindness by people in the Convention Center, even though she too reported that there was much violence, attempted rape, and looting. She told us that she was "adopted" by several people there who helped her.

These differing accounts illustrate the fact that even though the circumstances in which they found themselves were largely similar, survivors experienced the situation very differently. After several days, Smith managed to get on a military helicopter to the New Orleans airport and was eventually transported to Austin. It is interesting how this survivor focused as much narrative on the kindness of people at the Convention Center as on the harshness and poor conditions. At one point, she characterized it as "the most wonderful experience in my life because we had a lot of good people." These accounts of kindness and mutual aid support previous findings that reveal remarkable adaptability, resilience, and prosocial behavior in communities afflicted by disaster (Brinkley, 2006).

THE EVACUATION

Since the storm, a large number of books have appeared that portray the human tragedy and that document FEMA's failed response in New Orleans (Brasch, 2006; Brinkley, 2006; Brunsma, Overfelt, & Picou, 2007; Cooper & Block, 2006; Dyson, 2006; Hartman & Squires, 2006; Horne, 2008; Van Heerden & Bryan, 2006; Zakin, McKibben, & Jordan, 2006). Here we focus on the accounts of the evacuation by survivors who arrived in Austin, Texas, one of the many cities to which survivors were sent. The majority of the survivors who we interviewed had been forcibly evacuated from New Orleans and they arrived in Austin by air or bus. Upon arrival, they were taken to the Austin Convention Center, where they received shelter and other services. Of the seventy-three survivors we interviewed, nineteen had evacuated before the storm. In two cases, it is unclear how the survivors arrived in Austin.

It is impossible to know how representative the individuals we interviewed were of survivors in general or how they differed from those who found themselves in other cities. Those who evacuated after the storm were not selected in any way that we are aware of to come to Austin. In all likelihood, they were a cross section of those who were evacuated and who did not immediately return. Although we cannot be certain of the generalizability of the experiences of those whom we interviewed, the stories we heard provide useful information about the reactions of individuals exposed to this sort of stress and their experiences mirror those of other reports that have appeared in the literature. The storm and the events that followed it were clearly traumatic and left long-term scars regardless of where the survivors went. Studies of their mental health reveal that many remained at elevated risk of post-traumatic stress disorder and other mental and physical health problems even a year after the event (Gautam et al., 2009; Kessler et al., 2006, 2008; Mills, Edmondson, & Park 2007; Weems et al., 2007; Weisler, Barbee, & Townsend, 2006). In many cases, the trauma of the storm added to preexisting mental health problems. Many of those evacuated to Austin had preexisting physical as well as mental health problems (Brodie et al., 2006). As we will discuss in detail in Chapter 8, individuals with preexisting mental health conditions often did not get the care that they needed, which seriously undermined their ability to recover and begin a new life in Austin.

With sufficient social and material resources, one has a good chance of coping with the trauma of a disaster and recovering quickly, but for most of our participants, the storm destroyed the neighborhoods and tore apart the social networks that defined them. The strong bonds that might have provided practical and emotional support were gone and individuals were literally uprooted.

In what follows, we focus on the survivors' accounts of their experiences of loss of connectedness to familiar environments and social institutions that defined the familiar communities in which they lived before the storm. Despite their poverty, the low-income African American residents of the Lower Ninth Ward lived in functioning communities (Landphair, 2007). These neighborhoods represented the familiar social and cultural environments in which they had learned to operate. They were an integral part of what theorists might call their lifeworld (Bourdieu, 1977; Habermas, 1984). One's lifeworld consists of the intersubjective reality that defines community and social life at the most basic level. It is made up of the mutual understandings, meanings, and norms that humans learn and internalize in the process of socialization. It is also defined by institutions, including the family, kin networks, churches, schools, and much more. These institutions give meaning to and define community for its members. The evacuation severed the survivors' ties to that lifeworld and required that they reconstruct a new one in a strange place. The success or failure of that process, and the role of larger social structures in facilitating or undermining it, is the subject of later chapters. First, though, we must set the stage by defining the lost lifeworld of the community residents who found themselves set completely adrift on such short notice.

In the following sections, we focus on the stories of the families who remained in New Orleans through the storm and were forcibly evacuated afterward to Austin, as well as the few families that we interviewed who evacuated themselves before the storm struck. The situations of these two sets of evacuees reflect more than differences in judgment or understanding of the risk. The choices that families made were rational in terms of the risk involved in leaving as well as staying. Their choices reflect huge differences in material and social resources that determined whether evacuation was practically possible or not. Without adequate transportation or friends and family members with whom one might stay in some other place, families' options were limited. Those who stayed lacked the money, cars, or credit that would have allowed them to evacuate quickly. In addition, although many of those who stayed had strong ties and dense social networks in New Orleans, a fact that may have influenced their decision to stay, they did not have the weak ties and extensive contacts outside of the city or the state that might have facilitated evacuation.

Data from the Current Population Survey (CPS) indicate that one and a half million people sixteen and older evacuated from Alabama, Mississippi, and Louisiana after Hurricane Katrina (Dyson, 2006). The demographic characteristics of those who left reflected the racial composition of those states: Roughly 65 percent were white and a third African American. By October 2006, over 70 percent of those evacuees had returned to their pre-storm addresses. However, over four hundred thousand had not returned to their previous residences. There were significant differences between those who returned and those who did not. Those most likely not to return included African Americans, young adults, and never-married individuals. The majority of the survivors who evacuated to Austin, and the majority of those we interviewed, were African American. Although their accounts of their evacuations had much in common, there were significant differences. Only nineteen of those we interviewed evacuated by car or bus before the storm. Of these, five were homeowners and six lived in private-market rental housing. All but three of those who left before the storm owned or had access to cars. Ray Lee, a middle-aged white man, was evacuated from a hospital; Will Charleston, a thirty-one-year-old African American cook, and Donald Klein, a self-employed, middle-aged white male, evacuated by bus.

Most of those who evacuated before the storm had friends or family in other places with whom they could stay. They differed from those who were forcibly evacuated in terms of financial resources, social networks outside of New Orleans, and transferable work skills. For example, Paul and Jacqueline were white homeowners in their fifties who evacuated before the storm with Mr. Richardson's elderly mother, who was also a homeowner. They stayed with friends in Houston for three weeks. With the help of his business partner, Mr. Richardson continued working from a distance to get his business reestablished. Mrs. Richardson found a professional job in Austin, so the Richardsons moved to Austin. They eventually decided to destroy their heavily damaged home in New Orleans.

THE DECISION TO STAY

In many cases, families or individuals who self-evacuated to Austin traversed a circuitous route and spent time in several other cities before arriving in Austin. Those who evacuated before the storm clearly had more choice in their final destination than did those who were part of the mass evacuation after the storm. The voluntary evacuees were more likely to call upon family, friends, and business associates outside of New Orleans, and they had a distinctly different experience from those who evacuated afterward. The majority of those families we interviewed were evacuated after the storm. Our interviews with them were filled with stories of family separation and the loss of the strong ties that had sustained them in New Orleans. A typical experience among this group was that of Cynthia Knight, a forty-year-old African American woman, who during our initial interview recounted the consequences of her decision to ride out the storm.

Cynthia and her family had stayed in their home in the Ninth Ward during many other storms and nothing serious had ever happened. They expected this storm to be no different. Once the water began to rise, though, it was clear that the situation was more serious than they had anticipated. When their house flooded, they went to a relative's home in a housing project on higher ground. However, that apartment eventually flooded as well, leaving Cynthia and her relatives stranded in deep water with hundreds of other people for several days. They were eventually rescued by civilians in boats, who took them to a Catholic school where they spent several more days on the roof with hundreds of others until they were rescued by helicopters and eventually brought to Austin. During the evacuation, members of Cynthia's family were separated. Her son, who is disabled, was airlifted to another city, where he still lives. Her mother, who had been a mainstay of the family, was evacuated to yet another city. Her eighteen-year-old daughter, Danika, whom we met earlier, evacuated with her boyfriend to yet another city. Cynthia and several other relatives were evacuated to Austin.

The survivors provided a number of reasons for not evacuating. Xia Baker, whom we have already introduced, had no money; Flora Jefferson, a fifty-nine-year-old African American custodian, had no transportation; and others such as the Knights did not believe that the storm would be as serious as it was. Some tried to evacuate and found that they could not. Denise Johnston, a forty-two-year-old African American female, told us that before the storm arrived, she and her family had gone to a school where they understood buses would be waiting to take them out of the city. However, when they arrived, there were no buses, so they returned to her house. She stayed there with other family members until the water became too deep and forced them out. They were eventually rescued by boat and taken to a hotel on dry ground.

Susan Doyle, a forty-eight-year-old African American home health care provider, had planned to evacuate with her son, daughter, and four grandchildren, but the car windshield wipers did not work in the heavy rain and they had to abandon their plans. After the hurricane passed, for a brief period they, like many others, thought that they would be all right, but within a short period the broken levies caused their house to flood. The family waded across the street to a neighbor's two-story house, where they stayed for three or four days. Doyle, her son, and another relative walked to the Superdome to investigate, but returned to their home once they found out that it was, as they characterized the situation, like a war zone. Eventually the family was rescued by helicopter.

Most survivors had lived in New Orleans their entire lives and had lived through many hurricane seasons. As rational actors, they had to weigh the costs and benefits of evacuation. Some reported bad experiences with previous evacuations. Paul Richardson, a fifty-three-year-old business owner, detailed his thoughts as he prepared to evacuate:

I started doing some initial preparation....Saturday morning we got up early and went through pretty much the same drill that we had done almost a year, or right at a year, before, for Hurricane Ivan,...which was [to] back up the computer, because I ran my business out of my home, and collect and import files, a few of them, and this year, for Katrina I wasn't as organized as I was for Ivan. I was better organized for Ivan, but I did back up the most critical information that we had [and] we packed three changes of clothes....I was in communication with my mother, who lives alone and is completely dependent upon [my wife] and [me]....[I] told her to get ready, and I can remember being very, very angry [at] having to go through that drill yet again. It's the whole issue of having to evacuate, and having to make a decision as to what is important, what is not important, what can you take, and what you cannot take. It's just, it's mentally brutal, it really is, and the fact that I'd had to do it before, and have had to do it so many times, and for some reason for that, Katrina, I was just really, really angry to the point that I said, if it were just me, if...no one else were dependent on me, I wouldn't have left, I would have stayed.

Some clearly had been desensitized to the possible dangers by repeated experiences with hurricanes. Katherine Smith's son offered to evacuate her, but she could not bring herself to leave. Some New Orleans residents were and continued to be very philosophical about their choice to stay. Whitney Morris, who recounted her harrowing story of evacuation earlier in this chapter, told us,

I met this hairdresser...and she was asking me...what made you stay? She said that was very foolish. I said, "You can call it what you want....I wasn't financially able to go live in a motel [for] a week...so I stood where I was. I had everything, my valuables, my kids, you know, and I stood, I stood it out, I'm one of those people." So she said, "We had left like...three, four days before Katrina even, hit." [I said], "Okay, more power to you, but you know it doesn't make your situation any better than mine because we still lost everything, you know, you [were] able to save some things, I'm sure, like your supplies, your equipment, but you still lost everything like me."

Although most of those who stayed had few real alternatives, most of the survivors told us that they made whatever preparations they could to weather the storm. Many made preparations that included family and friends, often relocating to the house of the person in their social network located on the highest ground, and they purchased whatever emergency supplies they could. Sometimes these networks were quite large; some survivors reported waiting out the storm with twenty or more people. Immediately after the storm, survivors dealt with power outages by pooling food and grilling together and generally took care of one another. John Washington, a fifty-five-year-old African American male who was HIV positive, stayed in his apartment during the storm. He had just been released from the hospital, where he had been treated for pneumonia. After the storm, the electricity in the apartment complex went out. Washington described how people's apartments eventually flooded and the residents had to be rescued.

ARRIVAL IN AUSTIN

After the levees failed, nearly all of those who had stayed found that as the floodwaters rose, their homes quickly became uninhabitable. In response, survivors reported moving to higher floors in the same building, moving to taller buildings, seeking refuge on a bridge, or, as a last resort, going to the Superdome or the Convention Center. Eventually, though, even the heartiest and most determined were forced to evacuate. Some survivors arrived in Austin, Texas, a city that is very different from New Orleans. Most of them had not chosen to come to Austin and arrived confused and often traumatized. During the evacuation, many had been separated from family and friends who were, often defying all logic, sent to other cities. Support networks that had functioned in New Orleans were torn apart. As a result, many expressed deep cynicism and distrust of government and its representatives. The initial abandonment in New Orleans, the forcible separation of families and networks during the evacuation, and the disorientation that accompanied their arrival in a new and unfamiliar city no doubt affected their later relationships with governmental and nongovernmental agencies and their ability to start a new life in Austin. Survivors arrived in Austin in several ways. As we will see, those who evacuated after the storm had very different experiences and arrived with different levels of resources than those who left before Hurricane Katrina struck.

SURVIVORS WHO EVACUATED AFTER THE STORM

For most of the survivors who evacuated after the storm, the first glimpse of Austin was the Austin Convention Center, which served as the main shelter. The operation of the center and the response in general was a joint state and civil society effort, consisting primarily of the City of Austin and the Red Cross, with a great deal of assistance from the county and contributions from a range of additional organizations. After days of watching on television as survivors suffered in the Superdome, Austin citizens welcomed Katrina survivors with open arms. The mayor at the time welcomed each busload of survivors in person. After what they had been through in New Orleans, most survivors had glowing things to say about their first few days in Austin. As John Washington said, "…when I arrive in Austin and went to the Convention Center…[I] feel like, I don't know how heaven is, but I imagine this is heaven, [because] if we had stayed there [in New Orleans] I'd have died."

After intake and registration, survivors received initial assistance. They were tired and hungry and had not bathed in days. A number needed urgent medical attention. Tyrell Booker, a young African American male, had a huge gash on his leg acquired while wading through the water. The injury was treated as soon as he arrived. Sonya Davis, a thirty-six-year-old African American female, and her husband Darnell Davis, a forty-eight-year-old African American male, told us of the relief and comfort survivors felt at the Convention Center:

Darnell: They welcomed everyone with open arms.
Sonya: Yeah, [they] could eat and they could get a shower, they didn't know how to act. They [were] getting all kind of snacks for us.
Darnell: Got hot food for us.
Sonya: Yup, [they gave us] water every minute.
Darnell: Before you [could] even say anything.
Sonya: Toothpaste and everything....And they let us go pick out the little air mattress, you know, we had the little cot, we had to set air mats on them...[people were] happy to sleep.
Darnell: They didn't have no kind of attitude, you know. They treat us like....
Sonya: They had police there, watch over you and stuff... and they kept asking you what you need.
Darnell: Folks came [as volunteers] to help us.
Sonya:...I needed slippers, and a lady, she was nice enough to go get me two pair of slippers.

Many survivors told us of the gratitude that they felt at seeing helpful faces and having their basic needs attended to. Alfreda Simpson, a middle-aged African American woman, said that the morning after she arrived at the Convention Center, she was overwhelmed by how nice everyone was. She said, "Yeah, and it was [nicer] here than it was in New Orleans. [There] you were just on your own. You didn't know if you were going to get killed or not see another day." Unfortunately, in anticipation of the change in attitude that occurred later, one African American survivor remembered what her mother said at the time. The older woman observed that, "yeah these people are being nice to us because they think we [are] refugees, but it is not [going to] last."

As we have described before, the Convention Center was fully equipped and staffed with medical facilities, showers, sleeping areas, counselors, a post office, and an array of representatives from state and federal agencies, as well as local civil society organizations (Kulkarni et al., 2008). As Will Charleston, a thirty-one-year-old African American male, said,

It was like a world in itself. You didn't have to come outside for [anything]. Everything was free, it's like they had a clothing store, they had a shoe store, Bank of America was in there, um, security, police station, meals, everything. You didn't have to come outside. [It was] like a bubble, like the boy in the bubble, it was like a bubble, you know....

We would like to think that assistance was provided with dignity and in a humane way, in contrast to what the survivors recounted of the horrors of what happened immediately after the storm in New Orleans. However, members of our research team who volunteered at the shelter noted some of the limitations that may be inevitable in the case of massive disasters. The shelter was a huge closed building. The survivors' movements were monitored and there was little real privacy. Survivors slept together in several large areas, and they formed smaller groups in order to create more intimacy. There was constant police presence and continuous noise that made it difficult for many to sleep. As Reggie Vinton, a fifty-seven-year-old African American male, recounted,

You know [there were] children everywhere, all the people all in there...and all that noise...ten or eleven people went to jail at the Convention Center, yeah.... I was glad to get out....

As a result of the stress, some tempers flared.

Many of the survivors at the Convention Center had been separated from family members and were desperate to find out whether they were alive and safe. Survivors attempted to find their relatives and friends in any way that they could. Many consulted the Red Cross missing persons list. Survivors did their best to reconnect or create new relationships and they offered one another whatever assistance they could. We heard some dramatic stories of reunion. Janis Stephens, a forty-one-year-old African American female, had been separated from her children during the evacuation. She located a neighbor at the Convention Center who somehow knew where her children were and was able to provide invaluable information. Danika Knight, Cynthia Knight's daughter whom we were introduced to earlier, had evacuated with her boyfriend's family and wound up in Houston, while her mother evacuated to Austin. Her mother enlisted the assistance of a local news reporter who helped her locate her daughter, who was finally moved to Austin. When Danika arrived in Austin, she said that

...my mama hugged me for at least an hour and didn't want to let me go....And everybody that I know from the Ninth Ward was up in there and they [all said] "I'm happy you're here."...Because it was like [my mother] had told the whole world she didn't know where I was. And when I walked in the door, everybody was hugging me; she was hugging me, and everything.

While they were still at the Convention Center, the survivors learned about what had happened back home from news stories that were shown on big-screen televisions. Given the extent of the destruction, many realized that life as they knew it was really over and that they would not be returning to New Orleans any time soon. The reality of the situation began to sink in quickly and survivors realized that they had to become citizens of a new city, which meant connecting with state and local agencies and institutions. Much like new immigrants, they had to reestablish their citizenship, which meant dealing with identification issues, getting driver's licenses, obtaining mailing addresses, opening bank accounts, and so on. This often turned out to be a much longer and more complex process than anyone could have imagined in the early days at the Convention Center. Among the first things that survivors had to do was to register with the Red Cross and FEMA as disaster survivors. This allowed them to receive money in the form of debit cards that could be used to purchase necessities.

Some degree of chaos was probably inevitable in a situation in which so many individuals had to be processed and their eligibility for various services determined in a short time. It was not surprising that while survivors were grateful to be away from the destruction in New Orleans, they were anxious to get out of the Convention Center. Reggie Vinton worked hard to take care of everything quickly so that he could leave. As he told us,

I was the first one out of the place, they were calling names [alphabetically]. I mean, I was out of the Convention Center. I took care of everything early…[the lines [were] long, boy, it [was] packed. I can't remember [how many days I stayed at the Convention Center]….I'd say about…twelve…it might have been more….

Finding longer-term housing in the city of Austin was the primary goal for nearly everyone at the Convention Center. Survivors were assisted by NGOs, volunteers, realtors, and landlords. A local nonprofit housing organization presents a typical case. This organization had recently acquired a hotel that it was planning to rehabilitate and convert to a single room–occupancy complex. However, renovations would not start for several months, so staff went to the Convention Center to look for families or people with disabilities who could be housed there temporarily.

Flora Jefferson, a fifty-nine-year-old African American woman, told us that a volunteer from a church (she could not remember the name) took her and her family all around town to look for apartments. Whitney Morris, whom we met earlier, was in the Austin Convention Center for a week and a half. She told us that someone, possibly a realtor, took her around and helped her find an apartment. Katherine Smith, a seventy-eight-year-old white female, had wonderful things to say about the volunteers who helped her find an apartment. So did Reggie Vinton, who was at the Convention Center for eleven or twelve days. He told us that he met a landlord there who took him to see the apartment into which he eventually moved. Carlos Rodriguez, a middle-aged Hispanic male, told us about someone or some group that provided taxi vouchers that provided transportation so that survivors could look for apartments. He also told us about what it was like to set up a household:

…Well, before I left the Convention Center, FEMA helped me out with $2,000. So I used, basically used that money to furnish my apartment and get things that I felt like I needed. I would basically [get] whatever I felt…I needed. If I couldn't get it delivered, I would just [get] in a taxi cab and…cart it home…or I would hire somebody with a pickup truck or something to help me get it back to my [place].

As we have discussed elsewhere (Kulkarni et al., 2008), toward the end of the third week, the city began pressuring survivors to leave the Convention Center. By this time, many of the survivors who remained had serious problems and required additional assistance. Antoine Mosely, a forty-nine-year-old African American male, was among the last to leave the Convention Center. He said he hesitated because he did not want to experience another separation from familiar faces:

I was the last one left at the Convention Center….I left that Friday…it was almost empty….I found a little apartment…you would think that [I] would be happy, but [I was]…sad to leave….It was like a little unit, but when they bust, it burst, pop, so that was another hit…everybody going different ways…a lot of people didn't have no phone…so that was another blow for me. I got my place downtown for awhile because I still was trying to hang around downtown hoping I would see some people I had met along the way, you know.…

Although many organizations and volunteers had contact with the survivors at the Convention Center, the most central to the effort were the Red Cross and FEMA, and they were the organizations that most survivors remembered. Although the survivors we interviewed acknowledged that they had received help from many people, most could not identify other organizations or agencies at the Convention Center.

Our general observations, then, are that the survivors who were evacuated from New Orleans directly to Austin after the flooding did not know anyone in Austin, nor had they chosen to come to Austin. Many did not know where they were until they stepped off the plane. However, once here, most survivors who stayed at the Convention Center praised the assistance they received from volunteers and service providers. The assistance that they received, though, did not serve as a substitute for the sort of support that those with more human and social capital were able to call upon. Except for the few cases in which people from the same New Orleans neighborhoods were evacuated together or those in which they reunited with family and friends, most were not able to re-create the strong ties that sustained them in the old city. As we will see in later chapters, the strong ties of traditional neighborhoods are not easily transportable and are tied firmly to place, particularly for those with few material resources for travel and correspondence. The experiences of the few families who evacuated themselves before the storm arrived illustrate the difference in human and social capital.

SURVIVORS WHO EVACUATED BEFORE THE STORM

In contrast to survivors who were evacuated to Austin after they were forced out of their homes by the floodwaters, most of those who evacuated before the storm had more material, human, and social capital, including social networks that included members outside of New Orleans who could provide assistance. Most of those survivors who arrived in Austin on their own did so because they had friends or family here, or they chose the city on the basis of what they knew of its employment opportunities and lifestyle characteristics. Most did not spend any time at the Convention Center or any of the other local shelters.

For those who arrived voluntarily and on their own, their journey was often circuitous, and many spent time with friends and family in other cities. Louise Davidson and Nicholas Goldstein, a white couple in their thirties, left New Orleans by car and spent several nights on the road before they finally arrived in Austin to be close to relatives. When they arrived in Austin, they stayed at a motel for a few days until they found an apartment through an apartment locator. The couple received assistance from FEMA for rent, and also emergency food stamps and assistance from several local nonprofits. Like most of the other survivors who evacuated before the storm, this family had some material resources. Nicholas had just been paid by his employer and he was able to get the couple's credit limit increased. This financial power was important, as he told us,

I don't think I ever realized how powerful money is. I mean, you know you need it. I gotta pay rent, I gotta eat, blah, blah, blah. But, having a full bank account says you can survive for, with all of this unknown, for a little while. It was very comforting....

The Johnsons, the African American physical therapists we met in Chapter 2, also evacuated by car. Their first stop was in east Texas, but they immediately came to Austin, where they had relatives. After a week at the relative's home, they rented an apartment, where they received three months of FEMA assistance. As we detailed in Chapter 2, with the assistance of Mrs. Johnson's brother, the family eventually purchased and rehabbed a foreclosed home in Austin. They also received help with furniture from a faith-based organization, as well as assistance from the city government and another nonprofit organization, to set up the household. This family's experience highlights both the importance of bridging social capital (networks outside the disaster area) as well as capital in the form of financial resources and expertise. In addition, they received assistance from a number of civil society organizations as well as FEMA and HUD.

As was the case with the previous two families, Julia Mitchell, a sixty-year-old African American woman, along with her daughter and grand-children, evacuated by car and stayed at a hotel in Houston before moving on to Austin. They stayed at one of the smaller shelters in Austin for two days, before they found an apartment where FEMA paid their rent. Julia is a counselor and quickly found a job working with other evacuees. Here her social capital in the form of training and work experience, combined with federal assistance, eased the family's resettlement in Austin.

The situation of Jewel Banks, a sixty-three-year-old retired African American female, was unique. She was a grandmother and the matriarch of her family. She evacuated to Austin to stay with her son and daughter-in-law in an Austin suburb community. Eventually forty or fifty additional family members arrived at the son's home. The family's plight drew a great deal of attention and they received numerous donations from organizations in the local area. Jewel told us about how Austinites heard about her family's situation. As she said,

Austin played a beautiful part.... People that saw us on the TV...[someone] called Channel Eight, I believe it was, it was a news channel, and they came and interviewed [us] in front of the door, and...they got on the news and it went in the paper. So people knew the address and phone number and we start getting calls...food. [People asked]...what do you need? The garage was packed and that's a three-car garage, with clothes, with dishes, towels, bedclothes, whatever.

In this case, most of the help was from individuals, not agencies. When asked whether the family had received help from governmental agencies, Jewel responded, "no, there wasn't a lot of government agencies helping, this was natural people, we [weren't] communicating with a lot of government agencies." Jewel's resources included her extended family network in Austin, and through them the family drew upon the resources of the larger community of sympathetic neighbors and citizens.

However, not everyone felt that they had been received with open arms. Donald Klein, a middle-aged white male we introduced earlier in this chapter, arrived at one of the city's shelters ahead of the crowd of survivors and described his experience as "awful." As a white male, he was clearly in the minority and was obviously conscious of the fact that he was different from most of the other survivors. As he recounted,

[Shelter workers] weren't very nice to me, you know. I think most of the people there thought I was working there....'Cause I was white, I had my glasses, and I look intelligent, or I look like an oddball. I look like a bookworm probably. I don't know. People weren't coming up to me and like talking to me....Maybe they didn't think I looked so approachable. I don't know what it was. I felt very isolated there even among all the people. And it was very weird because when I first got there, there were just like...I was like about the third person there, so we had the whole place and it felt very strange. And so...I felt like there were three goldfish and there were all these people watching us, but they weren't coming up to feed us, something like that.

Donald Klein's experience notwithstanding, as we have mentioned and as we will see in later chapters, those who evacuated on their own typically, but with some exceptions, had a much easier time accessing services, primarily because they were more literate and had computer skills that helped them in the application process. They were also more likely to have brought identification and other important documentation with them. Although they often expressed frustration with the services provided, they were typically less dependent and relied on assistance for a shorter period of time.

In the next chapter, we return to an examination of social capital and illustrate the degree to which strong bonding ties are dependent on locality. As we will see, when the survivors left New Orleans, they left those strong bonding and supportive ties behind, and in most cases were not able to develop new ones in Austin.

5

The Limited Transportability of Social Capital

Companionship and intimate human contact are basic human needs even for the affluent. For those with little wealth and low incomes, the strong bonding ties and mutual support of family and local social networks are vital for survival (Edin & Lein, 1997; Stack, 1974). The affluent may have the option of isolating themselves since their material well-being is secure. The poor do not have that luxury. As we have seen in previous chapters, even among those survivors who told us about the serious problems that beset their old New Orleans neighborhoods, their stories also conveyed a sense of familiarity and community and, in many cases, social and material support. As important as weak ties are for information gathering, they are no substitute for the emotional and material security that only strong ties can provide. In this chapter, we address the question of how local or place-bound such ties are. Although weak ties do not depend on place, strong ties that are based on more intimate interactions and more frequent contact appear to be less transportable from one place to another.

The differences between the experiences of survivors who evacuated before the storm and those who evacuated after illustrate how varying levels of social capital influenced survivors' long-term outcomes. Those who evacuated on their own before the storm were in the minority in our sample and, as we shall see, consisted mostly of a group with higher levels of human and social capital than those who were evacuated after the storm. Much of the difference between these groups had to do with their ability to rebuild a sense of community in their new neighborhoods. Among the most important factors that affected that ability was access to adequate housing. Those with more human, social, and material capital had more success finding adequate housing than those with fewer of these resources. We will begin our discussion of rebuilding "community"; then we discuss housing policy in the United States. Before proceeding, let us examine aspects of community and the nature of the strong and weak ties that structure human interactions and define community.

Although the term *community* can be used to refer to individuals who do not share a common location, such as when we speak of the "community of scholars" or the "community of believers," in everyday use the term implies a defined geographic and social space. In the absence of a common location, the strong bonds that define supportive residential communities have a hard time forming, as does the solidarity that only those who live in close proximity to one another or who work together develop over time. Such geographically defined communities typically emerge spontaneously, as individuals with resources choose the neighborhoods in which they live and those with little income are forced to live in whatever neighborhoods they can afford. Federal housing policy, in addition to discrimination and other housing market forces, has historically limited the community options of low-income Americans. Beginning with the Housing Act of 1949, the federal government formally assumed responsibility for providing housing to low-income Americans (Orlebeke, 2000). Initially this responsibility took the form of promoting the production of low-rent housing, primarily through mortgage subsidies to nonprofit organizations and others who were willing to accept lower profit margins.

Beginning in the 1970s, federal housing policy shifted from subsidizing the building of low-cost housing units to a greater focus on vouchers that allow low-income individuals to find their own housing (Winnick, 1995). The voucher approach, most commonly referred to as Section 8 vouchers, a label that refers to the section of the Housing Act that authorized them, have had strong support and have been shown to cost less than subsidized construction (Ellickson, 2009–10; Orlebeke, 2000; Shroder & Reiger, 2000). The move toward vouchers was also fueled by the general desire to devolve responsibility for decisions concerning housing to state and municipal levels (Orlebeke, 2000). Regardless of the approach, though, the stock of affordable high-quality housing has remained woefully inadequate. Municipalities have inadequate resources to devote to affordable housing and many needy families remain on waiting lists for years (DeFilippis & Wyly, 2008; Mueller & Schwartz, 2008). Those who ultimately receive housing vouchers often cannot find a landlord who will accept them, and even if they find housing, it is often in low-income, disorganized neighborhoods (Basolo & Nguyen, 2005).

The general lack of high-quality affordable housing in U.S. cities undermines the possibility of solidarity and community as well as physical and mental health (Elo et al., 2009; Ross & Mirowsky, 2009). Low-income neighborhoods with low levels of residential stability and a decayed physical environment rarely develop high levels of social capital (Sampson, 2009; Sampson & Graif, 2009; Sampson & Groves, 1989). The lack of affordable housing in low-income neighborhoods is only exacerbated by disasters that damage or destroy existing housing stock (Comerio, 1998). Disasters that destroy property simply make an already bad situation worse and clearly call for an immediate and focused response from all levels of government and civil society. As we described earlier, after Hurricane Katrina, FEMA assumed the initial and major responsibility for providing such assistance. As a branch of the federal government, FEMA had the greatest financial and organizational resources and, given its mandate, it defined the general nature and extent of the response. Other agencies such as the Red Cross and other NGOs also responded, but FEMA was clearly the major player. Yet its housing policy was criticized for being inadequate, and in 2007 HUD assumed responsibility for long-term rental assistance through a program called the Disaster Housing Assistance Program (DHAP) (U.S. Department of Housing and Urban Development, 2007). Despite the huge sums of money devoted to the relief effort, the federal response proved not only inadequate, but it often interfered with survivors' recovery. Affordable housing remained a critical problem for Hurricane Katrina survivors, and the serious lack of adequate and stable housing became a major barrier to rebuilding community, either in New Orleans or in Austin (Carlisle, 2004; Kromm & Sturgis, 2008).

The story of Jackie Martin illustrates a number of the problems that many survivors experienced. This fifty-four-year-old unmarried African American female had been a homeowner and lifelong resident of New Orleans. After working for many years, she became disabled. She lived with a sister who was also disabled, and the two lived on their pooled disability payments. Martin was separated from her sister during the evacuation from New Orleans. The sister went to Dallas and was staying with relatives, whereas Martin was evacuated to Austin. When Martin arrived in Austin, a local nongovernmental organization helped her find an apartment, where she remained until the spring after the storm. Martin's FEMA claim was delayed because both she and her relatives had filed a claim on behalf of her sister, so they were both denied assistance due to FEMA's "shared household" rule, which prohibited assistance to multiple families that had been living in one household. Even though her home was severely damaged, her insurance company did not declare her home a total loss.

Martin received a settlement, but doubted that it would be enough to pay for the repairs that were necessary to make the house habitable again. After her initial claim to FEMA was declined, she applied for a FEMA trailer. She eventually received one, and at the time of our last interview in May 2006, she was planning to move back to New Orleans and try to rebuild.

Housing was clearly central to any attempt at rebuilding a normal life, either in New Orleans or in Austin. Martin's story revealed several themes related to housing insecurity that were common in survivors' accounts of their interactions with FEMA and their attempts to find a place to live. These themes include misinformation, insecurity about how long assistance would last, bureaucratic problems that arose from the shared household rule that denied assistance to multiple families living in one household prior to the hurricane, and the long process required to receive assistance. In the following sections, we examine the impact of these challenges on survivors' ability to reestablish themselves in Austin. We also examine the consequences of differences in individual human and social capital, including marketable skills, literacy, and social connections that affected the speed and extent of survivors' recovery, often in combination with housing problems.

We must begin with the observation, though, that major difficulties and inefficiencies were inevitable in the process of dealing with a crisis of this magnitude. Despite extensive and justifiable criticisms of its confusing and poorly coordinated response, FEMA provided invaluable long-term rental assistance and subsidized Austin's emergency shelter and the case management programs that we will discuss in this and later chapters. Yet both survivors and their service providers expended much unnecessary effort in their attempts to deal with the apparent irrationality of the system. Our interviews with both groups made it clear that FEMA was without doubt the most important resource that low-income survivors and providers could call upon, but at the same time it presented some of the most serious obstacles to survivors' recovery. One service provider characterized the agency by saying that "FEMA is its own monster." This characterization of FEMA as a Janus-faced monster that was at once savior and encumbrance to recovery requires some explanation.

FEDERAL DISASTER ASSISTANCE: AID AND OBSTACLE TO RECOVERY

President Jimmy Carter created FEMA in 1979, consolidating the disaster response responsibilities of a hundred independent agencies that had proliferated since the nineteenth century in response to numerous disasters. The result of this uncoordinated proliferation of agencies, complicated by the addition of responsibilities for nuclear power plants and dangers related to the transportation of hazardous materials, meant that states were forced to deal with multiple independent federal entities, each with its own set of rules and procedures. In response, the National Governors Association (NGA) requested that President Carter centralize federal emergency response functions, which he did through an executive order (Cooper & Block, 2006; FEMA, 2010; Roberts, 2006b). Subsequent administrations extended or contracted FEMA's responsibilities in response to specific disasters and the changing political climate. After forty years, the general view of the organization is that it responds effectively to routine disasters, but is overwhelmed by major catastrophes such as Hurricane Katrina (Cooper & Block, 2006; Roberts, 2006a).

After the terrorist attacks on September 11, 2001, President George W. Bush once again reorganized FEMA to focus its mission more on the response to terrorism and he staffed the agency with his own political appointees (Morris, 2006; Roberts, 2006a). Organizationally FEMA lost its status as an independent agency and became a branch of the newly created Department of Homeland Security (DHS). This newly reorganized FEMA, located in DHS and headed by the notoriously unqualified Michael Brown, was the agency assigned to coordinate the response to Hurricane Katrina (U.S. House of Representatives, 2006a, 2006b; White House, 2006).

As John Morris notes, the striking feature of the extensive and severe criticisms of FEMA after Hurricane Katrina was that none were new (Morris, 2006). The agency has always been a political football whose leadership has learned little organizationally or practically from its past mistakes. FEMA's current authority and functions are defined by the Stafford Act (Public Law 93–288), which was passed in 1988 (Bea, 2010). The Act directs FEMA to provide financial assistance for disaster-related needs, including the replacement of furniture, clothing, and occupation-related equipment. It also provides assistance for medical and dental care and with funeral expenses.

One of the most pressing needs of individuals and families after a disaster is housing. The Stafford Act authorizes two primary forms of housing assistance. The first is emergency assistance provided to local and state governments (Section 403) and the second is assistance provided directly to individuals (Section 408). Under Section 408, FEMA pays for rental housing, provides trailers, and also pays for the repair and replacement of owner-occupied housing. The result is that housing assistance can come from different levels of government and in different forms with different rules. As we discuss later in this chapter, this caused confusion as to who was providing housing assistance and for what purposes the funds could legitimately be used.

FEMA's mandate also includes the establishment of partnerships with other governmental agencies and nongovernmental organizations in order to facilitate the coordination of the emergency response and the longer-term recovery effort (Morris, 2006). However, those arrangements are often not true partnerships because they are not based on shared authority or decision making. Given its federal status and its control of resources, FEMA is clearly the dominant partner. After Hurricane Katrina, FEMA determined eligibility rules, established application and distribution procedures, and provided resources with little consultation with other agencies or organizations, except for very limited contact through the Voluntary Agency Liaisons (VALs) that are mandated by statute. State and local authorities had surprisingly little discretion in determining eligibility for assistance. As a consequence, the response lacked an effective chain of command and mechanisms for information to flow efficiently and quickly from lower to higher levels. Rather than dealing with local authorities, survivors as well as service providers and case managers had to deal with FEMA directly rather than with agencies closer to ground level. This structure clearly reflected a failure to appreciate the need to include local actors in dealing with local problems.

The inefficient and incomplete flow of information to local authorities and case managers was a major problem. Officials were often unaware of who was responsible for providing services to whom or whether they would be reimbursed by the federal government. For example, the City of Austin provided a great deal of housing assistance without any clear assurance that the expenditures would be reimbursed by FEMA. Local service providers, including governmental agencies in Austin as well as NGOs, found that the concept of partnership was nearly meaningless and that coordination was not feasible given the organizational arrangements and the overwhelming dominance of FEMA agenda setting.

The extensive criticism of FEMA after Katrina and other disasters leaves little doubt that basic structural and organizational problems, as well as the fact that the staffing at the highest levels of the agency is highly political, undermine the organization's ability to act effectively and efficiently in response to serious crises. Its failure to include local nongovernmental organizations represented a serious missed opportunity. In the end, though, we must reemphasize the importance of the federal government in defining and carrying out the objectives that lie at the core of FEMA's mandate. Although local agencies and nongovernmental organizations are important potential contributors, they are incapable of shouldering the rescue and recovery effort alone.

During the first three months after Hurricane Katrina struck, FEMA provided expedited assistance of $2,000 per applicant for emergency needs to over 800,000 individuals and families and provided transitional housing assistance in the amount of $2,358 each to 530,000 applicants. As of May 2009, FEMA had provided emergency housing to 143,000 families that had been displaced by Hurricanes Katrina and Rita. It provided $7.8 billion for housing and other needs, including transportation, clothing, and furniture (U.S. Senate, 2009). Its sheer size and federal mandate make FEMA essential to emergency response and there can be little question of withdrawing, or even greatly diminishing, the federal-level organizational response. As our study clearly reveals, local governmental agencies and nongovernmental organizations do not have the financial, organizational, or logistical capacities to deal with major crises, nor by extension can they deal with serious large-scale chronic poverty. An effective response to crises – and again by extension an effective response to the needs of chronically impoverished people in crisis situations – requires a less political and more professional and coordinated effort that pays far greater attention to the role of lower levels of government and includes nongovernmental actors as important partners.

FEMA's central role is illustrated by the fact that, while the majority of both survivor and service provider participants we spoke to focused on the problems that they encountered in dealing with FEMA, there were some families and providers who had good things to say about FEMA, and their experiences are quite informative (Beausoleil & Reid, 2007). Some of these families had high levels of human and social capital and were more able than families with less social and human capital to deal with FEMA's complex bureaucracy. Bill Smith, a white professor in his fifties, evacuated along with his wife before the storm and stayed with a relative in Louisiana for a short while before the couple came to Austin, where they again stayed for only a short while. This family had private insurance on their New Orleans property, and Bill's wife had an Internet-based business that could be continued from Austin. The couple returned to New Orleans after six weeks. Bill reported no problems with FEMA and summarized his family's interaction with the agency by saying that, "...the federal government was wonderful."

The Johnsons, the couple whose story we presented at the beginning of Chapter 2, received FEMA housing aid for three months. The range of options available to them was increased by their transferable professional skills (both are physical therapists) and by the fact that they had material assets, including proceeds from insurance on their relatively expensive, newly built home in New Orleans. James Long, a retired sixty-six-year-old African American male, reported numerous initial problems with FEMA, but with the help of a case manager, he applied for Section 8 housing and was able to move to a senior facility. He also qualified for disability payments. FEMA was clearly vital in providing temporary housing assistance until Long qualified for Section 8. With FEMA's assistance, a few survivors were able to return to New Orleans and restart their lives there.

Given such diversity in terms of recovery, one inevitably wonders about the factors that account for the differences. The few highly successful families that we have mentioned were clearly in the minority and, as we have noted, most brought high levels of human and social capital with them from New Orleans. Dealing with bureaucracies such as FEMA and other governmental agencies was clearly a major aspect of the experience of most survivors in Austin. Higher levels of education and previous experience with bureaucracies with complex application procedures no doubt enhanced one's chance of success in gaining access to services and other resources (Fothergill & Peek, 2004). Because of their association with differential levels of human and social capital, ethnic, racial, gender, and class differences no doubt influenced individuals' and families' ability to access disaster assistance (Quarantelli, 1991, 1999).

Research conducted following Hurricane Andrew confirms that "systems skills" and knowledge are important in dealing with bureaucracies and governmental organizations. These system skills were almost certainly more highly developed among the few middle-class survivors we interviewed than among lower-income and more socially marginalized victims (Peacock, Morrow, & Gladwin, 1997). Our experiences clearly revealed a major role for local actors in compensating for this lack of system skills. It was clear from the beginning of our field work that those survivors with limited human capital or system-level skills benefited greatly from the intervention of case managers. The case managers provided vitally important knowledge and assistance that represented important social capital.

This may be one of the central lessons of the study and a reason for some optimism concerning the utility of nongovernmental actors. Volunteers and local social service agencies, even when they are not formal experts or social scientists, can provide invaluable assistance in the form of very real social capital that can greatly enhance the quality of life of individuals in distress. The case management model has been employed, often by social workers, for decades in various domains, including mental health, rehabilitation, and other fields and it has been recognized by the federal government as important in disaster relief (Birnie, 2009; Martin & Browning, 2007; U.S. Congress, 2010). Although enhancing the case management model is an important objective in disaster relief, a more important focus should be on providing adequate basic services in a clear and transparent manner that does not require the kind of social capital that many recipients, by their very condition as survivors, do not possess.

In a situation in which survivors had little knowledge of Austin or FEMA and lacked basic knowledge of organizational entry points and bureaucratic requirements, case management proved to be vital. In general, such intervention is particularly important in mitigating the racially and ethnically based disadvantages that place minority individuals at particular disadvantage. The fact that the majority of our sample consisted of African Americans was only one indication of this groups' greater vulnerability. We heard hints of it from many sources. Mary Wilde, a forty-two-year-old white female who at the time of our interview was the only remaining Katrina survivor in an upscale hotel in North Austin, was keenly aware that the fact that she was white gave her certain advantages. She had this to say about how resources were distributed among survivors:

It became very clear to me that between the lines, I'm here because I'm white. I'm here because I'm not a mother. I'm here because I behave the way they think I should behave, and the only marginalized people that I've seen in this place have been the people who clean, the people who cook, the people who fix things.

Although low-income African Americans were at greater risk of recovery difficulties than middle-class individuals or whites, they were not the only ones who had a difficult time dealing with FEMA. Donald Klein, whom we met in Chapter 4, was a well-educated white male. He was quite atypical of our study participants. Earlier he had told us about how uncomfortable and out of place he felt at the shelter. Further, despite his considerable education and skill, he had very negative encounters with FEMA. He described a bad encounter in which he characterized FEMA representatives as poor listeners who provided misinformation that caused survivors to be denied benefits to which they were entitled. He recounted the frustrating experience of calling FEMA from a public phone booth in the middle of the night:

I said, "Okay, but you know, I'm out here, and it's late at night, and it's kind of dangerous, and I don't see why I should have to answer all these, I already did them all already, but if you want, but please understand this is not another application, I've already applied." To make a long story short, I found out later that she did me as another application, which made me look like I was dishonest, and then I was backlogged and I had to go back and explain it, and send all this information in triplicate and all this stuff, and it made the whole thing go three months later and all that because she didn't listen to me, you know, she was insisting on asking me.

Klein received six months of FEMA rental assistance, but understood that many other survivors received assistance for a year and believed that he would have as well had the process not been so complicated. Given his frustration, he did not apply for food stamps, even though it took him a while to restart his business, resulting in considerable financial insecurity and anxiety.

The problems that families and individuals faced were often interrelated and had serious practical consequences that pervaded their lives during the first year after the catastrophe. For many families, the instability and uncertainty persisted after their initial contact with FEMA and other service providers. Our interviews revealed that this instability and the sense of precariousness that it fostered emerged and persisted over time beginning with the initial application for assistance. In the following section, we go through these problems in sequence and identify points at which civil society and lower-level governmental organizations and agencies intervened, and describe how case management emerged as an important asset for vulnerable families.

THE INITIAL INSTITUTIONAL CONTACT: APPLICATION FOR ASSISTANCE

As survivors arrived at the Austin's shelters over the Labor Day weekend of 2005, they asked, "Where is FEMA?" For several days, there was no federal presence. A high-level city official we interviewed told us that FEMA representatives did not arrive at the Austin Convention Center, the city's primary shelter, for five to seven days after the first survivors began arriving, and when they finally did arrive, they only registered individuals for future assistance; they did not immediately issue checks or debit cards. This official told us that she had assigned city workers and NGOs to register survivors for FEMA's assistance online around the clock because FEMA's phone numbers were flooded with calls and its website overwhelmed with visitors; indeed, both the phone numbers and the website were inaccessible except in the middle of the night.

The assistance of city workers was vital because even though the most effective way to register was online, many of the survivors were not computer literate. As a result of these city efforts, most survivors at the Convention Center were registered before FEMA representatives even arrived.

After the Convention Center was closed to survivors on September 23, 2005, the city entered into a contract with FEMA to administer the 403 housing program and to provide longer-term housing to survivors. At first, there was a great deal of confusion concerning which survivors were actually eligible for this particular assistance. Because this assistance was formally an emergency shelter program, city officials were not sure whether survivors who had not stayed at the Convention Center were eligible, and for several weeks the requirements changed numerous times. As one provider we interviewed recalled,

> It [eligibility] was changing all the time. But it was things like, originally it [was] something really broad – like you stayed at the Convention Center. Then it was, you stayed at the Convention Center but you had to have stayed there by no later than September 7th. And then it was, September 6th....This is not really what it was but this is really close. It would change day to day, like, the dates within a week or it would change to...then you had to have stayed but had to have documentation that you stayed overnight. Then it would change that the documentation had to be X, Y, and Z. Then it would change, no, but you have to have this other documentation or, um, then you had to have a wristband and this. Then you had to have an ID. Then you had, I mean – it was crazy. It just changed all the time.

Another city official responsible for providing long-term housing to survivors told us about a serious problem in the process of signing survivors up for FEMA assistance and moving them into apartments:

> Now about the week before Thanksgiving is when FEMA lost their mind and the federal government once again just completely lost, and, again, I say FEMA, it was Homeland Security. They just lost their mind. We found out, unbeknownst to us, that FEMA had housed about six hundred and fifteen families in hotels in Austin in a separate program that we didn't even know existed. And they told those people that they had to be out of the hotels by December 1st, December 15th. Two weeks after Thanksgiving. Two weeks before, ten days before Christmas.

After a great deal of lobbying by host cities and other survivor advocates, this deadline was eventually pushed back to February 15 and city assessors eventually went to hotels that were housing survivors with FEMA "strike teams" to try to find other housing for hotel residents.

LOST IDENTITIES

The severity of Hurricane Katrina caught most survivors, and especially those who did not evacuate beforehand, by surprise; most left with little more than the clothes on their backs. There was no time to collect important papers, memorabilia, or much else. In the chaos of the evacuation, much of what survivors took from their homes was lost. Individuals arrived in Austin without driver's licenses, passports, or any other form of identification. These individuals were unable to provide documentation of leases, proof of insurance, titles to vehicles, or anything else that could have situated them socially. Most of us take identification for granted. We carry multiple identifiers on our persons, including driver's licenses, student and worker identification cards, credit cards, membership cards, and more. In normal times, we can easily get our hands on documentation of financial transactions, proof of home ownership, car titles, and so on. In reality, in the modern world our identity is what we can document formally. For many survivors, all that was lost and there was, in fact, no way of proving who they were.

Those who had evacuated before the storm and those with the most resources generally did not have this problem. This problem was much more common than we originally realized, though, among survivors. As John Wilson, a twenty-two-year-old African American, told us, "…the thing is I'm ready to find me a job cause I got a gas bill in my pocket and I have a check from FEMA that I can't even cash because I don't have an ID to cash it…" This problem was so serious and caused such complex problems that we will discuss it in greater detail in Chapter 7.

FEMA-TIZED

After the storm, individuals who dealt with FEMA coined the term "FEMA-tized," used to refer to the stress associated with dealing with the agency. According to the online Urban Dictionary, the term can be applied to individuals, governmental agencies, or even houses that are negatively affected by FEMA policies. FEMA-tization, if we may introduce yet another neologism, had clear negative consequences for the process of rebuilding community in Austin. Although FEMA emergency housing was critical to survivors' survival in Austin, FEMA-tization, especially in the form of constantly changing rules that were confusing to both survivors and service providers, created instability and precariousness in both the short and longer term. As one provider said,

...yeah, you're telling people for months that February 28, your rental assistance will end and you have to have a plan. And then it's March 31, then April and June and July. People are living very month to month and always unsure of what's going to happen next. And it just complicates – it's more stressful.

Teri Chandler, a forty-one-year-old African American female, wished to move from the apartment complex where she had originally been housed because the drugs and violence in the neighborhood made her feel unsafe as a single female whose unstable relationship with her boyfriend meant that she frequently lived alone. FEMA, however, refused to let her move. It was unclear why, but such FEMA-tization affected family relationships and sometimes kept families from being reunited.

The shared household rule that we mentioned earlier created family conflicts. Before the rule was modified, it meant that only some members of previously extended households qualified for assistance. The decision concerning who would apply often pitted individuals against one another. Denise Johnston, a forty-two-year-old African American female, had been recognized as the head of her household when she applied for assistance programs in New Orleans, but she was denied help by FEMA because other individuals who had lived with her filed competing head of household forms in order to collect benefits. Although she filed paperwork charging them with fraud, she reported that she felt sympathy for their situations: "...at the same time my heart goes out to them because I...do feel like in spite of all...[because] they went through with Katrina and had to be placed somewhere else, [they] should be compensated for something because it wasn't their fault."

Confusion over what specific federal programs could actually cover caused much ill will. The Katrina Disaster Housing Assistance Program (KDHAP) was designed to provide a seamless transition for residents of public housing in New Orleans who needed public housing in Austin. Unfortunately, as was the case with the Section 8 housing program, the KDHAP program paid rent but not utilities. FEMA housing assistance, on the other hand, paid both rent and utilities. Participants in KDHAP were sometimes resentful of their neighbors who were receiving the more inclusive FEMA benefits. Many assumed that they would not have to pay utilities only to have their utilities terminated.

The story of Henry Baker and his wife Xia illustrates the problems that arose when utility bills could not be paid. This African American couple had lived in New Orleans their entire lives. They had five children and before the storm had been living in a house they rented with Section 8 assistance. Both Henry and Xia worked at a variety of informal jobs. When flooding forced them to evacuate their home, they waited for rescue on an interstate and were eventually airlifted to Austin. They stayed at the Convention Center for several weeks and then moved to a hotel while they searched for a home large enough for their family. As part of the process, they attended the required meetings offered by the Austin Housing Authority. The family eventually found a house and moved into it, but neither Henry nor Xia was able to find employment, so they were quickly overwhelmed by utility bills that they could not afford to pay. As a result of their limited income, the family was without natural gas from time to time and also experienced food shortages, even though they received food stamps and Supplemental Security Income (SSI) payments for two of their children. Henry and Xia also appealed their FEMA award for property losses, which was only $2,000. This amount did not come close to paying for their losses. At the time of our last interview, the family was still struggling with utility bills and had not resolved their FEMA award claim.

Voluntary organizations and individual assistance providers and case managers were vital in dealing with FEMA's complex documentation procedures. Even they, though, were often challenged to understand those procedures. The problems with rules governing which programs would pay for what services continued to create much confusion. In November, for example, the FEMA Disaster Recovery Center (DRC) site manager informed the case management director for the City of Austin that FEMA checks could be used only for rent and nothing else. To ensure that this rule was followed, FEMA required that all receipts had to be kept and presented to its agents when clients reapplied for an additional three months of assistance. For some reason, applicants were not told of this restriction when they applied nor when they received their initial rent checks of $2,358. They simply received a check in the mail. Those who used the money for expenses other than rent were told that they would not be eligible for additional assistance. Many recipients were unaware not only of the restriction on the use of the money but of the requirement that they keep receipts. Clifford Thompson, an African American male in his late forties, described the experience of being asked to provide proof of how he had spent the FEMA money when he applied for additional assistance. His expressed a clear sense of injustice when he said that, "…I know how to manage when I know what I have to do." Being told after the fact that he had violated the rules undermined his faith in FEMA. Had he been told of the requirements, he would have complied.

Being accused of willfully violating the rules when one was not even aware of them clearly caused much resentment. In the worst cases, FEMA sometimes attempted to recoup assistance paid to survivors. In the case of Justine Betts, the thirty-nine-year-old African American female we met in Chapter 1, FEMA payments for housing were stopped in June because the family used the money they had received for rent to buy household items. Justine explained that the family had not been aware that FEMA funds were to be used only to pay rent, and that they had used some of the money to purchase other things they desperately needed. She told us that "we were just buying stuff to try to live again." The family purchased an inexpensive car for transportation to errands and appointments. Although Justine offered to produce receipts to show that the family had spent the funds on necessities, FEMA refused to continue rental assistance and sent a letter requesting that the family return the $2,700 they had received originally. At the time of our last interview, Justine was planning to appeal. Service providers explained that Justine's situation was common because survivors did not understand or could not comply with the documentation requirements of FEMA.

The providers also corroborated survivors' accounts that FEMA communications were opaque. One provider explained that,

> …they didn't understand the, the letter that FEMA sends, stating why they're ineligible for certain assistance, it's very difficult for even, it was difficult for me to read and, they, they themselves call it FEMA-ese. It's written in FEMA-ese. It's similar to legalese but it's specific to FEMA. You know, it's hard to even understand, it's not made clear. It's not, like, you know, brought down to the lowest common denominator. You know, it's not made, it's not simple.

This entrapment by bureaucratic procedures was also revealed when providers who were accustomed to interpreting official documents and rules found FEMA's rules to be confusing. If professional assistance providers found the rules and procedures opaque, individuals with little education and little experience in dealing with bureaucracies no doubt found them much more so.

One research participant summarized a common complaint of both survivors and providers by saying, "FEMA tells you different things every time you call." Both survivors and service providers complained of FEMA's confusing rules. The logic of what FEMA provided was unclear. Survivors received different amounts of money to replace personal property with no clear explanation of the amount granted. Providers could not understand the rules either and described many frustrating encounters with FEMA officials. One provider told us that

I can call FEMA four times in one day on the same client, and each four times, ask the same question, and every time get a different answer. So they don't really know. There's lots of conflicting information on the ground with the FEMA people.

The rule changes had serious implications for the City of Austin, which paid landlords in advance without firm guarantees that they would be reimbursed. City officials also reported having to "turn on a dime" to deal with rental issues every time FEMA changed the rules, resulting in staggering overtime for city employees. In addition, the incessantly changing time limits and termination dates associated with FEMA programs increased uncertainty. The original FEMA deadline for the termination of 403 housing assistance to the city was the end of February 2006, but it was then extended to March 31, then to May 31, then to June 30, then July 31. It finally ended on August 31, 2006. The extensions were necessary and welcome for survivors who had not been able to find jobs but required living with uncertainty as to when the real end would come. As with the 403 program, the 408 program, direct housing assistance to individual families, was also extended several times from February 28, 2007, to May 31, 2007, then to August 31, 2007. These extensions were also communicated in an unclear way, generally only days before the assistance was due to expire, compounding stress for survivors, apartment landlords, and nonprofit advocates working with survivors.

The ever-changing FEMA deadlines created additional stress for survivors and service providers who were trying to make plans for survivors' futures. As one provider said,

...they [survivors] get an eviction notice every time FEMA or the city changes their mind. You know, the city says, "Okay, we're not paying no more." And everyone will get an eviction notice. And then the city will say, "Okay, we're going to pay a couple more months."

Nonprofit organizations were also affected by the changing deadlines. For example, at the time of our first interview with her, one survivor who had received FEMA assistance for six months was terminated. Luckily, a local charity stepped in to help her pay her rent. The survivor appealed the FEMA decision and her housing assistance was eventually reinstated, but in the meantime she fell behind in her utility payments because she mistakenly thought FEMA was paying them as well. Again a local charity had to step in and pay her utilities. In this case, as in many others, the lack of clarity of FEMA rules not only created instability for the survivor, but also drained limited local private funds.

DELAYS IN ASSISTANCE

Delays in assistance were a recurring problem and occurred at multiple bureaucratic decision points. Survivors had to wait for assistance for weeks for no apparent reason; there were delays in receiving word on their cases and clarification of those decisions, and appeals of decisions took time even when assistance was ultimately approved. The sense of being in limbo prevented survivors from reestablishing themselves in Austin or moving back to New Orleans. Denials of assistance caused serious problems because most survivors had no visible means of support. Among these problems, our interviewees had been denied expedited assistance, rental assistance, and personal property/damages payments. One of the most serious problems that they encountered resulted from the shared household rule that we mentioned earlier. Under the shared household rule, the household was considered a unit, like a family, and members of that household could not separately receive assistance, even if they had been forcibly separated. As one provider noted, "…it's really sad about the shared household rule. It just looks like whoever gets to FEMA first gets benefits and the other people, you know, they're homeless." This policy was challenged in federal court, and although the judge ruled that the case did not meet the standard required to sue the federal government and refused to invalidate FEMA's practices, the agency eventually stopped attempting to enforce it (U.S. Senate, 2009).

This particular rule, although perhaps logical in terms of avoiding duplication of benefits, caused serious strains and even conflicts among family and social network members. At the same time that their support systems had been disrupted by the storm, a FEMA regulation kept some from qualifying for desperately needed housing assistance. The fact that FEMA finally recognized the irrationality of the rule is not surprising. However, survivors faced other obstacles to financial recovery. Many were denied Individual Assistance, a program that provides funding for critical expenses to individuals and businesses without insurance whose property has been damaged. In many cases, FEMA determined that there had been insufficient damage to individuals' property in New Orleans. Mayor Bill White of Houston sent an envoy to New Orleans to investigate these insufficient damage judgments and claims and determined that thirty out of forty-five houses that had been deemed habitable by FEMA were in fact completely destroyed (Carlisle, 2006).

In general, the most vulnerable survivors felt that the assistance they received was not sufficient to deal with the extent of their material loss and their daily subsistence needs. As Cynthia Knight, the forty-year-old African American woman we introduced in earlier chapters, grimly noted, "...FEMA think[s] my possessions and my life was worth four thousand nine hundred and seventy-two dollars. That's the price they put on millions of people life[s]." Low-income homeowners also faced unique barriers to recovery. The Road Home Program was a federal grant program operated through HUD that provided assistance to homeowners and small rental property owners who were un- or underinsured (https://www. road2la.org/). The program was not implemented for some time, and meanwhile homeowners with no or inadequate insurance had few options for repairing their homes and faced many obstacles to recovery. Esmeralda Guttierez and her husband, a skilled craftsman, were middle-aged Central American immigrants who had been purchasing their New Orleans home. Esmeralda had worked in New Orleans as a housekeeper. The couple had only flood insurance and at the time of our first interview, which took place in Austin two months after their evacuation, they were waiting for a settlement that they believed would pay off their existing home loan.

Lynn Hughes, a sixty-two-year-old white woman whom we first met in Chapter 5, became involved in a drawn-out struggle with her insurance company to obtain a settlement on her New Orleans home. She wanted to rehabilitate the property and rent it so that she could afford to remain in Austin. The delay kept her in limbo since the New Orleans property was uninhabitable and not generating income and there was no guarantee that the final settlement would be sufficient for repairs.

For those without insurance, governmental programs were often inadequate. According to a 2008 report, 80 percent of Road Home recipients in New Orleans did not receive adequate funding to cover repairs; statewide there was a gap of $46,000 per household between what the program provided and what repairs would cost. This inadequate compensation disproportionately affected low-income and African American communities, which had few resources with which to rebuild (Rose, Clark, & Duval-Diop, 2008). In addition to providing meager compensation, the process in general was slow and families had to wait long periods before they received even the inadequate funds. A Rand Corporation study (Rand Gulf States Policy Institute, 2008) found an average waiting time of eight months for applicants to receive funding.

RESIDENTIAL INSTABILITY AND COMMUNITY

Frequent moves clearly undermined stability and the ability of survivors to form or become part of new communities. Nongovernmental organizations did what they could, but FEMA's rules and procedures dominated. The difficulty of transporting social capital was revealed in another way that reflected social class and culture. Survivors' attempts to rebuild the sorts of communities that they were accustomed to in New Orleans were often met with disapproval in Austin, where behavior that was acceptable in lower-class neighborhoods in New Orleans often violated neighborhood norms. A provider gave the following example:

> New Orleans is pretty rough and a lot of our clients came from public housing and from the projects and, you know, they're wonderful individuals, they just, they're – we have a lot of clients who are very loud, and the apartment managers are just like, "They're outside all the time, they're loud," and that's just – they're not harming anybody, that's just the way they are. That's just – they spend a lot of time outside. So it's just little things like that, that people are like, "Why do they do that?"

Although survivors were often represented as "passive" and "helpless victims," in reality neither survivors nor service providers were passive in the face of the obstacles that they faced. As one African American survivor said, "you got to speak up for yourself." A white survivor offered a similar assessment when she said, "…you have to fight to stay on top of all this stuff, or it will just slip between the cracks." Local agencies and case managers were vital in ensuring that the survivors were able to act as effective agents on their own behalf. Finding relevant information about how the system worked was very important from the beginning. Researchers who volunteered at social service agencies in the weeks after the evacuation witnessed cell phone networking by survivors standing in lines to receive assistance. One might hear about a resource (or more likely, the lack of a resource) at a certain agency and pass that along via cell phone to family and friends. Although it was not always accurate, this sort of information was passed constantly among members of social networks. Janice Lyons, an eighteen-year-old African American female, explained that with the assistance of volunteers and staff of a not-for-profit organization, she was able to figure out how to "take care of business." She eagerly sought as much information as possible from the beginning and made good use of volunteer and nongovernmental resources.

Acting as effective agents included appealing negative decisions. One survivor enlisted the help of a lawyer in order to resolve her shared household case in which she had been denied benefits. She helped her attorney present a detailed explanation of the situation and why housing assistance was justified. The appeal took time but was ultimately successful. Harriet Gibson, a white survivor who was an attorney, was employed by a local legal aid association and became a powerful national advocate for survivors.

As further illustration of their active rather than passive roles, survivors made contingency plans. They sought assistance from family members and friends as well as assistance from governmental and nongovernmental agencies and organizations. One African American grandmother had a disaster housing voucher valid until June 2007, but was worried that her daughter and her daughter's five grandchildren might be evicted at any time. The family had discussed moving in together in case such an outcome occurred. The daughter was high on the waiting list for subsidized housing, but her situation required planning in case the housing did not materialize in time.

Local agencies and case managers were vital in ensuring that the survivors did not become helpless victims and were able to demand benefits to which they were entitled. Service providers also developed communications networks, both among themselves and, as we describe in the next chapter, among survivors. A local agency set up a listserve to keep providers abreast of new developments with FEMA and the availability of specific sources of funding and services.

THE ROLE OF CIVIL SOCIETY: REALIZED AND POTENTIAL

Dealing with FEMA required a huge amount of work and skill on the part of survivors and service providers. Here the social theory concepts of "agency" and "structure" that we introduced in Chapter 3 are instructive (Ritzer, 2008; Ritzer & Gindoff, 1994). Our interviews with both survivors and service providers revealed numerous examples of *agency*, attempts to engage in action to impact the situation (Ritzer, 2008; Ritzer & Gindoff, 1994). However, over and over we saw that the low-income, primarily African American survivors encountered structural barriers – such as social class, income, wealth, education, ethnicity, and social norms – that limited their options and undermined their ability to control their lives.

As a result, advocacy was not an experience that was empowering or positive either at the individual or collective level. On the contrary, dealing with arbitrary decisions and opaque and illogical administrative barriers created widespread mistrust of FEMA, of local agencies, and of government as a whole. It eroded trust in local agencies and institutions that were not part of FEMA but that got caught up in the agency's irrationalities. As we have documented, the situation generated resentment among survivors who saw others receiving assistance that was denied to them. Justine Betts, whom we met earlier, believed that FEMA was "taking care of [people they are] not supposed to be taking care of. The one's that need it, we can't get it. My mom [hasn't] received no kind of help since she been here." This perceived injustice undermined possibilities for building community and forming new relationships.

From our perspective, one of the worst consequences of the clumsy bureaucratic response was the negative light in which it placed survivors. It in effect turned law-abiding citizens into criminals who were punished for not understanding and complying with utterly confusing rules. The practice of providing money without clear instructions concerning what it could be used for resulted in a form of bureaucratic entrapment. Local government and nongovernmental agencies attempted to help by providing information, housing, or financial assistance. Given the magnitude of the need and the overwhelming role of FEMA, these agencies' capacity to address the survivors' most serious needs was severely limited and their ultimate effectiveness undermined.

The events and situations that we have described clearly demonstrated the central role of FEMA and the federal government. State and local authorities, NGOs, and even private citizens can respond effectively only in the context of an effective governmental response at the highest level. Crises that affect thousands or hundreds of thousands of people require extremely high levels of coordination to deal with logistical and other problems. In the end, our study clearly demonstrates that civil society organizations and even local levels of government cannot function effectively in the leadership vacuum that excessive devolution of federal authority to local levels implies.

We must note that many of the problems that our sample of survivors faced had their basis or were exacerbated by race and their social class positions. The uncertainty that pervaded their lives and their interactions with FEMA was a consequence of historical processes that placed them in danger in the first place and that undermined their capacities to recover and rebuild. Our data, in addition to governmental statistics, make it clear that much of the formal federal response to the crisis represents short-term solutions to long-term problems of poverty, marginalization and racism, and the lack of affordable housing in most metropolitan areas.

Survivors faced not only the fear of homelessness and uncertainty about the future; they also often felt disrespected and looked down upon. Some characterized their overall experience with FEMA as inhumane. Some, as we have shown, felt unwelcome and distrusted by the citizens of their new city. Antoinette Thereoux, a twenty-four-year-old African American female, framed the survivors' experiences in terms of class and talked about how FEMA focused its efforts on those who were least in need. As she said,

...And sometimes I think they're just...the word I want to use is just [not] humane....FEMA has you under a certain status, and I think they are picking and choosing who is eligible under that status....I think they just kicking the poor people to the curb, you know.

These sentiments point to more than simple bureaucratic problems. They reflect more deeply entrenched problems of social and racial inequality, disempowerment, institutional traumatization, and the absence of citizenship rights (Somers, 2008).

The experience of both survivors and providers illustrates how the organization and structure of the emergency response system hamstrung various organizations at every level. Survivors' lack of social capital was accompanied by a lack of cultural, political, and economic capital. Although they evacuated with family and friends, survivors were forcibly separated from the major part of their most important resource, their social networks, and placed in situations in which they could not regroup. The requirements for receiving assistance were impossible to meet, irrational, and at times abusive. Civil society organizations, and even local-level governmental agencies, were unable to compensate for or negate FEMA's failures. The consequences included protracted delays in survivors' ability to return to normal as well as the waste of resources, expertise, and time by formal and volunteer responders.

Rebuilding community in a strange place, especially when the survivors are scattered and separated from those individuals on whom they rely, is inherently difficult, if not impossible. Civil society organizations, including NGOs, churches, and other organizations, as well as individuals, were constrained in their abilities to help rebuild social capital and material well-being by the overwhelming size of the crisis and their limited human and material resources. The serious lack of coordination was clearly central to the limited role of civil society organizations. Although FEMA is mandated to form partnerships with local agencies, those partnerships exist basically in name only. The information that we have gathered suggests that FEMA appears unable or unwilling to include civil society agencies in a truly meaningful way. As a consequence, civil society agencies are themselves unable to coordinate their efforts, and their potential contribution to the alleviation of suffering is consequently compromised. In the next chapter, we will examine the organizational ecology of Austin more closely and discuss the attempts of local governmental agencies and nongovernmental organizations to coordinate their efforts. As we will see, those efforts, although admirable, were again inherently limited by larger structural factors.

6

Civil Society, NGOs, and the Grassroots Response

The Eastside Community Support Association (ECSA), a local faith-based, nonprofit organization located in a small office behind a church in a low-income section of East Austin, illustrates the potential positive role of voluntary efforts in dealing with crises. It also reveals the limitations faced by small-scale organizations in dealing with large-scale and complex social problems. The organization was run by Pastor Gerald Jackson,[1] a dedicated middle-aged African American who believed that the church had a special mission to minister to the poor. ECSA had been in existence for a few years before Hurricane Katrina struck, and the association administered a number of programs, including a breakfast program, HIV testing, and a children's summer camp. Given its history of ministry to an impoverished African American community, responding to the needs of the mostly African American Hurricane Katrina victims was an irresistible moral imperative.

The storm and the arrival of survivors in Austin evoked an outpouring of sympathy, and a large number of church members volunteered to help. Somewhere between fifty and one hundred church members provided assistance at the Convention Center and solicited donations of money and goods to provide to survivors. Some of the volunteers were from another church in a more affluent section of the city. Given the large number of donations that were made, the organization was forced to

---

[1] The names of organizational participants and local organizations have been changed to maintain their confidentiality.

move its operation out of the small church office into a larger facility. ECSA provided assistance with transportation, food, and access to medical care and helped survivors who had FEMA housing vouchers contact local landlords. The organization raised nearly $50,000 to provide gift cards to survivors. During the first few weeks, ECSA helped over six hundred families.

Within three months, the initial enthusiasm began to wane and the number of volunteers declined. ECSA closed its extended facility and returned to its old location behind the church. The organization continued to maintain a database of survivors and refocused its efforts toward helping survivors with longer-term adjustment. Even with its experience in providing assistance, ECSA, like other organizations, found that addressing the needs of Katrina survivors was a daunting task. As Pastor Jackson told us, "…when we jumped in, it was just going so fast that we never had time to plan for anything because we were just trying to meet the needs of people." The number of individuals and families in need was far greater than ECSA and other small organizations could easily deal with.

Housing, of course, was an immediate and pervasive need. ECSA used its knowledge of the community and contacts with local landlords to help evacuees find housing. Even when they had housing vouchers, it was difficult for survivors who did not know the city to find available rental property. Pastor Jackson told us that both survivors and landlords found the service that ECSA provided valuable. As he said,

…we knew some contacts in the area [and] we began to become a conduit for housing.…What happened when people got out of the Convention Center, they would call us and say, "Do you have any housing?" And because…everybody…knew that we were sending folks to some of the landlords, that was a goldmine because somehow, some of them [the landlords] didn't have high occupancy in some of the areas, so what they did, they call ECSA [and] say,…"I got two duplexes"…[or,]…"I got four places in my apartments." So what we started doing is writing those things down. As people came in, we would tell them to call this landlord or this place or this apartment.

Because many evacuees had no transportation, ECSA used its vans to transport them to view the various rental properties. ECSA also attempted to help survivors with medical problems. Pastor Jackson explained that,

…we dealt with a few people who had HIV issues. One that hadn't eaten and had no medication…came up to ECSA throwing up and everything…so we called the Human Resources, I know a guy…sent some young ladies to take care of her, kind of nurse her back to health, feed her and everything, and then they put her in a place, I haven't heard from her since.

Pastor Jackson told us that he was aware from the beginning that the survivors' situations were complex and that providing assistance to them would be a long-term enterprise. They needed help with getting transportation and food, finding work, and much more. It was clear, though, that a small, local nonprofit organization could make only a small difference, despite the dedication and enthusiasm of its director. Pastor Jackson told us that, "…we also understood this was going to be long-term recovery and not just two or three months where you can put a Band-Aid on it and think it would go away." The initial enthusiasm and desire to help in the larger community had other short-term beneficial effects. As we mentioned earlier, members of other congregations volunteered to help. Pastor Jackson explained that this was not usual and that volunteers from East and West Austin, two very different and historically divided areas, found that they could work together. In the absence of a formal organization, though, such cooperation lasted only temporarily.

Despite promises, the agency received no reimbursements or assistance from FEMA or other government agencies, even though some of ECSA's expenses covered what seemed to have been government responsibilities. The organization paid for a funeral for a woman's daughter and it paid for prescriptions for others. As Pastor Jackson explained,

…we spent over thirty thousand dollars of our donated money and we sent some information to the city and FEMA, and FEMA says, "We [are] going to reimburse you." That hasn't happened yet. And then out of the thirty some-odd thousand, they said, "Well, we can't reimburse you for a funeral. We can't reimburse you for U-Haul," or whatever. So, they said, "We can only reimburse you for eight or ten thousand." I said, "Well, whatever you do, it'll be fine." But we hadn't received anything from FEMA.

Pastor Jackson said that as the initial sympathy waned, the public began to feel that survivors should find work and get back on their feet, but that expectation, he explained, was not realistic. The problems that survivors faced were long-term, and without governmental assistance, there was little that voluntary agencies could do to assist with major problems such as employment and serious medical issues. When asked about the organization's longer-term objectives, Pastor Jackson replied that,

That's a good question. Because every time we try to focus on something, we expand what we focus on. …We [were] focusing on aftercare, that means just to call, let them know we haven't forgotten about them, and just say, how [are] you doing? But what is happening, we believe is that…the empathy…I would say, is beginning to fall in the community. What I'm saying is, and I did an interview with [local radio station] a couple weeks ago…and the main question was…why should people still pay tax dollars for people that should be working? And, that is the general consensus now, which is troubling because, as a pastor, I do funerals. And doing funerals, I've done, I'll check on the families, six, eight months later, during the holidays, they're still grieving. So now, for someone to lose their family, their home, the church, the community, their relatives, their kinfolks, to be separated because they're not together as a family anymore, you don't get over that in a year's time.…The apathy [of the Austin community] there is really…it kind of bothers me for the fact that we've become so insensitive that we give folks a time when they should be over their grieving process of that situation. And that's…tough. But to answer that question, where are we, right now, we are doing aftercare.

Pastor Jackson was clearly driven by a sense of mission. As he put it,

…I think that the church has always been there to help in the community, to meet the needs of the community. That was the assignment of the church over two thousand years ago.…I believe that it's going to come down to the churches. The first year our donations were given to some of the nonprofits and social services to do certain things. But what happens when FEMA or the city says, "We're not doing that anymore"? Then the money runs out. Who has to step to the plate? And I think it's going to be the community that's going to say, hey, we need to help.…

Pastor Jackson's and ECSA's efforts were important and revealed the depth of sympathy for the survivors that people felt immediately after the hurricane. Ordinary people, professionals, and entire groups volunteered to do what they could. Often, in fact, there were too many volunteers to be employed effectively. Unfortunately, that outpouring of sympathy and the truly generous donations that were made did not alter the fundamental vulnerability of the survivors. Sympathy is short-lived and is no substitute for structural integration in the form of employment opportunities and adequate housing. Charity, in fact, can detract from what is really needed, which are longer-term investments in people and neighborhoods that fundamentally alter individuals' life situations. Although civil society agencies can help and even enhance aspects of the community, as was the case when volunteers from East and West Austin cooperated in voluntary efforts, those benefits can also be short-lived and, in the absence of support from the state, leave vulnerable populations in the same situation in which they have found themselves historically.

CIVIL SOCIETY AND LARGE-SCALE NEED

An efficient and effective response to a widespread crisis that results in the almost complete breakdown of the normal social order in reality requires an almost military level of command and control. Yet in the case of most large-scale disasters, such centralized command and control, or anything approximating it, is usually absent. In the immediate aftermath of the event, someone or some group should ideally have the authority and expertise to direct and coordinate the actions of those on the ground. Some central authority should coordinate rescue and evacuation operations, address emergency medical needs, and deal effectively with basic logistics to make sure that personnel and equipment are deployed to where they are needed and to ensure that precious resources are not wasted and efforts duplicated. In most major disasters – such as the 2004 Pacific tsunami or Hurricane Mitch, which caused massive loss of life in Central America in 1998 – centralized command and control is missing and multiple international, governmental, and nongovernmental organizations respond in an uncoordinated manner that often fails to include local groups (Glantz & Jamieson, 2000; Rocha & Christoplos, 2001; Telford, Cosgrave, & Houghton, 2006). The result is a massive duplication of effort, the neglect of certain vital needs, and a delayed and incomplete recovery.

As we have documented in preceding chapters, although FEMA is formally charged with coordinating disaster response, the political realities that define its mandate, its organization, its funding, and its real authority limit its capacity to direct and coordinate the efforts of lower-level agencies and organizations effectively. Immediately following Hurricane Katrina and during the longer-term recovery effort, FEMA occupied the central coordinating role in a situation in which there were many other organizations responding to the crisis, each of which might have benefited from some direction. As we have mentioned, many of the survivors were further traumatized by the militarized response. Although the rescue may have had a military feel, it lacked the coordinated command and control of an effective and efficient military operation. State and local governments offered various forms of assistance and numerous nongovernmental organizations responded as well, both in the short and longer term, but their effectiveness was clearly undermined by a lack of coordination. In this chapter, we examine the role of those lower-level agencies and organizations, paying particular attention to the role of nongovernmental actors in dealing with both the short- and longer-term needs of the survivors. We pay particular attention to the problem of the coordination of efforts by different agencies and organizations at multiple levels and we document the consequences of a lack of coordination for the survivors.

As has been widely documented, in the immediate aftermath of the storm the lack of coordination among various responders resulted in chaos and death. Yet even after the evacuation from New Orleans, lack of coordination continued to undermine efforts to return the survivors to some semblance of normality. In the longer term, the response evolved beyond emergency needs to include assistance with housing, employment, education, medical care, transportation, and more. Reestablishing the survivors in Austin required rebuilding their lives in every detail. Relatively soon after their arrival, the magnitude and complexity of the task became apparent. It involved numerous governmental and nongovernmental actors whose efforts were largely uncoordinated. In response, NGOs in the Austin area developed structures to facilitate the sharing of information and resources in an attempt to employ scarce resources more efficiently and to better coordinate their efforts. These attempts were a great improvement over a situation in which each agency and organization pursued its own internally defined objectives in the complete absence of knowledge of what other agencies and organizations were doing. Yet these efforts came up against the inevitable limitations of voluntary efforts in which individual organizations pursue their own agendas that they for the most part have defined for themselves. FEMA's legislative mandate includes encouraging coordination among local agencies and organizations, but in the absence of real centralized authority, these attempts often have only limited success. Although limited government and a maximal reliance on local authority may reflect core values in our political culture, in times of crisis or for dealing with large-scale social problems, the absence of an effective federal presence limits the possibilities for response.

DEVOLUTION AND DISASTER

As we outlined in the introduction, since the Reagan administration, a philosophy of devolution has dominated American social and public policy (Wineburg et al., 2008). From the perspective of proponents of a minimalist governmental approach, big government directly threatens individual freedom and local authority (Reisch, 2009; Schram, Fording, & Soss, 2008; Soss, Fording, & Schram, 2008). Welfare reform and devolution in the United States are perhaps extreme versions of the more general fiscal crisis of the welfare state that has resulted in calls for reducing the entitlements in most developed nations (Esping-Andersen et al., 2002; Hacker, 2002; Pierson, 1994, 2001a, 2001b). Critics of big government and proponents of greater austerity argue that local institutions are best suited to make decisions about local needs and how they may be most effectively addressed. From this perspective, NGOs, including faith-based organizations (FBOs), are ideal mechanisms for mobilizing the social resources of civil society and useful organizations through which to funnel government funding.

One of the supposed strengths of NGOs is that they are more agile and less bureaucratic than federal agencies and more able to respond to crises quickly (Fremont-Smith, Boris, & Steuerle, 2006; Homeland Security Institute, 2006; Olsasky, 2006; Steuerle, 2002). In reality, though, NGOs and FBOs face serious limitations in resources, accountability, and coordination that can undermine their efficiency and effectiveness and limit their ability to deal with complex problems. Accountability is an ongoing issue since at the same time that they are concerned with clients' needs, they are accountable to donors who have their own funding priorities (Fremont-Smith, Boris, & Steuerle, 2006; Steuerle, 2002). Those who need assistance most often do not receive charitable donations, resulting in potential inequities (Fremont-Smith, Boris, & Steuerle, 2006; Moore, 2006; Steuerle, 2002). In addition, private donors tend to be interested in immediately visible disaster relief rather than longer-term recovery. Private donations rarely build infrastructure, enhance human capital through education and training, or provide overhead for daily organizational operations (Fremont-Smith, Boris, & Steuerle, 2006; Goldman, 2006; Moore, 2006). Perhaps most important is the lack of coordination, which in the absence of an adequate emergency response organization results in inefficiencies, the inappropriate use of resources, major frustration among helpers, and unmet needs among victims (Kapucu, 2007).

The terrorist attacks on the World Trade Center in New York on September 11, 2001, provided an important, if tragic, illustration of the challenges involved in coordinating a response to a major event (DiPerna, 2003; Government Accountability Office, 2002). As is usually the case in major disasters, no single agency was responsible for tracking funding distributions to different organizations (Government Accountability Office, 2002). In recognition of the coordination vacuum, the government developed a National Response Plan for a coordinated response to domestic disasters. The American Red Cross and the National Voluntary Organizations Active in Disaster (NVOAD) were assigned specific responsibilities for coordination in future emergencies. Seven of the largest disaster response charities, in partnership with FEMA, formed the Coordinated Assistance Network (CAN) with a database designed to facilitate collaboration and data sharing for future disasters (Government Accountability Office, 2005).

Despite these efforts to create a structure for collaboration for NGOs during a crisis, the 2005 hurricane season, which included not only Katrina but also Rita and Wilma, strained the financial and organizational resources of the American Red Cross (American Red Cross, 2006). The confluence of three serious storms revealed the limitations of even a massive NGO such as the Red Cross in dealing with major crises. The needs created by disasters such as hurricanes are similar to those presented by long-term poverty. Although emergency NGOs may be experienced at short-term emergency assistance, they are ill-equipped to provide complex social services such as job training, mental health counseling, or community rebuilding (Smith, 2006). To address the need for case management after Katrina, FEMA contracted with a national faith-based service organization in 2006 to establish a case management consortium. This federally funded case management initiative also suffered from coordination challenges, though, and was overwhelmed by large caseloads, high turnover of personnel, and limited community resources, including housing, transportation, and employment possibilities. Investigators found that Katrina case management clients were likely to have had their cases closed even before their needs were met (Stough & Sharp, 2008).

The availability of assistance varied from one agency or organization to another, forcing survivors to shop for services, often resulting in duplication. The case management consortium used the previously mentioned CAN database. Even with this resource, though, complicated bureaucratic barriers interfered with recovery (Stough & Sharp, 2008). The system suffered from the normal problems involved in a major data collection effort. Organizations reported that the process of cooperating with the consortium was more time consuming and burdensome than they had expected and the pressure to maintain high caseloads impeded in-depth case management and created competition among agencies and organizations (Stough & Sharp, 2008).

THE MAJOR NONGOVERNMENTAL PLAYERS

Nongovernmental organizations responded immediately to the crisis in New Orleans and many continued to assist survivors in the longer term in other cities, including Austin. The Red Cross was of course among the first to respond both in New Orleans and in the cities to which survivors were evacuated. Because of its long history of disaster relief, within a short time the organization received well over $1 billion in donations for hurricane victims, far more than any other NGO. Because of the size of the disaster and despite its experience and reputation, the Red Cross was crit-icized for a disorganized response and for not forming partnerships with other local Gulf Coast nonprofit organizations (Salmon, 2006). Serious accusations of impropriety were leveled against the national organiza-tion, including the theft of relief supplies, failure to follow established procedures for distributing and tracking supplies, and clear violation of Red Cross rules, such as allowing felons to work as volunteers in the disaster area (Strom, 2006). Although the Red Cross's mission includes community services to assist needy individuals and families, its focus remains primarily on disaster relief. The longer-term task of rebuilding lives is far more complicated and difficult and largely beyond the organi-zation's mandate or capacities.

Other NGOs in New Orleans and the Gulf Coast region assisted in rebuilding neighborhoods (Chandra & Acosta, 2009). Some were estab-lished organizations, whereas others were created in response to the crisis. One grassroots organization that was formed in response to the storm was the inspiration of the family that formed it to provide infor-mation on recovery to property owners. The organization, which began in the family's own partially restored home, provided Internet and phone services and referrals to reputable contractors who could repair storm damage. The organization held seminars on topics such as mold reme-diation and power restoration. The home became a resource center and a place where neighbors could begin to rebuild networks and their local communities. What began as a small operation in someone's home spread throughout the city, and after one year there were eight neighborhood resource centers. The mission has grown to include several community building programs, and the momentum, in response to ongoing need, shows no sign of diminishing.

Given the extent of the physical damage, restoring homes so that peo-ple could return to some semblance of normal was a first priority. Another NGO that had been working for several years on home renovation proj-ects was intended to improve the lives of elderly and disabled persons as well as single parent households with minor children. The impact of Hurricane Katrina led this NGO to focus its efforts on the restoration and often the complete rebuilding of damaged homes. The list of non-governmental organizations that responded to the human needs created by the storm is too long to list completely. It includes well-known orga-nizations such as the United Way and its affiliated agencies and smaller agencies, some started in response to the disaster.

As well-meaning and successful as many NGOs were in addressing the needs of the survivors, there were clear problems of role definition and coordination both with government agencies and NGOs. The result was often duplication of effort, wasted resources, and the failure to address needs in an effective and efficient manner (Chandra & Acosta, 2009). The problem largely reflected the fact that the major federal emergency management apparatus has not developed plans for the effective use of NGOs in rescue or in recovery. A study by the Rand Gulf States Policy Institute that consisted of interviews with the CEOs of several Gulf Coast NGOs revealed a serious lack of recognition of the potential role of civil society organizations (Chandra & Acosta, 2009).

THE ORGANIZATIONAL ECOLOGY IN AUSTIN: PROBLEMS OF COORDINATION

Although we would have liked to present a diagram of these local agencies with clear lines of authority and resource flows, the reality is that the organizational and funding environments were changing so rapidly that a concise and accurate organizational chart or a static description of resource and information flows is not possible. The fluidity of funding and the changing roles of specific organizations would have required monthly or even weekly flow charts. As we have explained, organizations adapted their missions on an ongoing basis in response to the fact that funding from different sources was unpredictable both in timing and amount. Organizations engaged in whatever activities were possible when funding was available and then turned people away when funding dried up. Planning and coordination were undermined by uncertainty concerning future funding. Large organizations such as the Red Cross were resource rich and provided funding to other organizations. Smaller organizations were at the mercy of unpredictable funding streams. In all of this confusion, much duplication was evident while many needs went unmet.

As the case study with which we began this chapter showed, the initial response of the Austin community to the humanitarian crisis was overwhelming (Gajewski et al., 2011; Lein et al., 2009). Concern for the survivors' welfare was genuine and donations poured into national and local organizations. Many individuals volunteered to help in any way they could – so many, in fact, that many were turned away. NGOs, including many FBOs, were key players in the response. In Austin, these organizations provided furniture to eight hundred households and placed fifty families in private homes as part of an interfaith housing program. With funding provided by FEMA, the city signed contracts with over four hundred landlords to provide housing to survivors. Some citizens sponsored survivor families through "adopt a family" programs, while others donated to food pantries. Many NGOs and FBOs were providing services to survivors in Austin nearly a week before FEMA officials arrived at the Convention Center. Unfortunately, as we have noted, this influx of new residents and the overwhelming community response created serious coordination problems (Gajewski et al., 2011; Lein et al., 2009). The Red Cross received between fifteen thousand and twenty thousand volunteer applications to help assist survivors of Katrina and Hurricane Rita, which struck the Gulf Coast a few weeks after Katrina. This number of volunteers was far more than the organization could train and employ effectively. Relatively quickly, the volume of donations and volunteers overwhelmed many of the volunteer organizations.

Pastor Jackson's observation that the initial response was short-lived was true generally. Within a few weeks, many survivors were facing food insecurity and were struggling to get food stamps. Although it is impossible to document exactly how much money was raised locally for Katrina survivors, we estimate that at least $5 million from churches, individuals, foundations, and corporate sponsors came into Austin, in addition to the funding provided through FEMA and HUD (Gajewski et al., 2011). The resources that flowed into the community after Katrina added considerable complexity to the service delivery system, as each source of funding had its own start and end dates, eligibility criteria, waiting times, and application paperwork. Keeping informed about available funding required considerable effort by case managers. It also added additional barriers for hurricane survivors because they had to navigate this complex system to get the help they needed. Additionally, changes in federal disaster and income maintenance policy created an unstable service environment that was often challenging for both survivors and service providers to understand and navigate.

The clear need for greater coordination and communication among agencies and organizations was quickly apparent. Several organizations and governmental agencies became involved in coordination efforts and eventually held regular meetings and devoted resources to the effort. As we describe later on, certain organizations and agencies were more central to the effort. Others did not participate or did so only peripherally even though they were working with survivors. This necessary effort was not without significant costs, not the least of which was staff time. Yet the changing nature and complexity of the survivors' needs forced the issue. As survivors moved from temporary shelters to hotels and more permanent housing, NGOs rapidly expanded and refocused their efforts to respond to emerging longer-term needs. Given the complexity of these needs, case management quickly emerged as the assistance paradigm of choice. The objective of case management, however, is not to address the more basic problems, such as low educational levels and limited work experience, that survivors had before the crisis. Disaster case management, as defined by NVOAD, focuses on returning clients to their pre-disaster level of functioning (Bell, 2008; National Voluntary Organizations Active in Disaster, 2004). It does not involve an attempt to deal with preexisting social or personal problems and is not focused on improving the client's pre-disaster social or economic condition. The objective is much more focused on immediate problems that are the direct result of the disaster (National Voluntary Organizations Active in Disaster, 2004). With this objective, the case manager works with the client to develop a recovery plan. The approach very clearly stresses the importance of client responsibility and the development of self-sufficiency. Disaster case management is also concerned with the optimal use of resources and preventing clients from receiving government money and private assistance for the same problem (Bell, 2008; National Voluntary Organizations Active in Disaster, 2004).

Given the objective of avoiding duplication of funding and service delivery, the need for some means of coordination and information sharing among the many organizations involved became apparent. In mid-October, United Way instituted the Centex Disaster Response List Serve on which service providers could share information. Other local agencies also served coordinating functions. Numerous meetings were held in October and November of 2005 to explore possibilities for the coordination of response efforts among organizations. Individual service providers involved in the emerging case management effort had their first meeting in October. These regular meetings eventually resulted in the assignment of case management efforts by postal code. As the information about various programs became available to service providers, the focus moved to helping case managers with individual cases. Some organizations raised private money and were able to start developing caseloads early.

Although a detailed organizational chart of the relationships among organizations involved in the coordination of the case management efforts is not possible, Figure 6.1 presents a general schematic of the various

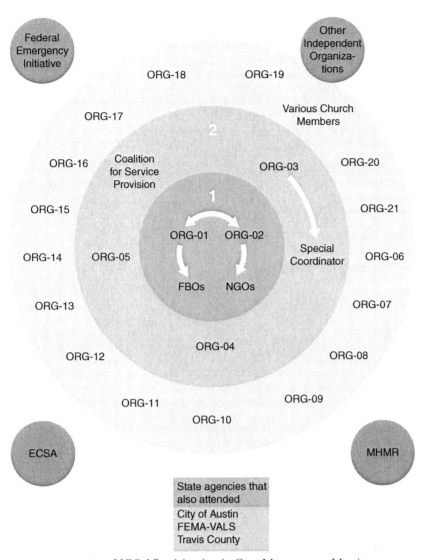

FIGURE 6.1. NGOs' Participation in Case Management Meetings.

organizations in the Austin area that participated to varying degrees, as well as their relationship to one another. The figure is intended to illustrate the fact that several organizations were involved, but that their commitment to the coordination effort varied significantly. The roles of the organizations and their relationships changed frequently, so the schematic is only a general guide to understanding the organizational ecology in Austin. The diagram is organized as a series of concentric and overlapping circles, with the organizations that assumed the greatest responsibility for providing services and case management in the center and those that provided fewer services or that participated less in the effort farther from the center.

Within the inner circle, two organizations served as the major motivators and administrators for bringing NGOs and FBOs into the coordination effort. Several other organizations in circle two were active participants. Various coalitions and other special recovery assistance organizations were also fairly active. In the third circle, we locate several organizations, many with specific clientele, such as children or the elderly. Others included specific congregations or organizations focused on specific health conditions, such as AIDS. The figure makes it clear that many more organizations were specialized or less centrally active in the coordination effort than those organizations in the core. The figure also includes other organizations that did not actively participate in the coordination of case management. This group also included the local mental health agency, as well as other organizations that had a focus that overlapped with disaster services but were not subsumed under it. The box at the bottom of the figure notes that several governmental agencies sent representatives to the coordination meetings.

This coordination effort evolved over time. When survivors first arrived in Austin, the operation at the Convention Center was managed primarily by the City of Austin and the Red Cross. Many other agencies and organizations were involved, but many survivors, service providers, and those members of the team who volunteered at the Convention Center and other shelters described the first few weeks as so chaotic that it was hard to tell who was doing what. Figure 6.2 presents a schematic of the flow of funding from major funding sources through intermediary agencies and finally to front-line service providers. The figure is reproduced from a study of organizational flows carried out by four members of the research team. More detail concerning the specifics of the flows can be found in the published article (Gajewski et al., 2011). The figure does not include the amounts transferred and it may not include all flows, but it serves to illustrate the complexity of funding streams. We do not know how decisions on allocation were made or why particular agencies were funded. Funders were attempting to distribute the money that they had in ways that in their judgment would benefit the most people and do the most good. The criteria on which their specific decisions were made remain unclear.

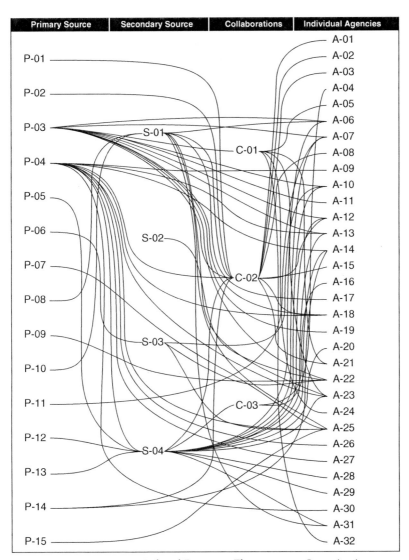

FIGURE 6.2. Katrina-Related Resource Flows among Organizations.

Unfortunately, the large number of players and the complex funding flows caused much confusion. The service providers we interviewed commented on the extent of confusion at a number of levels. Describing the initial relationship between the City of Austin and the Red Cross, for example, one service provider described confusion and contention about who would be in control of particular areas. She explained that "…it seemed that nobody was clear about where the buck stopped." Some of the difficulties involved the need to manage rapidly changing missions. She continued,

...the instant change, day [to] day...your first forty-eight hours were a pure emergency evacuation situation...we were triaging patients at the airport, transporting directly to the hospital, making [decisions on the go], we actually opened two facilities, we opened Palmer [auditorium] and the Convention Center. Palmer became our acute care [facility]...so many different decisions had to be made...you have a completely different [situation] your first forty-eight hours...then you're transitioning into [something] we'd never been in before, long-term sheltering of a community.

The need to coordinate the efforts of all the agencies and organization involved, and the serious consequences of the failure to do so, became obvious in the first few months after the evacuation. Resources were not used optimally and survivors' needs went unmet. The leadership of various organizations, especially those involved in case management that required contact with multiple agencies and organizations, recognized the problem. In early meetings of the case management group, a local pastor assumed a leadership role along with various city and county officials in an effort to better coordinate their efforts. A branch of a large NGO assumed the role of the fiscal agent for that group of organizations and managed the flow of funds to member organizations. The pastor played an important role in establishing lines of communication and in organizing meetings of providers.

Unfortunately, differences in the service missions and service delivery operations of various organizations interfered with coordination efforts. There was no agreed upon standard operating procedure. Providers from faith-based organizations that were working with the emerging network of providers met at one place, and NGOs that were affiliated with a second group met at another. The separation was not complete, though, as a number of participants attended both meetings. The two groups eventually decided to meet together to better deal with the issues related to case management. These case management meetings were co-chaired by the emerging leaders of the two groups. Case managers continued to meet weekly until August 2007, when the majority of the organizations involved lost their funding. A few organizations continued to meet bimonthly after that.

Although organizations were the major focus of organizational efforts, certain individuals stood out as key players. They mobilized nonprofit organizations to adapt their missions to disaster response and facilitated the efforts of others to achieve specific objectives. One such individual was Harriet Gibson, who worked for a legal aid association. In Figure 6.1, the legal aid association appears in the second circle because it was not as central as other organizations, but was certainly very important, especially in providing seriously needed legal aid to survivors. Gibson was herself a survivor and an attorney. She familiarized herself with FEMA rules and regulations and assumed the role of advocate for survivors. She educated the case managers on legal issues so that they could provide accurate and useful information. Gibson was in contact with individuals and organizations in other cities to which survivors had been sent, and she developed a number of forms that allowed survivors to comply more easily with FEMA rules. She also attended every case management meeting for over a year and provided invaluable input. Indeed, without her legal knowledge and advocacy, FEMA procedures would have remained much more opaque and obscure for case managers and survivors.

Another key player was Sandra Long, who was also a survivor. In the spring of 2006, the United Way received some funding for survivor assistance and hired Long as a long-term recovery coordinator. However, by the time that Long was hired as the coordinator, the case management system had already coalesced around two other organizations, resulting in some role confusion. Eventually, Sharon Wilson, who worked for a local community organization, helped negotiate an agreement concerning the division of responsibility between the case management group and the long-term recovery committee. Long noted that confusion arose because as she said, "…providers are normally used to working short-term and this is something that has been overwhelming for them."

In the third circle of Figure 6.1, we have placed the organizations that regularly participated in the case management meetings but were less central than those in the inner two circles. Many of these are well-known organizations with broadly defined missions, as well as church-related initiatives. Most received funding from various sources to provide case management to survivors. A few organizations provided services to survivors but did not participate in the case management meetings. For example, ECSA, whose story we presented at the beginning of the chapter, originated in an African American church on the predominantly minority east side of the city. As volunteers for a faith-based organization, ECSA workers did not think of themselves as case managers.

Despite the influx of funding and resources, some basic needs went unmet. As we have noted, affordable housing was and remains in short supply in Austin. Survivors who were not eligible for FEMA housing assistance had few options other than to apply for federal public housing assistance or the Section 8 program. NGOs could offer little other than short-term rental assistance, usually for only one month. Transportation, both within Austin and for survivors who wanted to return home, was a clear need, but was supplied by NGOs only on a limited basis. Given the socioeconomic profile of evacuees, many who arrived in Austin had lived in persistent poverty in New Orleans and had multiple needs not related to the storm. Pre-storm vulnerabilities, coupled with the trauma of displacement and the loss of the social supports that had sustained them in their old neighborhoods, meant that many survivors would struggle to resettle in Austin (Lein et al., 2009). Nongovernmental organizations were important in providing short-term emergency assistance, but longer-term resettlement required a much larger governmental response. As in the case of the complex problems of chronic poverty, that response did not materialize.

SERVICE PROVIDERS' PERSPECTIVES OF KATRINA SURVIVORS

Professional and voluntary service providers were clearly central players in the post-crisis drama. They represented a major source of social capital for the survivors, and the assistance that they were able to provide, even when it was inadequate, was invaluable. The providers' largely middle-class knowledge of federal, state, and municipal bureaucracies facilitated the survivors' ability to get the help they needed. As we have shown, survivors with more education, more material resources, a more sophisticated understanding of bureaucracies, and computer literacy were less dependent on such service providers. Yet despite their greater familiarity with the system, providers also had difficulties dealing with the system. Difficulties also arose as the result of the very social class differences that made providers helpful to survivors. Despite their best intentions, service providers often found survivors hard to engage in case management. Sometimes their efforts were rebuffed. Clients had to be sought out and convinced to avail themselves of services; they did not seek case management. As a result, caseloads built slowly. One supervisor described resistance among survivors. As she explained,

It seems like logically that case management would be a helpful tool for folks, but this group of people, by and large, does not recognize case management as a coherent meaningful interaction [...and as a consequence] it doesn't work tremendously well....This sense of partnering up with a professional...[does] not...always make a tremendous amount of sense...it's actually kind of annoying to lots of evacuees....They're really not interested in having extra people in their life to tell them what to do, which is what that feels like.

Case managers complained about clients' apparent lack of motivation to work toward self-sufficiency. Cultural differences were invoked to explain client motivation, engagement with service providers, and outcomes in ways that both highlighted and concealed issues of race and class. A common observation made by the primarily white providers was captured in a statement by one provider who expressed the opinion that "...these people are different." As far as we could tell, little effort was made to address these serious social class and cultural differences in understanding and behavior in the public meetings that we observed. In case management meetings, cultural competence training typically focused on relatively superficial aspects of New Orleans culture such as Creole food and Mardi Gras rather than on structural discrimination or race-based barriers to human capital development or labor force success. Excerpts from an interview with a white case manager illustrate the problem. As she described,

...You know we had lunch with the lady that we adopted [the agency had an "adopt-a-family" program], or, you know, kind of mentored. She's a twenty-four-year-old with a ten-year-old daughter and a three-year-old son, single, black lady, and...she's never graduated from high school, but I don't know what level she finished. I would imagine around ninth or tenth grade and...she's staying at one of the apartments. I [asked her,] "Well, how are you going to pay for one of these apartments?" And she said, "Section 8, whatever."...it was striking to both of us, ...getting a job and paying her own rent was not a thought for her....Section 8 was a given. [Her attitude was] "It's mine, it's an entitlement....I deserve it, it's mine." Getting out of that situation is not a thought, and I thought, "How is that so different? Why is that her mindset and that's not my mindset?" And then I thought, "Well, her sisters, her mom, her cousins, the entire extended family and friends and neighbors all have that same thought."

This excerpt illustrates some of the differences between case managers and survivors in terms of expectations and beliefs about self-sufficiency and personal responsibility. The concepts of "agency" and "structure" that we introduced in Chapter 3 may help to explain these differences. For the mostly African American survivors, their attitudes most likely reflected real limitations to social mobility that had defined their lives and those of their ancestors. Structural barriers such as low levels of education, impediments to effective parenthood, and multigenerational poverty and marginality resulted in worldviews and behaviors that placed survivors at odds with providers and very quickly also with middle-class white observers, who had generally fewer experiences of structural barriers and more experience of personal agency, at least in their personal lives.

African American and white service providers often had different understandings of clients' behavior. White providers were well aware of and mentioned the numerous structural barriers to recovery that survivors faced, including a lack of housing and other resources, the slow rebuilding of New Orleans, FEMA's irrationality and intractability, post-traumatic stress, and the disruption of social networks. Even when they acknowledged major structural barriers, white service providers often moved immediately to a discussion of self-sufficiency and lack of motivation. An excerpt from one interview with a provider illustrates this view:

Provider: …with the clients I think there is more a sense of urgency now, because when I was first meeting with them, their rent was still being paid and they were pretty, you know, confident even if sometimes they weren't sure…now I think there's more a sense of urgency to get work. That motivation has not always been there and that's been really frustrating as a case manager because, you know, you can't [find work] for your clients. You can tell them how important it is, even look at their budget and show them that employment and income is very necessary…
Interviewer: Can you tell me more about that motivation, lack of motivation?
Provider: Yeah….there's another element to it. Part of it is…if they are not sure whether they're going to go back…it's part mental health and it's part, like, the planning issue. Okay, if they think they're going to go back at the end of the summer, what is their motivation to try to find work?…Some of my clients, not all, [also have] mental health [problems], you know, [they are] still dealing with what's going on, maybe have post-traumatic stress disorder, depression, anxiety, everything that comes with something that huge….we've been trying to get them hooked up with a counselor and things like that, but even the motivation to see a counselor isn't always there. You can give them the numbers, you can tell them this is a great place to go. We have a volunteer now that's on staff who can work with trauma. She's a licensed clinical social worker and she's just great, but…it's the motivation.…I tried to set up three of my clients with her. I don't think any of them have met with her at this point.

An African American case management supervisor had a different view. She emphasized the point that, "…it's not about being unmotivated, you know. It's about being motivated very differently and not, we're not understanding [what motivates survivors] and that's okay. I mean, we can't understand everything." This supervisor realized that impoverished families and minority individuals who have lived in very different situations than middle-class and white individuals have had very different experiences with government and bureaucracies and cannot be expected to act in the same way.

Another African American case manager felt that some case managers were inexperienced and did not understand their clients or appropriately follow through with them. She felt that some case managers' fear of their clients, which had been discussed in the case management meetings several times, made it hard for them to get to know their clients. This case manager said that she understood that there were many barriers that survivors had to overcome to find work, but she felt that a good relationship with a case manager helped greatly in addressing those barriers.

One notable example of a sensitive and productive intervention that was informed by an understanding of the importance of culture and race was a program developed by ECSA, the African American faith-based organization that was discussed at the beginning of this chapter. Shortly after survivors began arriving in Austin, the city housing director, who was white, contacted Pastor Jackson to enlist ECSA's assistance in dealing with survivors' needs. This organization had begun providing emergency services to survivors shortly after their arrival. When it became clear that survivors would be in Austin for a while, the United Way targeted this organization for ongoing funding for a program based on a program that had been successful in New Orleans. The program started in June 2006. The new program built on survivors' strengths, hopes, and future plans and focused on rebuilding their social networks, both with other survivors and with their new Austin neighbors. Three survivors were recruited as door-to-door visitors who met with survivors in designated apartment complexes. Rather than focusing on collecting information and developing a case plan, this "visiting" approach was more informal and personal. The program also held community gatherings where food was the focus. Survivors brought their favorite dishes and interacted while they prepared and ate the meal. Both the New Orleans and Austin programs emphasized spirituality as well as community because they were sponsored by faith-based organizations. The program was designed to help bridge differences between Austin's African American community and African American Katrina survivors, who were significantly different culturally.

As valuable as this program was, it was limited in its impact. Such efforts were small-scale and, like the majority of voluntary nongovernmental efforts, provided short-term and temporary assistance to a small number of people. It was not just individual voluntary efforts that were limited. The case management system that developed in response to the long-term needs of Katrina survivors had a limited impact for a number of reasons. To begin with, the focus on disaster-related needs formed a kind of Catch-22 for survivors. Many were victims of Katrina precisely because of their pre-disaster structural vulnerabilities. Disaster case managers, as we have explained, were prohibited from addressing those needs even though there was probably little they could have done to redress them. In addition, we observed a mismatch between case managers' and survivors' expectations about the goals of service delivery. Given the lack of basic services, particularly transportation and affordable housing, and the mismatches between survivors' work skills and the employment market in Austin, the middle-class goal of immediate self-sufficiency was probably unrealistic for most. It was not clear from our interviews with survivors that "self-sufficiency" was even a concept or a goal they understood or valued. In New Orleans, they had relied on networks of mutual support. They looked to the group, rather than the individual, for sustenance and support.

SURVIVORS' PERCEPTION OF SERVICES

As we detailed in earlier chapters, survivors who arrived in Austin were initially overwhelmed by the response of local residents and their kindness and generosity, particularly compared to their dreadful treatment in New Orleans. Esmeralda Guttierez, a Hispanic woman we met earlier, told us that her family was able to settle into Austin quickly because of help from the community. As she said, "…yes, thanks to God, we had everything on time. Many people donated clothing to us, food also. They treated us very well…the community here treated us very well. We did not lack any food." Sonya Davis, a thirty-two-year-old African American woman, commented that her family quickly received donated items that helped them replenish their wardrobes.

However, as time wore on, Katrina-related funding diminished and it became clear that for many survivors, returning to New Orleans would be difficult if not impossible. As they remained in a limbo from which they could not escape, survivors became more and more frustrated with the services or lack of them. Mary Wilde, a forty-two-year-old white female, made this comment about the Red Cross:

…like the Red Cross is the biggest sham on the planet.…Ninety-nine percent of the Red Cross people that I dealt with were completely ignorant about how to talk to someone in crisis, how to give them information, how to treat them with respect. I mean, I have story, upon story, upon story of insults that the Red Cross heaped upon me.

Cynthia Knight, whose situation we presented earlier, reported that her difficulties with providers led her to fear that she and other survivors would become homeless. After negative experiences with service providers, she concluded that, "…a lot of us victims are gonna be [in] homeless shelters. I'm serious, though, under bridges." By the first Christmas after their arrival, some survivors were talking about a backlash against Katrina survivors. Some attributed the backlash to those who they described as "trashy people," referring to individuals from New Orleans who behaved badly and made a negative impression. They felt that these few individuals gave rise to a stereotype that resulted in negative attitudes and discrimination against all survivors. Whitney Morris, whom we first met in Chapter 3, reported difficulty with several service providers. She told us that,

> …I tried calling…they never returned my call, and I called the 2-1-1 [a social service information and referral line] trying to get different things, I went to apply for medical at the human resource, they denied me food stamps and medical. So you know, it kind of depresses you and makes your motivation go away.

Survivors also had to learn to interact with service providers in a new way. Some were unused to being recipients of charity. Justine Betts, the African American female who we have met before, initially had wonderful things to say about her adoptive family, but was insulted by the low quality of donated items she was receiving. Although the family was helpful early on, taking her to the dentist and providing other help, they distanced themselves later, and Betts became convinced that they had provided help only to receive charitable tax deductions. In her opinion,

> …they did it for tax reasons. They left us alone. It was just tax reasons. We had to, like everything that they gave us, they had to mark it down for tax reasons. They [were] all using my tragedy for tax [purposes]. I'm thinking they are all doing it from the kindness of their hearts but you all get something in return off of my tragedy.

Justine described the "adopted" family's increasing distance from her:

> They didn't even much call and wish me, wished us a Merry Christmas or nothing. And I tried to get in contact with them. And when we finally got settled, I called them, I said, "Hi, Mr.….I told you once we get settled in, I was gonna call and fix you all a nice dinner." He gave me the cold shoulder.…

A STRUCTURAL DILEMMA

Although many funders, as well as national and local NGOs and FBOs, responded quickly and creatively to the crisis, the major attempt at coordination among the various volunteer organizations in Austin was only moderately successful. The attempt was costly in terms of time and overhead and appeared to be unable to completely eliminate duplication of services. No clear accountability for all the resources spent was achieved, and no organization or coalition of organizations was able to provide three of the survivors' most basic needs: housing, transportation, and access to jobs. It became clear quite early in our study that the focus of disaster case management presents both victims and service providers with a fundamental dilemma. As we have shown in previous chapters, the victims of Hurricane Katrina, like those in other disasters, suffered serious disruption and its negative consequences in close relationship to their long-standing structural vulnerabilities. Due to low levels of human capital, limited work-related skills, few material resources, and strong ties to networks that can provide only local support, impoverished families cannot easily escape either the poverty in which they live or the negative consequences of large-scale disasters. But disaster case management specifically avoids addressing those basic structural vulnerabilities. It focuses on returning victims to normal even when what is normal is seriously suboptimal. In addition, the response in Austin and nationally was based on a model of individual self-sufficiency that was alien to many of the low-income survivors given their group orientations, and which was unreasonable given the many barriers to employment and incorporation that the new environment presented. The focus on individual agency and self-sufficiency, rather than on the numerous structural barriers that survivors faced, sometimes led to negative attitudes toward survivors. At the same time, encountering those structural barriers was frustrating for service providers.

Among the most helpful forms of assistance that case managers provided was advocacy. As we mentioned, survivor and attorney Harriet Gibson became a national expert on FEMA and assisted survivors with their legal problems and educated case managers in FEMA's rules and procedures. As a result, case managers were much better prepared to help survivors respond to FEMA requests for information, to help them appeal denials, and to maintain the appropriate documentation for continuing applications. Given FEMA's massive and nearly incomprehensible bureaucracy and the agency's often seemingly arbitrary application of rules, without this informed advocacy from case managers, it seems clear that many survivors would not have received the assistance for which they were eligible.

The response by civil society organizations to the human tragedy created by Hurricane Katrina illustrates many of the strengths and limitations of the nonprofit sector in dealing with large-scale social problems. What we discovered in Austin corroborates the findings of studies of Katrina case management services nationwide (Bell et al., 2010; Jenner et al., 2008; Stough & Sharp, 2008). Nongovernmental organizations, including faith-based organizations, moved quickly and began providing services to survivors well before FEMA arrived on the scene. Their sponsorship and advocacy were critical in assisting survivors in gaining access to FEMA assistance. In this chapter, we described the extent of coordination that NGOs in Austin achieved voluntarily. Although we cannot assign a dollar amount to any potential savings, our observations made it clear that some duplication and waste was avoided.

Although these efforts at sharing information and coordinating service delivery efforts were useful, it would be a mistake to overestimate their value. It appears that certain agencies and organizations with established mandates, administrative procedures, and service delivery mechanisms did not see the need to collaborate with other nongovernmental organizations. Nor, as we learned, was the coordination effort costless. As we noted, a new organization emerged to provide critical coordinating functions, but as a new organization it required staffing and incurred new overhead costs for offices, furniture, and associated expenses. The case management meetings themselves required additional time and effort by the already stretched staff members of the participating organizations. The question remains as to whether the benefits outweighed the costs or whether the coordination effort actually resulted in significantly greater efficiency.

As we have shown, problems were often complex and compounded. Health problems interfered with work, which caused housing problems, which fed back into poor health, and so on. In addition to identifying and diagnosing problems correctly, knowing what people and materials must be moved where is critical for effective logistics. Placing individuals in available housing requires knowing where units are available and how close they are to other vital services. During crises, information is often in short supply (DiPerna, 2003; Kapucu, 2007; Renz & Marino, 2004). Problems with incompatible databases and inconsistencies in their use are common (Government Accountability Office, 2009; Homeland Security Institute, 2006). The result is often duplication of services or the failure to provide needed services. In Austin, as in other situations, some survivors received services from multiple organizations while others received none.

The lack of a centralized information repository not only made research concerning resource flows difficult, if not impossible, it undermined accountability. Many NGOs could not provide a clear accounting of money received or services delivered to Katrina survivors. The exact value of gifts and in-kind services donated to charities and nongovernmental organizations remains unknown. In the absence of a common set of accounting procedures and criteria, each organization employed its own methods, making it impossible to assess the efficiency of different aspects of the collective operation. Since the disaster, some attempts to address aspects of the problem have been adopted. In 2008, the National Response Framework transferred responsibility for coordinating disaster intervention from the Red Cross to FEMA in recognition of the fact that an effective response to major disasters is too large for nongovernmental organizations (Government Accountability Office, 2008). After Hurricane Katrina the seven largest FBOs in the nation have devised plans to improve communication and coordination with one another, as well as with government organizations (Government Accountability Office, 2008).

The City of Austin also learned from its experience and has better integrated secular and faith-based organizations into the city's disaster plan. A local nongovernmental organization was assigned the role of serving as a clearinghouse for volunteers during future disasters. Another faith-based organization was given the role of coordinating NGO activities during disasters, and those functions were called upon during hurricanes Gustav and Ike, the second and third storms of the 2008 hurricane season. Unfortunately, this organization was forced to close as a result of the recession, but one hopes that the lessons that were learned will inform the response to future disasters. In addition to these attempts at assigning greater responsibility and authority for coordination, the local Voluntary Organizations Active in Disaster (VOAD) continues to function and city officials have improved their working relationships with nonprofit organizations.

These improvements reflect a greater understanding of the problems of coordination. That greater appreciation of the problem resulted in the Post-Katrina Emergency Management Reform Act of 2006, which charged FEMA with implementing a more consistent disaster case management program and greater collaboration among relief agencies among states (Government Accountability Office, 2009). For all of the shortcomings that we and others have documented, FEMA remains central to any disaster response. In recognition of that fact, the agency has been given primary responsibility for assessing the capacity of voluntary organizations to respond to mass disasters. It has also been directed to make Homeland Security Grant Program funding available to voluntary organizations and local VOADs to improve their disaster preparedness. Unfortunately, even with this greater appreciation of the importance of information and coordination, future disasters will no doubt reveal further shortcomings. Although preparedness is essential, governmental and nongovernmental agencies must focus on a wide range of major social problems on a routine basis. At some level, major disasters will almost inevitably catch us somewhat off-guard.

Ultimately, like the survivors and case managers in our study, researchers, policy analysts, and care providers are faced with a serious and fundamental dilemma that emerges from the very nature of large-scale social problems that require large-scale coordinated responses. We began the chapter with the suggestion that a centralized level of command and control is necessary to deal with the widespread impact of situations in which the normal social order is destroyed. Such a centralized and authoritarian level of command and control, though, is incompatible with a basic desire for maximal local control and a reliance on civil society. Yet crises of the magnitude of Hurricane Katrina make obvious the limitations of a local response and the devolution of major social welfare and support functions to lower levels of government and the voluntary sector. Civil society organizations can provide useful assistance in the case of a limited or fairly isolated crisis, and they can serve an ancillary role in larger crises. In the absence of an effective state response apparatus, though, civil society organizations cannot fill the vacuum or address such pervasive problems as chronic poverty or a major disaster.

7

Housing, Employment, and Identification

In Chapter 5, we examined the role of the state in providing affordable housing and disaster services and traced the devolution of federal housing policy that has occurred over the past forty years. We also reviewed the history of the Federal Emergency Management Agency (FEMA). In addition, we discussed the differential impact of those programs and policies on two loosely defined groups of survivors: those who evacuated before the storm, most of whom had transferrable resources and social capital; and those who were forcibly evacuated after the storm. This much larger group was largely impoverished and brought limited social capital with them. We examined the very different barriers that these two groups faced in obtaining FEMA housing assistance in Austin. In that chapter, we also highlighted the importance of identification in obtaining assistance and the serious disadvantage that lost identification documents created.

In this chapter, we turn to the role of civil society in addressing survivors' basic needs. We return to a discussion of housing policy and its impact on low-resource versus higher-resource survivors and to the critical role of identification in accessing services of all kinds. Housing, identification, and employment proved to be interconnected in survivors' efforts to reestablish themselves in a new city. Low-income survivors encountered a number of structural barriers to recovery, and as we show, local civil society organizations were limited in their ability to deal with problems that had their roots in long-standing social disadvantage. We examine the role of social capital in terms of networks of mutual support that many low-income survivors relied on in New Orleans that were disrupted during the evacuation.

CASE STUDY: HOME IS WHERE THE HEART
CAN AFFORD TO BE

Before Hurricane Katrina, Cynthia Knight, whom we have introduced earlier, rented a house in New Orleans. The composition of the household was fluid and changed frequently as members of Cynthia's extended family moved in on a temporary basis. Cynthia's teenage daughter, Danika, was the only other full-time resident. Cynthia's disabled teenage son lived with Cynthia and Danika part time and spent the rest of his time with Cynthia's mother. Cynthia also shared custody of her teenage brother with other family members. The brother spent time at various relatives' homes and occasionally stayed with Cynthia. At any one time, therefore, the household could look very different. At the time that Katrina struck, she was receiving SSI because of a serious illness. Her disabled son and brother received social security disability benefits, which helped support the family.

This short snapshot makes it clear that even though her household was at times small, Cynthia's was a large extended family that pooled resources and supported one another practically. Unfortunately, the storm and evacuation dispersed this somewhat fragile support system. We spoke to Cynthia about her family in New Orleans before the storm. She told us that several family members lived within four miles of her. She told us that

...my mother [has a large number of] sisters and brothers. I have [several] sisters....I have like [several] nieces and [that many or more] nephews, you know, and we're a close family. We all live[d] close [to one another], you know, and we [would] all get together...now we have to take like planes and bus trips, you know.

As we recounted in Chapter 4, during the process of the evacuation, Cynthia was separated from her daughter, her son, and her mother, who were evacuated to different cities while Cynthia and her brother and her nieces were evacuated to Austin. Cynthia learned of her children's where-abouts through the Red Cross and was eventually able to arrange for her daughter to come to Austin.

Cynthia's ties to her extended family were severed by the evacuation, leaving her with only a few of the strong supportive ties that she had relied upon in New Orleans. After two days at the Austin Convention Center, Cynthia, her brother, and her nieces moved to a hotel, where they were later joined by her daughter. Cynthia spent about a month going to various agencies to try to find a place for the family to live. Eventually she was successful, but despite her success in locating housing, the high cost of living in Austin caused her great concern, and in our initial interview she told us that she intended to return to New Orleans. As she said,

...I love Austin, but I'm going to leave...because our cost of living up here is a mess and I just can't afford to live here. Uh-uh, that's the only thing. Like the rent here is six hundred dollars and my light bill, my gas bill, now is like a hundred dollars, had like a two hundred and eighteen dollar light bill...and my income is nothing but six hundred dollars a month.

Danika, Cynthia's daughter, also described the differences in the cost of living between Austin and New Orleans. She told us that "...in New Orleans we only paid $375 for a two bedroom [apartment]." Danika helped her mother with the apartment search in Austin, and found that "...all the other apartments [were] $850 a month." The apartment that they finally found for $600 a month was located far from the downtown area. Shortly after she settled in her new apartment, Cynthia faced a dilemma. FEMA called to ask her to relocate back to New Orleans, but even though she had said earlier that she intended to return, she had changed her mind because she was afraid of another storm and other problems that the family had faced in New Orleans. Staying in Austin had its drawbacks, though, primarily because she was afraid that she would not be able to afford housing in Austin once her FEMA benefits ended. During the first interview she told us that

...now we [are] on our own as of March. It costs me, I think, from eight to a thousand dollars [a month] to live here, you know, and I don't have money like that. This is my greatest fear now. This is my biggest fear now that I'm going to become homeless up here....I will become homeless and, and it's hard because I don't know what it is to be homeless. I don't know what it is to be without, you know, and that's my biggest fear 'cause...I cannot afford to pay these bills here and I can't work. I just want affordable housing.

Cynthia was anticipating a rent hike because she had rented at a "hurricane special" rate that would soon be ending, raising her rent to $700 a month. Her search for cheaper housing was complicated by her need for three bedrooms to accommodate all of the family members. Her finances were further strained because she had not been able to get food stamps. She had been to the food stamp office six times with no success. As was the case for other survivors, Cynthia's problems in obtaining benefits were exacerbated by her lack of identification and her inability to provide required information. Because she had been able to manage without food stamps in New Orleans, she had never been required to produce this information. She told us that

...they want to know where my kids' father's at. Why after eighteen years, why I don't know his social security number? Did I know where he worked at in Louisiana? And like I expressed to them, I've always [taken] care of my kids in Louisiana. I've never even received any kind of government benefits in Louisiana because I could afford to take care of me and my kids in Louisiana. I just can't do it here.

Many survivors were confused about which agency would pay for different things. FEMA paid the rent, but did not pay for certain utilities. This caused great confusion and financial difficulty. Cynthia told us that

...FEMA told us they would pay this rent for six months...they were going to pay the rent and utilities for six months. See, we thought the utilities meant the gas too. It meant only the electric, and we just found that out. So, a lot of people were complaining that we didn't know that we had to pay the gas. How am I going to tell my kids, "Okay, well you cannot run heat, or you know, it's a certain time, we all have to bathe at once." And things we thought was a luxury to us, it's really not...they keep sending me threatening bills to cut the gas off....They told us the City of Austin would pay for the electric and gas. So, I come to find out they [are] not paying for the gas, and I have an almost three or four hundred [dollar] gas bill, and every...day we're scared to cook, or we're scared we won't have hot water, things like that.

In later interviews, Cynthia told us that in an effort to support herself, she had begun looking for work in Austin and had registered with the local governmental employment service. Despite spending many hours a week traveling to the agency and to potential job interviews, she had not found work, although she had found casual work by going door to door. The lack of food stamps and her inability to pay bills made food an ongoing concern. Cynthia continued to feel that her situation in Austin was much less secure than it had been in New Orleans, but her options were limited. As she told us, "...we just try to survive, at least [in New Orleans], we knew we could survive month to month, now we just trying to survive...day to day."

By our third interview, three months after our first meeting, Cynthia had received a lump sum of several thousand dollars from FEMA to replace lost personal property, but still had not received food stamps and was concerned because her rent was only a few dollars less than her SSI payment. Despite these concerns, Cynthia had decided to remain in Austin, in part because she felt that the environment was safer than in New Orleans, but also because she felt that she lacked other options. Unfortunately, the transition to Austin continued to be difficult. The chaos of the storm and the disruption of her previous life left Cynthia and her family in a limbo from which there seemed little chance of escape. She continued to face health challenges and was facing an accusation of assault in a case where she said she had been defending her children.

As Cynthia's story illustrates, those hurricane survivors who remained in Austin for long periods had little to return to in the old city. A history of urban development policy that encouraged building in unsafe areas meant that their homes were largely uninhabitable. This reality in combination with the fact that they had no employment opportunities in New Orleans meant that they had few options other than to reestablish themselves in Austin. When they first arrived, their most immediate need was for emergency shelter, which they received at the Convention Center and at other locations around the city. That solution was only temporary, though, and almost immediately it became necessary for the survivors to find longer-term housing. Eventually, as it became clear to some that the move might be permanent, employment also became a major concern. Yet as we have described, building a new life in a new and unfamiliar city was challenging for individuals with little material, human, or social capital. In addition to problems with emergency response, the survivors' ordeal revealed important shortcomings in U.S. housing policy. As we have pointed out, crises often introduce strains that expose more fundamental systemic weaknesses in social intuitions. Debates over the fates of Fannie Mae and Freddie Mac, the government guarantors of private mortgages, bring into question a housing policy that makes homeownership the ultimate objective and marker of success for everyone. Large segments of the population, including individuals with limited resources or short-term ties to an area, require livable rental options, yet for the most part the low-rent housing market remains inadequate to the need.

In the United States and even in Europe, neoliberal housing policies have favored the private market and homeownership as a basic objective (Van Zandt & Rohe, 2006; Weber, 2002). During the second half of the twentieth century, homeownership became a core middle-class goal, and indeed it became one of the core markers of middle-class status. In addition to the clear profit motives that drive the real estate market, homeownership was widely believed to have multiple positive social as well as individual benefits. High rates of homeownership have been shown to enhance a neighborhood's quality and stability and to improve the well-being of its residents (Galster, Quercia, & Cortes, 2000; Herbert & Belsky, 2008; Hill, Ross, & Angel, 2005; Leventhal & Brooks-Gunn,

2000; Rohe & Stewart, 1996; Rohe, Van Zandt, & McCarthy, 2002). Renters have more tenuous ties to a neighborhood and community and are therefore supposedly less invested in maintaining or improving neighborhood amenities. Measures of neighborhood quality or desirability include some measure of the residential stability, usually measured as the proportion of owner- or renter-occupied residences (Beyers et al., 2003; Boggess & Hipp, 2010; DiPasquale & Glaeser, 1999; Wood, Frank, & Giles-Corti, 2010). In the common wisdom, homeownership also fosters a greater sense of responsibility for one's own property and a greater concern for neighborhood and community institutions.

In addition to providing collective community advantages, homeownership has immediate and longer-term financial benefits that increase family stability. Homeownership allows one to accumulate equity (Herbert & Belsky, 2008). For most working- and middle-class families, housing equity represents the largest fraction of their total net worth (Díaz & Luengo-Prado, 2010). Faith in the value of home equity is widespread even outside of the United States. Hernando de Soto, a popular and influential Peruvian economist who is president of the Institute for Liberty and Democracy in Lima, attributes the poor performance of developing economies to the lack of clear housing titles and the resulting inability of individuals to tap into their home's equity (de Soto, 2000). Because they cannot use their housing equity as collateral, the supposed owners are unable to borrow to improve the dwelling, educate their children, begin businesses, or assist other family members.

If ownership is indeed superior to renting, the inability of individuals with limited incomes, including minorities, to purchase a home represents a serious inequity. In response to such practices as red lining (that is, the practice of lenders to refuse mortgages for home purchases in certain neighborhoods), a liberal housing agenda embodied in the Fair Housing Act (Title VIII of the Civil Rights Act of 1968), the Redevelopment Act of 1977, and subsequent legislation encouraged lenders to provide mortgages to families with modest means (Rohe, Quercia, & Van Zandt, 2002; Van Zandt & Rohe, 2006). Debate continues as to whether excessively inclusive housing policies contributed to the housing bubble that finally burst in 2008, taking the world economy with it. What remains clear, though, is that reasonable rental options are not always available, especially for individuals with limited incomes, and that government subsidized units are in short supply.

Earlier attempts to provide housing to low-income people in high-rise residential housing projects such as Cabrini Green and Robert Taylor

Homes in Chicago were massive failures and resulted in a rejection of the ghettoization of low-income people in conditions that often led to crime and social dysfunction. Alternative policies were designed to house low-income families in existing units or subsidize smaller-scale congregate housing (Olsen, 2008). Currently, the Section 8 housing voucher program, which refers to the section of the Housing and Community Development Act of 1974 that established the program, provides rental vouchers to low-income families that they can apply toward rental units that they locate themselves (Varady & Walker, 2007). Finding desirable units and landlords who will accept the vouchers or who wish to rent to Section 8 families can present a challenge. The rental housing market in most cities remains seriously inadequate relative to the demand from low- and moderate-income renters (Katz & Turner, 2008). In Austin, although Katrina survivors were able to find rental units with FEMA and city assistance, when that assistance ended survivors faced rents that they could not afford. As a consequence, some faced eviction.

In what follows, we delve more deeply into the housing dilemma that survivors faced in Austin and investigate the nature and sources of their housing vulnerabilities. As we have shown in previous chapters, finding stable housing represented a major problem from the very beginning of the crisis, and it represented a major focus of those who attempted to help. Rents in Austin are higher on average than in New Orleans, and individuals who had owned their homes in New Orleans now found themselves forced to make high weekly or monthly rental payments. In addition, there was serious confusion as to who was responsible for utilities and other housing-related expenditures. With no income and few assets, survivors were almost completely dependent on the support that they had received and needed to find new sources of housing support immediately.

Ideally, once they found stable housing, survivors would have found new jobs and become active participants in the Austin economy. Finding work, though, represented a major challenge that was exacerbated by housing difficulties. Those few survivors with transferable skills, such as the physical therapist couple we met in Chapter 2, quickly found work and settled in. They were able to buy a new home in a desirable neighborhood and get their lives started again. Others with high levels of human capital probably returned home relatively quickly and never stayed at one of the shelters and were never part of our sample. Those who stayed in Austin often had no job to return to in New Orleans, and their difficulties in finding work in Austin were often made more serious by problems such as poor health, lack of basic documentation, lack of transportation, or criminal records.

Housing and employment problems were made even more serious for some survivors by the fact that they left New Orleans without identification. Most of us take identification for granted and when we are asked for a driver's license in order to board an airplane or cash a check, we readily produce it. Without a driver's license or birth certificate, or even a permanent address, one has a difficult time renting an apartment, applying for telephone or electrical service, or finding work. Without identification, one becomes, in effect, a nonperson. Various agencies and nongovernmental organizations attempted to help with these interrelated problems of housing, employment, and identification and did so with varying degrees of success that were largely determined by formal legal and bureaucratic regulations and procedures.

FINDING A PLACE TO LIVE

For humans, a home is more than a dwelling. The place in which one lives is nested within a neighborhood and a community. Ideally, one's house or apartment represents a haven into which one can enter to escape the noise, the crowds, and the general hubbub of everyday city life. In his book *La Poétique de l'Espace* (The Poetics of Space), published in 1957 and republished and translated many times since then, French philosopher Gaston Bachelard pointed out how symbolic and intertwined with our sense of self the physical spaces that define our homes are (Bachelard, 1957). Home protects us from the outside world, but it is also reflected in the intimate spaces of our minds, and it affects how we feel about ourselves and the larger world. The rooms, attics, vestibules, nooks, and other familiar spaces in which we spend our childhoods and intimate special times become part of our identities. One need not take as psychologized or romantic a view of one's intimate physical environment as Bachelard to appreciate that one's home is more than just a location, and its loss requires that one reconstruct those internal as well as outside spaces anew.

Familiarity with one's neighborhood and a feeling of belonging were part of a sense of place that many residents of New Orleans clearly felt for their city (Chamlee-Wright & Storr, 2009; Landphair, 2007). Unfortunately, as we have described in previous chapters, for many survivors who lived in disorganized and dangerous neighborhoods in New Orleans, home was not necessarily the haven that Bachelard described. As we have recounted, some of the survivors felt less than comfortable or secure in their old neighborhoods. Abandoned and dilapidated structures, gangs, and violence can undermine the basic sense of trust and safety that define community. A growing body of research documents the fact that individuals who live in deteriorated neighborhoods or those who perceive their neighborhoods to be unsafe are more likely to report poorer physical and mental health than those who perceive their neighborhoods to be free of serious problems (Franzini et al., 2005; Gary, Stark, & Veist, 2007; Hill, Ross, & Angel, 2005; Mair, Diez Roux, & Morenoff, 2010; Schieman & Meersman, 2004; Stockdale et al., 2007). The picture of New Orleans that emerged from our interviews was complex in that certain survivors longed to return and described a familiar place with unique and desirable characteristics, whereas others focused on crime and corruption and saw the storm as an opportunity to leave. Even without romanticizing the survivors' accounts of the old city, we can recognize that it was a familiar home to many.

In addition to affecting one's sense of physical and mental health, one's residential location determines one's potential immediate social network. Neighbors often assist one another in difficult times and the simple fact of having social support can serve as a buffer to the negative health and other consequences of neighborhood disorganization (Aneshensel, 2008; Edin & Lein, 1997; Kim & Ross, 2009; Mair, Diez Roux, and Morenoff, 2010; Stack, 1974). For the survivors of Hurricane Katrina who were evacuated to other cities, residential and neighborhood familiarity ceased to exist, at least in the short term. In Austin, the Convention Center provided a place where individuals from similar situations and often the same neighborhoods were together initially. But that proximity was quickly lost as survivors were assigned housing in different parts of the city. Rather than finding themselves together with others with similar backgrounds and experiences, they ended up in smaller groups, often consisting of a single family, in neighborhoods that were nothing like the Lower Ninth Ward or other neighborhoods in New Orleans.

These individuals found themselves among strangers in a city with a very different culture and in which they often felt isolated. Survivors were often resettled in apartment complexes that were far from potential jobs and stores, a problem exacerbated by Austin's fragmented and limited public transportation system. Being assigned to housing units far from job opportunities clearly exacerbated a survivor's employment difficulties in a mutually reinforcing cycle. If one has a good job, one is usually able to find adequate housing and one's chances of finding a job are enhanced if one lives close to work opportunities or transportation that allows one to get to work without excessive difficulty. Two cases clearly illustrate the difficulty of coordinating housing and work. Justine Betts, whom we have met before, lived in a complex that was accessible to some stores but was a long way from any job opportunities. Justine was able to find employment in an outlying area that could not be reached by public transportation. When we asked her how she managed to get to work, she said, "my boss used to come get me every morning....I would never have made it out there." Susan Doyle, a forty-eight-year-old African American female who had been a nursing assistant in New Orleans, reported that, "...I have had three job [offers], but I couldn't take them because they were located in [another city outside of Austin's city limits], and buses don't run out that way."

NGOS AND HOUSING

A major focus of our study has been on the complementary roles of NGOs in directly providing assistance or acting as intermediaries that facilitate their client's access to services provided by municipal, state, and federal governments. In the case of housing, NGOs were conspicuously absent in the role of direct providers of housing. When the crisis occurred, one nonprofit organization that was in the process of renovating a hotel it had purchased to provide housing units for low-income Austinites made them available to survivors for a few months, and one organization that focused on the homeless received some short-term housing that it made available, but no other organization controlled or provided actual housing units. NGOs' main roles consisted of acting as intermediaries in helping survivors access housing through official agencies or providing some temporary financial assistance for rent for a few families. The limitations that NGOs face in providing housing become obvious rather quickly in a crisis. The response of national housing NGOs to the devastation caused by Hurricane Katrina makes this point painfully clear. Habitat for Humanity has built over twenty-two hundred homes since 2005 as part of its response to Hurricanes Katrina and Rita (Habitat for Humanity, 2011). Brad Pitt's Make It Right Foundation has built fifty houses (Make It Right, 2009) and Oprah Winfrey's Angel Network built or restored nearly three hundred homes in eight communities in four states in the two years following the storm (Building Oprah Katrina Homes, 2011). These clearly represent great

efforts, as well as the decency and generosity of those who have contributed their resources to help, but they have made only a small dent in
replacing the three hundred thousand homes lost along the Gulf Coast.
Indeed, even in normal times NGOs are ill-equipped to provide enough
low-rent housing to make even a small dent in demand. If the federal
government has been unable to do so, how can civil society organizations that have far fewer resources deal with such a broad and resource-
intensive need?

The Red Cross was perhaps the major actor in housing, although
even it did not directly provide rental units. With its historical focus
on emergency response, the organization paid the first month's rent for
many survivors. The organization did not locate the units that survivors
rented, though; it only provided transitional support once a survivor
family found a rental unit through some other means. As we have mentioned before, the Red Cross had far more resources than other nongovernmental organizations and even its role was limited in providing
housing to survivors. For the most part, NGOs simply could not provide housing or help with rent for extended periods. The organization
that we mentioned earlier that was renovating the hotel ultimately made
a few additional apartments available to survivors according to need.
Survivors could apply for those units, but the organization's occupancy
rules were very strict and disqualified applicants who were unemployed
or had a criminal record.

Initially, the City of Austin entered into contracts with about four
hundred landlords to provide housing paid for by FEMA rental assistance funds. Unfortunately, this assistance was temporary, and when
survivors lost FEMA support, they were left with few options. Some
NGOs occasionally helped with part of one month's rent, but they were
unable to provide more. Case managers who were helping survivors in
their recovery could do little directly to find housing for their clients. At
the time of the evacuation, Austin had a very low rental vacancy rate,
and to the best of our knowledge, case managers could do little more
than refer survivors to other sources, such as the public housing authority or to senior complexes. In the end, the most effective actions that
case managers were able to engage in was to act as advocates in getting
survivors signed up for Section 8 housing vouchers. As we will discuss
in greater detail in the final chapter, in the absence of resources with
which to provide direct services, advocacy aimed at mobilizing governmental action represents a major function of civil society organizations.

In guaranteeing the welfare of populations, the state is the ultimate guarantor of adequate housing, and civil society organizations cannot substitute in providing this basic need.

In addition to making it possible for an individual to afford an adequate residence in a neighborhood of his or her choice, a good job or career provides a sense of responsibility and buttresses self-esteem. Work forms the basis of individual and family routines and places one in contact with another important community, that of coworkers. Although some of the survivors were remarkably successful in finding work and reestablishing themselves in Austin, for the majority finding adequate employment was exceedingly difficult. A lack of personal identification documentation was a major barrier for many. For the most part, the jobs they could find paid low wages and offered few benefits. As with housing, nongovernmental organizations did what they could to help survivors find employment. They faced serious barriers in doing so, though, because many of the survivors had low levels of education, lacked familiarity with computers, and had checkered work histories.

WHITNEY MORRIS

Whitney Morris, whom we have met in earlier chapters, was an example of a low-income African American survivor who found it difficult to maintain employment in Austin even given an apparent advantage. In New Orleans, she had worked for a national restaurant chain and was hired by the same chain in Austin the first week that she was in the Convention Center. Unfortunately, the lack of adequate public transportation in Austin made it difficult for her to get to work. She could not work night shifts, when customers tend to tip more. Whitney took some time off in the spring of 2006 because of stress, and also to visit her family in New Orleans. She was anxious about her future and missed her family. Her managers at the restaurant, though, were very understanding and allowed her to take the leave.

Whitney took another break that summer to visit her family in Louisiana. Although she had a job, Whitney had no medical or dental insurance, and she suffered from major health problems. These made it necessary for her to take another leave of absence from the restaurant until she felt better. By the summer of 2006, Whitney had quit her job. Like many other survivors, she had problems getting a permanent identification card. She relied on her Louisiana ID and the Temporary Texas ID card that she was issued in the Convention Center. During the summer of 2006, while she was unemployed, she cared for her grandson so that her daughter could work full-time. She received financial help from friends as well as local charities and churches, and she relied on local food banks. During the summer, she looked for work in her neighborhood. She applied at a local grocery store chain but had no luck. She felt that "all the spots are taken," and it was hard for people without college degrees to find work. Whitney also felt that the grocery store chain discriminated against African Americans in favor of Hispanics.

Finally in March 2007 she found a part-time home health care job, but soon after was admitted to the hospital for a serious health problem. At the time of our last interview in March 2007, she was in the hospital, but her new employers were holding her job for her. Despite Whitney's good start in the Austin labor market, various barriers prevented her from keeping a steady job. The lack of transportation, a lack of identification, health problems, perceived job discrimination, and the need to deal with the remains of her life in New Orleans all posed barriers to her successful integration into Austin.

Whitney's story hints at one of the barriers that resulted from the unique nature of the Austin labor market. Austin has a large Mexican-origin service-sector workforce. Many employers in Austin are reluctant to hire workers who do not speak Spanish, or at least many survivors felt that this was the case. Cynthia Knight, the African American woman whose situation in Austin we have recounted in some detail, reported that she had been discouraged from seeking work because of the availability of Hispanic workers who were willing to take lower wages. She told us that,

I'll work anywhere. It's just so hard....It's so hard, and then, these people down there at the resource center down there. They make it a joke. [They say,] "Well, you know, you all can't find jobs because the Mexicans have all the jobs....You know, the Mexicans work, [we don't]." And you know, I don't feel like that. I really don't. They gonna tell us, "If you work for ten dollars, the Mexicans will work for $5."

Justine Betts felt that she faced discrimination in her job search: "You see, what the problem is, [is that] they [are] hiring more Mexicans than anything. You go there, the job is filled. You come back, it is a Mexican or something."

Survivors reported that some employers were reluctant to hire individuals who they believed would be leaving to return to New Orleans within a short period. Some survivors also experienced what they felt was discrimination. Johnetta Hays, an African American female in her late fifties, believed that this had cost her and her husband at least one job. As she said, "We got a job two days after being here in Austin. You know them people that took that job away from us and told us they couldn't hire us because we were the 'refugees' and 'contaminated.'"

THE ROLE OF CASE MANAGERS

Helping survivors find employment was a primary concern of case managers, who ranged from professional social workers to volunteers with nonprofit agencies. Data published by the Bureau of Labor Statistics indicated that of the approximately eight hundred thousand evacuees sixteen and older, just over half were in the labor force in October 2005, and nearly a fourth of those in the labor force were unemployed (Bureau of Labor Statistics, 2006). The employment situation in Austin reflected the general experience of survivors. At a case management meeting on June 7, 2006, one of the representatives of a large NGO asked case managers how many of their clients were employed and only a few people raised their hands. Case managers and others who were responsible for assisting the survivors find work identified various barriers to employment and told us of various programs available to assist survivors. A few providers also mentioned successes.

The barriers that case managers identified were those that we observed ourselves and that the survivors told us about. As we have noted, most survivors who stayed in Austin had low levels of education and most had no experience with computers. The case managers also noted that the inability to speak Spanish placed survivors at a disadvantage in finding jobs in fast food and construction. The language barrier was described during a focus group with case managers. As one case manager, who had worked both for the Red Cross and for another NGO, explained,

Something that I hadn't thought about that a couple of people had mentioned to me is getting jobs that you would think would be simple like fast food or things like that [is hard] because they don't speak Spanish. Several people have told me...I couldn't work here if I don't speak Spanish....[I am] qualified to be a supervisor in construction, and they said, "Well, you can't do that if you don't speak Spanish because everyone you're going to be managing is Spanish-speaking!" So I've heard a lot of frustrations from hurricane survivors about that.

Another case manager pointed out the problems that a lack of computer literacy caused:

Because I was told that the people at [a public employment service] just send them to the computer lab, but they don't know how to use a computer, so they can't know....I'm thinking of the Convention Center. We would have them fill out the forms, tell them have a seat and fill out the initial paperwork. Some people, we would call them, and they would just sit there with it, just sit there. And then we would ask, "Do you want us to help you with it?" Or you could see them trying to do it. And these were, not like older people, but everyone.

One case manager described the discrimination that the survivors experienced because they were from New Orleans:

A lot of people were denied jobs because when they went to be interviewed, the first thing someone would say is, "Are you from New Orleans?" And if they said yes, [they would be told,] "Well, you're gonna leave in a month or two months, so no."...[They would] not even finish the interview with them. I heard that happened a couple of times.

Another provider, who worked with one of the NGO consortiums, described the differences between job requirements in New Orleans and Austin:

The types of jobs that a lot of folks had in New Orleans were either in the service industries or they were in like fishing, shrimping, those kinds of things, especially for our Vietnamese folks, there was a whole pocket of Vietnamese folks who came. So they tend to be in those areas that their skill sets tend to be in those areas,...and the community was very much a community where people, it was very much a more affordable community, you could live. You could get a six-hundred-dollar-a-month social security check but you had a three-hundred-dollar-a-month rent, and so you could just make it. You weren't comfortable by any means, but people lived as a community – family, friends look after each other – and then they've come to this state. Even though we see ourselves as a caring community, it's very much that individual Texan mentality and our skills that we need for even entry-level jobs in this town tend to have some component of technology to them. You know, even at McDonald's you've got to be able to push certain buttons and we tend to have a higher, we've already got a higher level of education in this community. And so you know, if somebody was describing a person who was thirty-five years old who was able to survive on welfare in Louisiana, never really had a job, well, maybe had odd jobs coming into this community, there's not a whole lot of that kind of work available.

As we have mentioned, for those without identification documents, obtaining proper identification presented huge problems. Although identification cards were issued at the Convention Center during the early days of the evacuation, there was massive confusion concerning who was eligible and what the procedure was for issuing the documents. Without identification, one found oneself in a Catch-22. To obtain an ID, one had to prove one's identity, which was impossible without an ID. A description from the focus groups of providers reveals some of the problems:

…it's sort of a circular thing, in order to get a birth certificate from Louisiana, you have to have some level of identification. In order to get Texas identification, you have to have a birth certificate or some other form. And so we get into this kind of circular thing. And Louisiana is incredibly backed up with getting at their birth certificates. So, then the other thing that we found out was at the Convention Center, this is something we found out last week at a meeting, at the Convention Center the city sent off for a whole bunch of birth certificates, giving people the P.O. boxes to get, have them sent back. Well, unfortunately, instead the state of Louisiana sent the batch back to the city. The city couldn't receive them because they're official documents, so they turned them over to the state. So there's now, we don't know how many, whether it's fifty or five hundred birth certificates sitting at the state level that they can't release.…So now they're going to send them back to Louisiana to get them destroyed.…So we're trying to figure out, are there ways that we can intervene in that process?

Another provider, who worked at a faith-based NGO, compared survivors to individuals seeking political asylum, noting that when displacement is added to poverty, there is no good solution:

…my boss just went to a big conference in New Orleans that was specifically about displacement and migration, many people who have done this work in foreign countries who are talking about it, now they weren't just focused on Katrina, they were focused on disaster in general and talking about how that uprootedness just throws people off and like seeing it in other countries. So now they're saying, oh, well, this might be a helpful way to think about what's happening, and I think it's that the relationship of poverty and displacement, because I've worked for fifteen years with political asylees and many political asylees, not all, but they come either educated or with clear skills. Things to bring to our country that would translate. They don't come looking for a handout, they come expecting to work and to build a new life. When you throw in the issue of poverty in displacement, then you're probably also, not necessarily, but you're probably also going to have lack of education, lack of job skill, disability, or age in there and so it's, it's a group of people that's only going to survive in some kind of public-assisted way, and there's no good solution for that group.

Some case workers did not feel that difficulties finding employment were solely a reflection of the barriers we have mentioned. They did not see the survivors as helpless victims. Some mentioned a lack of motivation as a serious barrier to employment. A provider from a faith-based nonprofit organization told us that some of her clients' motivation to find a job and work would wane at times because they were unsure about their future or whether they wanted to return to New Orleans. Some clients experienced symptoms of PTSD, which clearly undermined their ability and motivation to work.

Given the difficulty that the survivors faced in finding jobs, employment services were vital to those who intended to remain in Austin for extended periods. Many organizations and individuals attempted to help survivors find employment. These included governmental agencies and NGOs. Given their unique situation, survivors were granted extended unemployment benefits (FEMA, 2006). Another federal program was National Emergency Grants (NEG). These grants provide funding to states in response to large, unexpected economic events that cause significant job losses. As their webpage explains, "NEGs generally provide resources to states and local workforce investment boards to quickly reemploy laid-off workers by offering training to increase occupational skills" (U.S. Department of Labor, 2011). An administrator at the County Human Services agency told about her experiences with this program, as well as the role of an NGO in administering the program:

…one other thing that we did during the process was [a large NGO] was a recipient or the grant monitor of…a national disaster workforce grant…[which they used to employ] evacuees at a temporary capacity to work in different areas. Initially it was to only work with other evacuees and so we hired some folks here and at [a nearby town] and at one other center, I don't remember which one, to help with the food pantries and the intakes and the data entry and so forth. And then…they expanded it and they said, "You can hire them for not just evacuee to evacuee work." [I said,] "Great. Can I have an admin person to help me?" And they said, "Yeah."

Some employment programs provided work incentives. A provider from a large faith-based NGO told us that

Right now we just started an employment or education incentive, so once they start school or once they start a job, then we get them a fifty-dollar Wal-Mart card and then like within the first two weeks after they start and then if they keep the job or if they keep going to school, then within like four to six weeks after that, we give them another fifty-dollar Wal-Mart card, so it's up to a hundred dollars in that Wal-Mart card, which is a pretty good incentive for them. Not that it's not already an incentive to have income but…that's something we've added.

Nearly two years after the evacuation, this same faith-based organization hired a job coach. The NGO was now working mostly in counties outside Austin. Another large NGO provided some job training for survivors, which they announced at a case managers' meeting on April 5, 2006. According to the NGO's spokesperson, the agency's primary objective was to get jobs for people who faced barriers to employment, including ex-convicts, welfare recipients, and others. The organization sponsored a career fair on May 10 at a major Austin exposition center. The NGO also had intake offices all over town. Survivors who sought services were required to participate in a mandatory orientation, after which their job readiness was assessed by case managers before they went on to job placement. Case managers often drove clients to job interviews and provided other assistance to help them stay employed. The case managers provided gift cards at thirty, sixty, and ninety days as incentives to encourage survivors to continue their job search. Another civic organization also provided employment services, including one aimed at young adults.

For-profit groups also provided employment-related services in Austin. However, some case managers reported that clients did not find these services helpful. As one case manager for an interfaith NGO told us,

…so many people are at the point where they can't pay their rent, they're not trained to do a job, and, you know, you can get all this training, but how do you support yourself while you do this training? I mean, it's nice to say you can get training for six weeks to do this or to do this or do this, but if you've got a family and nobody's working, how do you go to school to be trained in something if you don't have the resources to be able to sustain yourself during that time?

Several case managers told us that their clients did not want to go to the state employment agency because they did not find it helpful. One employee of a nonprofit organization who was also a survivor told us that the organization's job placement efforts were largely ineffective because they did not deal with issues of work preparedness and networking. As she said,

When I saw a client come out of a[n] office with a…piece of paper and a[n] address on it saying go here…that blew me away. Why did we waste that client's time, whether he was [a] Katrina [survivor] or a regular Austinite?…We serve as a job developer…we mold you to get jobs. I could've [given] him that number, where is a job referral letter?…Where's the networking with these employers to build job relations so we can win the reputation that anybody [organization's name] send, it's a, it's a hire.…We haven't done [that], we haven't done a service to this person.…

Despite all the challenges, providers did report some successes. One case manager at an NGO described an instance of a woman who found employment, even though her husband was still unemployed. As the case manager explained,

...this couple made it...to Austin, and I talked to her, she had...been hired through a grant...it was a National Emergency Grant fund, and she was an employee of [organization's name]. And she was, you know, she's doing fine, her husband's still looking for work, but he's qualified to work,...he's been working as a boat-builder for, for quite a while. But there was some way he could get training at Goodwill or other places and transfer those skills, and they looked to be like, you know, like they were gonna be okay as long as they stayed on top of things. It wasn't gonna be easy, but they were both willing.

Another NGO case manager said that many survivors found that they were more able to work than they thought:

I think I have a lot of clients who thought that they wouldn't be able to work because of, um, disabilities or educationwise, I think here, they found, I think, a lot of them have realized that they can as far as like working with [a specific training program] or different training programs that will help them fit their needs, 'cause I have a couple clients who are kind of just thinking about they were gonna, they were okay, maybe able to live off of their SSI checks every month and they realized here it's a lot harder to do, but never thought they'd be able to work, and I had two clients who went through [job training program] who've really found that they actually, there's a lot they can do and kind of enjoy getting out of the house and being able to work for the first time in like twenty years or so.

IDENTIFICATION

As we have mentioned before, a major barrier to both housing and employment for certain survivors was the lack of identification. For survivors who evacuated during the chaos after the storm hit, documents were often lost or abandoned during the confused evacuation process. Clifford Thompson, a forty-seven-year-old African American man who evacuated after the storm, reported that the need to leave quickly in the midst of flooding caused him to lose his personal documents:

You don't have your folder with all your papers....Yeah, nobody's thinking on that, you know what I'm saying? Nobody thinking about that, you just grab what you grab and get out, you know, yeah, you know, but you have to go through water and if you had a bag, it's going to be wet up and that kind of sewer water and all that mixed up together...

Many survivors had been able to function in New Orleans without ID, but found the situation very different in Austin. Ray Lee, a forty-one-year-old white male, had been without a government-issued photo

ID for four years before the storm. Louise Wilkins, a forty-one-year-old African American female we first met in Chapter 2, contrasted the requirements for identification in New Orleans with those in Austin. As she told us, "…like in New Orleans I could have got a job with a copy of my ID, a copy of my birth certificate, a copy of my social security card, some jobs you don't even need it as long as you there, but down here, I mean, you need original birth certificate, original social security card, original ID, everything got to be original down here, it can't be no copies of nothing…."

Charlotte Hendricks, the fifty-one-year-old African American woman we first met in Chapter 4, was a college graduate, but was unable to find work due to identification problems. In her first interview one year after Katrina, she told us that she had finally gotten her birth certificate by traveling to Baton Rouge and that she was waiting to be able to afford the $15 fee to get a permanent Texas ID so she could work. As she said, "…I need to get a job, I have jobs lined up, I need an ID, I really need an ID, and basically that's what keeps me depressed because I don't want to sit at home, I have fifteen years of schooling, I have a [college] degree…, I don't want to sit here, understand?"

Louise Wilkins reported that, "I can't get a good job because I don't have a certain ID…every time I try to go out and get work, I have my feet in the door, and when it time for me to get the job, they ask me to present an ID." Louise had been hired for a job in law enforcement, but was unable to take the job without ID. Like other survivors whom we interviewed, she had been given a temporary Texas ID at the Convention Center, but when that expired, she was unable to replace it with a permanent one because she had no birth certificate. She had filled out paperwork to order her birth certificate several times with no result. Fifteen months after the storm, she remained without current ID and was still unemployed. Nongovernmental organizations provided assistance in some cases, but survivors reported that caseworkers were not always helpful. Whitney Morris, whom we met earlier, complained that her caseworker had not helped her get an ID.

The lack of identification also affected survivors' abilities to obtain housing, particularly subsidized housing. Although she was high on the list for Section 8 housing, Louise Wilkins was also concerned that because she lacked birth certificates and social security cards for her children, she would be ineligible for an apartment once her name came up. Xia Baker, a thirty-three-year-old African American female, whose housing situation we discussed in some detail in Chapter 5, also reported that she was concerned about her ability to obtain Section 8 housing because she did not have birth certificates for her sons. For Ray Lee, lack of identification became a Catch-22 that hampered his attempt to find housing. The absence of ID made it difficult for him to rent an apartment. After he completed the paperwork for an ID, he lacked the money to pay for it. This lack of identification initiated a spiral: Lee was unable to rent an apartment without an ID, and could not get an ID without a mailing address.

Replacing IDs was difficult for a number of reasons. Some survivors, such as Charlotte Hendricks and Ray Lee, lacked the money to pay the application fees. Although the fees seemed low in the context of a middle-class budget, meeting replacement costs of $15 and higher required saving and careful planning for unemployed individuals. Others were given conflicting information about where to send forms for replacements, or they were told that they would need to travel back to Louisiana to request them in person. Janice Lyons, an eighteen-year-old African American female whom we met in Chapter 5, reported that she had been told first that she would have to go to New Orleans and later that she would have to go to Baton Rouge. As we mentioned earlier, Charlotte Hendricks actually did travel to Baton Rouge to get her birth certificate.

COMPOUNDED PROBLEMS

These stories clearly illustrate the interrelatedness of identification, housing, and employment problems. Indeed, these problems were related to and exacerbated by health problems and other difficulties, including low human and social capital. The cases show the Catch-22 that a lack of proper identification creates. As the survivors told us, without identification, they could not find work or apply for an apartment. Without identification, survivors were a nonperson without an address or a social identity. We may often feel that we are just numbers rather than people, but without a social security card or driver's license, survivors had a difficult time functioning socially or in the labor market. Occasionally one hears calls for a national identity card that would define citizenship. In the context of immigration, such a proposal can be seen as positive or negative.

Whatever the merits or lack thereof of a national identification system in the context of immigration, in the case of a disaster of the magnitude of Hurricane Katrina, it is clear that as part of the coordination that we have called for, some centralized capacity to facilitate the replacement of identification for those who have lost it is imperative. Those individuals who are at greatest risk of finding themselves without identification are those who are at highest risk of suffering the loss of their homes and property. They are most likely to have low incomes and lack safe deposit boxes or online data storage capacities. Most of us take identification for granted, much as we do a permanent address. It is only when the taken-for-granted nature of identity and residence is lost that the precariousness of identity itself becomes clear. For the survivors of Hurricane Katrina, that precariousness had serious long-term consequences.

Even with proper identification, though, the displaced survivors of Hurricane Katrina faced serious barriers in finding housing and work. Nongovernmental and faith-based organizations, as well as goodhearted citizens, did what they could to help, but the success of those efforts was limited. Full employment is an ideal of most governments, but it is rarely achieved. Where governments fail, NGOs are unlikely to have greater success. They may help a few individuals, but they do not have the capacity to deal with large-scale unemployment or homelessness. In the case of the victims of disasters, as in the case of individuals with little education or work-related skills and experience, the tasks of providing employment and housing are daunting given the number of people in need. As we have seen, survivors were often placed in housing units that were chosen for their availability rather than for considerations such as proximity to jobs and everyday necessities. This was perhaps inevitable given the magnitude of the crisis and the number of individuals involved, but it once again illustrates the massive coordination effort that is necessary for a successful response to crisis. Uncoordinated NGO efforts are simply not up to the task.

The difficulties that survivors faced in finding housing and work and the instability that these problems introduced into their lives had a substantial negative impact on their health. Even the most resilient individual is bound to suffer some demoralization as the result of the loss of his or her home, familiar social networks, and hope for the future. As we will see in the next chapter, many of the survivors arrived in Austin with serious preexisting health conditions associated with the poverty in which they lived prior to the storm. When they arrived in Austin, these preexisting health conditions, as well as the trauma that many experienced in the evacuation, further undermined their ability to reestablish themselves. Again, nongovernmental and faith-based organizations attempted to help, but as we shall see, the magnitude of the need seriously limited their success.

8

Health Care and the Limitations of Civil Society

CASE STUDY: FALLING THROUGH THE CRACKS

Just before the storm, John Washington, a fifty-five-year-old HIV-positive African American male, had moved into a subsidized apartment in a complex for elderly and handicapped individuals in New Orleans. Getting the new apartment was a major achievement and, John hoped, the end of his homelessness. Before moving into his new apartment John had been living at a shelter. It was there that he received assistance in applying to the housing voucher program that finally enabled him to get his own place. Prior to that, he had at times been homeless and often slept in the streets. Just before Katrina struck, he had also begun receiving social security disability payments. Unfortunately, John's newly independent living arrangements were short-lived.

The residents of the apartment complex were old and disabled and thus most suffered greatly as a result of the storm and its aftermath. According to John one resident died during the storm. Because of his illness, John also had a difficult time. He had recently been hospitalized and had been taking medications for several HIV-related health problems. The storm disrupted his medication regimen, and when he was evacuated, he left without his medicines. As he told us, "...I was on...[inaudible] and Bactrim 'cause I have pneumonia...and some other kind of medicine, but I can't think of the name of it....I don't know the...name of the medicine." We interviewed John only once within a few days of his arrival at the Austin Convention Center, where he should have immediately been placed in contact with HIV services. We do not know why he was not. Perhaps he did not inform the Red Cross or others of his condition. In any case, he was not taking his regular medications and was confused about how to get help. He told us that he "…[didn't] know how to get [my medicines] 'cause I [came] with [only] the clothes on my back…the only way I [knew] how to get [my medicines]…is if I call…[the medical center in New Orleans]….I don't know if they reopened or not."

It appeared that John was still expecting to receive care from the clinic in New Orleans from which he had received medications before. He was clearly overwhelmed and confused by the situation. He told us that he had not taken his medicine since he arrived in Austin and that he was suffering from health problems and was not eating properly. He said that, "…I feel kind of sick a lot of times…'cause it's been quite a few days [since he took his medication]….I haven't eaten….I've had one egg…water and some food a lady gave me downstairs."

John was overwhelmed by the new city in which he was a complete stranger. He may have been confused as well because of his disease, which in some cases has serious cognitive effects. He told us that he had particular difficulty with the transportation system, which he said interfered with his ability to get HIV treatment in Austin. When the interviewer offered to investigate HIV services for him John was appreciative and in response to the offer of assistance, he said, "…yes, ma'am. I really do 'cause I can't, I'm not functioning….I don't know the buses….I don't know…about Austin, how to take these buses…[they're] different from New Orleans."

To complicate matters, John had lost his driver's license; it had been in his wallet, which he lost somewhere during the evacuation. Despite the difficulties that he was forced to endure, though, or perhaps because of them, John expressed great satisfaction with the Austin Convention Center. As for most survivors who found shelter there immediately after their evacuation from New Orleans, the Convention Center provided at least a temporary respite. In John's words, it "seemed like heaven." As with many other survivors, the situation during the first days after the evacuation was so chaotic that many needs went unmet and survivors' own understanding of the situation was often confused.

After our one interview with John, we left him information concerning HIV services and he indicated that he would get in contact with the list of agencies that we gave him. It was clear that his medical care needs were serious and complex. Whether John ever made contact with HIV services, we do not know, nor do we know what happened to him. His case, though, illustrates the severity of many of the untreated medical problems from which survivors suffered and the difficulty that many had in accessing care.

THE HEALTH CARE SYSTEM

The disruption of the normal social order that we have documented was hardly unique to Hurricane Katrina. Natural and man-made disasters are common occurrences, and in addition to undermining the social order, such disasters destroy infrastructure and vital institutions. Among the major institutions affected are hospitals and clinics, many of which, as in New Orleans after Hurricane Katrina, are badly damaged or destroyed. With the loss of infrastructure, many individuals, particularly low-income people, are unable to get the medical care they need because not only is transportation disrupted, the medical facilities they depend upon are not functioning and medical professionals lack the tools they need to practice effective medicine. As individuals gather together in refugee centers and shelters without adequate sanitation or medical care, a situation common in developing nations and even in developed nations after serious disasters, the risk of infectious disease increases (Spiegel et al., 2007; Watson, Gayer, & Connolly, 2007). Vulnerable individuals, including pregnant women, the elderly, children, and the chronically ill, face particularly serious health threats (Callaghan et al., 2007; Jhung et al., 2007; Kessler, 2007; Miller & Arquilla, 2008; Tulin, 2007). Although the victims of Hurricane Katrina were not confined in refugee centers for months, as is often the case in the developing world, the appalling conditions at the Superdome clearly held the potential for the spread of serious infectious disease.

In this chapter, we focus specifically on the health and health care access among the survivors. As in any low-income population, physical and mental illnesses were common and seriously undermined functioning and well-being. Poor health seriously diminished many survivors' ability to establish new and productive lives. In the United States, as in the developed world generally, middle-class individuals take access to doctors and hospitals for granted. Because health care coverage in the United States is largely an employment benefit, unemployed working-age adults or those employed in jobs that do not offer affordable health plans are at elevated risk of having no insurance of any sort. Jobs that do not offer health insurance are unlikely to pay enough to allow an employee to purchase a private individual or family plan. Given our focus on civil society and the nongovernmental sector, in this chapter we investigate the role of NGOs and charitable activity in facilitating survivors' access to health care. In the developing world, health care systems are often inadequate and cannot be relied upon to provide even basic levels of care to the poor. As a consequence, in many nations NGOs play a major role as health care providers (Doyle & Patel, 2008; Peters et al., 2008; Pfeiffer et al., 2008). In these situations, NGOs attempt to compensate for serious shortcomings in the state's ability to provide basic care to citizens. Where adequate systems of health care are lacking, the contribution of NGOs may be crucial and even limited assistance may represent a major asset.

In developed nations, though, insuring adequate health care is a major state responsibility, and as our interviews reveal, in the absence of a well-functioning and coordinated state system of care, civil society organizations cannot serve as an effective or adequate substitute. High-quality physical and mental health care must be provided by trained professionals with access to modern hospitals, clinics, medical equipment, and pharmaceuticals. Nonprofessionals have a clear role in health care as they do in other areas of human need. They are particularly useful in terms of providing companionship, transportation, and information to socially isolated and vulnerable individuals. As important as such human contact and assistance might be, though, it is clearly ancillary and is no substitute for professional intervention. Modern health care systems are complex and consist of primary, secondary, and tertiary facilities, as well as extensive training capacities and highly skilled specialists. In this context, civil society organizations and voluntary action are best suited to a complementary role focused on providing social and material support and bringing individuals into contact with formal health care providers. As our interviews show, even this is a challenging task, and even outside of the context of a disaster, many vulnerable individuals find that their access to health care is limited or inconsistent.

TRAUMA AND A DISRUPTED HEALTH CARE SYSTEM

Immediately after the storm, several studies of the mental and physical health status of Hurricane Katrina survivors were carried out in situations that, like those in Austin, were characterized by great urgency (e.g., Texas Health and Human Services Commission, 2006; Wilson & Stein, 2006). As we noted in Chapter 2, the immediacy of the situation and the desperate need of the evacuees required rapid intervention and did not allow for the careful methodological planning and detail that would have been possible with a longer planning period. Nonetheless, information was vital, and in the weeks following the Hurricane, a number of rapid needs assessments or "cot surveys" were conducted by the Centers for Disease Control (CDC) and other public health and community service organizations (Appleseed, 2006; Brodie et al., 2006; Centers for Disease Control & Prevention, 2006a, 2006b, 2006c; Coker et al., 2006; Ghosh, Patnaik, & Vogt, 2007; Ridenour et al., 2007; Rodriguez et al., 2006). These studies clearly showed that a large proportion of survivors who were forced to evacuate from areas most seriously affected by Katrina experienced some level of post-traumatic stress.

The fact that many survivors suffered from preexisting physical and mental health conditions only added to the difficulty of the situation. Studies of survivors of Hurricane Katrina and other disasters document a high prevalence of chronic physical conditions among the victims, who are often the most vulnerable residents of disaster-prone areas (Jhung et al., 2007; Kessler, 2007; Miller & Arquilla, 2008). A survey carried out at the Houston shelter immediately after the evacuation revealed that 41 percent of survivors suffered from at least one chronic health condition, including diabetes or hypertension, diseases that are prevalent among low-income and African American populations (Brodie et al., 2006). Subsequent studies of the victims revealed that they remained at risk of post-traumatic stress disorder and other mental and physical health problems for protracted periods (Gautam et al., 2009; Kessler et al., 2006, 2008; Mills, Edmondson, & Park, 2007; Weems et al., 2007; Weisler, Barbee, & Townsend, 2006).

Our interviews corroborate research that reveals that individuals who experience traumatic events often need counseling and other mental health services long after the actual event (De Vita & Morley, 2007). A study of individuals who received supportive recovery services following the terrorist attacks on the World Trade Center on September 11, 2001, found that these individuals experienced an ongoing need for services several years after the attack (Morley, De Vita, & Auer, 2006). As the evacuation after Hurricane Katrina turned into a long-term displacement, many survivors began showing increasing signs of emotional distress, including higher rates of mental illness and substance abuse (Kromm & Sturgis, 2008; SAMSHA, 2008). Survivors also experienced physical ailments related directly to the evacuation, which were compounded by chronic poverty and by disruption in medical care during the evacuation.

Like evacuees elsewhere, many of those who evacuated to Austin had preexisting physical and mental health problems (Brodie et al., 2006). These preexisting conditions, often exacerbated by the disruption and stress of the storm and evacuation, presented serious health care access challenges to survivors and taxed the health care delivery system in Austin. Individuals often did not get the care they needed, which seriously undermined their ability to reincorporate and begin a new life in Austin. The most vulnerable suffered greatly, including pregnant women, older people, and those with chronic illnesses, such as John Washington, the HIV-positive individual with whose case we began the chapter. Whatever continuity of care that individuals had enjoyed in New Orleans was disrupted and was difficult and often impossible to reestablish in Austin. Medical records were not available, individuals did not know where to seek assistance, and providers were unfamiliar with these new patients.

The disaster clearly revealed the centrality of the state in health care. In the absence of a system of universal care that could immediately respond to the needs of the survivors, different governmental programs and voluntary groups provided often uncoordinated and discontinuous coverage. Civil society organizations were clearly ill-equipped to deal with the needs of individuals with complex and challenging medical problems. The experience made it clear that health care is not a social welfare state function that can be devolved to local agencies or voluntary organizations. Although most survivors had access to physical and mental health care services at emergency shelters, they had few accessible and affordable options after they left the shelters. Our interviews with survivors in Austin illustrate the structural sources of the lack of adequate health care. In the absence of a universal and comprehensive public health care system, individuals do not automatically qualify for care, especially when they have problems with identification and are unfamiliar with complex health and welfare bureaucracies. In the absence of electronic health records, medical professionals lack vital information that they need to treat new patients effectively, especially when they have limited time to evaluate each case.

Although civil society organizations are limited in their ability to provide direct medical services, one potentially major role of such organizations is in helping individuals with limited skills navigate complex health care systems. Health and mental health issues pervade the survivors' accounts of their difficulties in Austin. We did not directly focus on health care access per se, so these accounts appear indirectly and emerge in the context of discussions of other issues. These accounts demonstrate not only how pervasive and complex health problems are in low-income and marginalized populations, but how inadequate our current health care system is in addressing them.

Although physical and mental health problems were common, some groups of evacuees were particularly at risk. Older persons were, of course, among those. The Richardsons, whom we met in Chapter 2, evacuated from New Orleans in their own car accompanied by Mr. Richardson's mother. The long drive to Houston was an ordeal for the older woman and her health remained precarious. In the weeks and months following the storm, her declining physical and mental health finally left the Richardsons no choice but to place her in a nursing home. They were eventually able to grant the older woman's wish to return to her home in New Orleans, where she could be cared for by home health aides. At the time of our last interview, the Richardsons were still struggling to find a way to manage the mother's care long distance.

Although those survivors who weathered the storm were subjected to potentially greater stress and more health risks than those who evacuated before the storm, both groups suffered from significant preexisting medical problems. Those with potentially life-threatening illnesses faced unique challenges because they often needed immediate and extensive care. Ray Lee, a white male in his early forties, had been hospitalized for cancer and was medically evacuated from a hospital in New Orleans before the storm. He arrived in Austin without any of his medical records. During several interviews, he described his ongoing efforts to get his medical records transferred and continue his care in Austin, but he had encountered many barriers. In addition to this medical ordeal, he experienced most of the financial and housing problems reported to us by other survivors.

Beverly Dawson, an African American grandmother in her fifties, had been left partly paralyzed by a stroke earlier in 2005. She evacuated to Austin with her daughter. At the Austin Convention Center, the medical team found that she had dangerously high blood pressure and immediately hospitalized her. She remained in the hospital for ten days. When we interviewed her a few months later, she had had a second stroke and had undergone surgery to reduce the risk of further strokes. Although the experience had been an ordeal, she was generally satisfied with the care she received. Luckily, she had family members, including a daughter and a sister, available to provide emotional and practical support.

Beverly's daughter, Chantal Henderson, one of her mother's main caregivers, was pregnant when she arrived in Austin. Although Chantal was greatly concerned for her mother, she was not feeling well herself. The long drive from New Orleans while she was pregnant had taken a toll on her. Her blood pressure was elevated and in the months following the storm she had problems with Medicaid that interfered with her prenatal care and treatment for other medical problems. Chantal lamented the loss of her old family network and the aunt who would have helped her through the pregnancy. Chantal's health problems were a great concern to her mother. In our second interview with her, Beverly expressed particular concern about the possible negative effects of the stress that Chantal was experiencing on her and the baby.

Other women had different problems in obtaining prenatal care as well as care for their newly born infants. Kita Godwin, an African American in her twenties, was also pregnant when she and her family left before the storm. Her first child, who was five at the time of our first interview, was born prematurely and had serious health problems. As the storm approached, Kita was pregnant with her second child and the pregnancy made the trip to Austin difficult. She was nauseated and vomited during the journey and had a cold and fever when she arrived. Despite her pregnancy and illness, she had difficulty getting Medicaid. She told us that "...you wouldn't believe the trouble I had to go through to get coverage here." She had Medicaid in Louisiana, but said of Austin that "...it was hard when we came here. They [weren't] giving any medical assistance to Katrina victims." She was eventually able to obtain benefits and to find medical care, but she was still having health problems at the time of our last interview. She told us that she was not feeling well and expressed concern for her baby.

Aisha Bell's water broke while she was stranded on a bridge for nine days. The twenty-three-year-old African American woman did not mention it to anyone. While stranded, she contracted an infection that was not treated until she arrived in Austin. Luckily, both mother and child emerged from the ordeal healthy. For Janice Lyon, an eighteen-year-old African American female, the stress associated with the storm led to a premature birth. The newborn was extremely sick and required three surgeries. As we recounted in Chapter 2, Mary Powers, an African American female in her forties, gave birth in Houston before rejoining friends in Austin a few weeks later. Evidently she had been completely lost in the system and had received no prenatal care, nor had she been in contact with any social service agency.

In addition to pregnancy, chronic conditions challenged the system. As is the case for all low-income populations, diabetes and hypertension were common. These conditions, which are relatively manageable with the appropriate monitoring in normal times, were complicated by the disruption that followed the storm. As a result, a number of acute crises occurred among individuals who required constant monitoring while they were still in New Orleans. These problems were often in a crisis stage when survivors arrived in Austin, as the example of Beverly Dawson illustrates.

In addition to these common chronic conditions, some survivors suffered from other life-threatening conditions, such as HIV and cancer. Some cases presented serious challenges to the emergency health care system because of their complexity. The huge number of survivors with multiple health problems nearly overwhelmed the capacity of the health care system to respond. Although many survivors received health care, a few did not, and many others did not receive adequate or complete care. For many, care was delayed. The situation of Tiffany Wilkins, a twenty-one-year-old African American woman we introduced earlier, was particularly tragic. She contracted HIV in Austin and found out about it after learning that she was pregnant. Tiffany described her experience in detail and expressed great fear that her son would be born with the disease. She was able to get the health care that she needed, though, and with proper prenatal treatment, her baby was not infected.

PUBLIC HEALTH INSURANCE

Survivors' preexisting conditions, in combination with the illnesses they suffered as part of the storm and evacuation, made immediate access to professional health care crucial. In the absence of a universal health care system, obtaining and paying for health care presents a major problem for low-income individuals and families. One of the main concerns that survivors expressed during our interviews related to difficulties in obtaining care in Austin. Almost none were able to find jobs that offered health insurance, so for most evacuees public programs and charity were the only options. Some had received such assistance in New Orleans whereas others faced the necessity of applying for the first time. Ideally, the survivors would have transferred from one health care system to another with little disruption and their electronic medical records easily accessible. No such smooth transition occurred. Once they left New Orleans, any continuity in their medical care that they might have enjoyed was lost. Their experiences made the structural shortcomings of our expensive, yet incomplete, health care system obvious. Low-income survivors faced health care access problems that were similar to those faced by the low-income population in general, including bureaucratic hurdles, discontinuity of health coverage, and inadequate access to providers.

Largely because the health care system is fragmented, survivors' experiences with the health care in Austin were diverse. For some, as is the case for the population in poverty generally, emergency rooms and public clinics served as a source of routine care. Because Texas has different eligibility criteria as well as compensation levels than Louisiana, survivors had to learn a new system. Their abrupt departure from New Orleans meant that few survivors had the necessary documentation with them that might have made application for program participation in Austin easier. Our interviews revealed various bureaucratic paths to health care coverage, some of which were more efficient and successful than others. Overall, the picture that our interviews reveal is one of discontinuity of care and inadequate or incomplete care that neither the state nor civil society organizations were able to address effectively.

Although survivors did not receive all of the care they needed in a timely manner, the federal government did respond with programs such as Emergency Medicaid. This program allowed individuals with serious acute illnesses or injuries to receive immediate attention without preapproval. Survivors who were covered by federal programs such as Medicare and social security disability benefits before Katrina faced fewer problems with interruptions in coverage. Those survivors whose applications had been in process when the storm struck, however, often faced complications and delays in receiving benefits.

Medicare recipients were of course able to maintain continuous coverage given the universal nature of the program. Some, though, expressed concern that they might not find a doctor who would accept Medicare. Those who lived in senior housing found it easier to access care. Katherine Smith, a seventy-year-old white female, was dual-eligible, a term which refers to low-income individuals who receive Medicaid to supplement Medicare. At our second interview, she expressed doubts about the receptiveness of doctors in Austin. As she said, "…here the doctors don't want to accept Medicaid.…" Despite her fears, she eventually found a doctor who provided services at the assisted living facility in which she lived and she seemed quite pleased with the care she was receiving.

James Long, a sixty-six-year-old African American male, had multiple health problems, including depression, chronic back pain, and difficulty walking because of a weak leg. He told us that he had found a doctor who came to the senior citizens' complex where he lived. James was pleased with this doctor and told us that, "…I got a doctor [who] comes right here." When the interviewer remarked that she was surprised that any doctor makes house calls, James said,

…well, when you in a[re], you a[re] victim of a catastrophe, these doctors like him, they know that people can't get out, they can't get around. This is an elderly community, this is a community when he [is done with] me he's going to see somebody else. He's that kind of doctor, "I'll bring it to them since they can't come to me." I really like the doctor.

THE ROLE OF CIVIL SOCIETY

Although issues related to health and health care emerged frequently in our open-ended interviews with the survivors, we did not ask specifically about the survivors' contacts with civil society organizations in reference to health-related issues. Although the survivors mentioned nongovernmental organizations' assistance in health-related matters on several occasions, their discussions of illness and health care focused mostly on their experiences with the formal health care system. This is not surprising, as health care is such a basic state and market function and not thought of in terms of nongovernmental or faith-based organizations. Even when such organizations are involved in helping individuals obtain health care, the overwhelming presence of the formal health system makes their role less prominent or essential. Doctors, clinics, and hospitals are the focus in discussions of medical conditions and treatment. Although survivors found voluntary organizations' assistance with health-related problems to be useful on those few occasions when they received it, nonprofessional and nonmedical actors were not major players in dealing with health problems or health care access, just as they were not major players in providing housing.

The story here, then, is one of the absence of civil society organizations in providing direct health care to low-income individuals. Community hospitals and health care foundations certainly played a role, but they are part of the formal system even if they are nonprofit and nongovernmental. Aside from these core medical organizations, no civil society entity played a major organized role in survivors' accounts of their health care. Because of the scale of the task and the complexity of population health issues, health care for low-income people remains essentially a welfare state function.

Because our interviews were not focused on health or on the role of civil society actors, their presence is probably somewhat hidden. We cannot conclude that such organizations were not concerned with or involved in dealing with survivors' health care problems. They did so, though, in the context of responding to a far wider range of problems. As we discussed in Chapter 6, some survivors had extensive contact with a wide range of case managers. As part of their function, these case managers routinely asked about health care needs and concerns and provided basic information and support. Volunteer doctors and other health professionals provided care at the Convention Center and other shelters immediately after the evacuation. The few cases of civil society input in health care that we observed, though, suggest that such assistance was limited, discontinuous, and difficult to obtain. No nongovernmental organization appears to have defined its core role as that of providing support or direct health care.

The support that NGOs provided survivors took different forms and was defined by structural factors related to health care. That system is capital and personnel extensive and expensive. As in the case of housing that we discussed in the last chapter, the potential role of civil society organizations is limited by the sheer scale of the task. As we have noted, NGOs, FBOs, and other voluntary organizations are best suited to ancillary and supportive services, such as helping individuals in need gain access to the formal system. As we have shown, in the case of the survivors of Hurricane Katrina, supportive assistance was provided by the case managers, often in the form of general information about the availability of services. Survivors received some direct mental health services as well as some limited financial assistance for medical treatment and prescriptions, but little more.

In addition to case managers affiliated with NGOs, more informal organizations, such as neighborhood associations and individual congregations, had a potentially important role in providing information on where and how to access professional health care in Austin. Although we did not witness a great deal of involvement of such organizations, they could conceivably serve as a source of information concerning eligibility criteria, potential problems with particular sources of care, and the existence of other nongovernmental sources of information or care. For individuals in a strange situation who may not be used to dealing with medical bureaucracies, such assistance could prove vital. In the post-Katrina context in which there were frequent changes to the complex set of rules that determined eligibility for benefits, these local agencies could potentially have served as intermediaries and helped individuals navigate complex bureaucratic environments. Although some of these functions were mentioned, they were, as we have said, largely hidden.

CIVIL SOCIETY AND CASE MANAGEMENT

As we have explained, case management was the intervention model used in Austin to assist evacuees with their many needs. Ideally, in addition to dealing with other problems related to income, nutrition, child care, employment, and housing, case managers should have been able to ensure that survivors obtained the medical care they needed for their medical problems. However, case managers were limited in what they could do given the extent of the survivors' other needs. For the most part, they could only provide information and were not more actively involved in helping survivors access care. Only a few of the survivors explicitly mentioned having benefited from this type of assistance. A case manager offered to assist Clifford Thomson, a forty-seven-year-old African American male, to get to his doctor's appointments, but Thomson never seemed to have taken advantage of the offer.

In a few instances, survivors told us that they had received information about health care services. Whitney Morris, whom we met earlier, told us that she had received information about emergency psychiatric services that were available on a walk-in basis from an agency that provided employment services. The limitations of this sort of assistance were obvious because information alone was usually not enough to ensure that survivors obtained the care they needed. One case manager at an employment service did what he could to help MaryAnn Hoskins, a white female in her midforties we first met in Chapter 3, find affordable health care. Hoskins did not have health insurance, and although the case manager gave her a list of health care providers that she might contact, she found none that would accept her without insurance. She told us that, "…I went into [the employment service] and I got the [referral] sheet and I tried calling…trying to find affordable health care.…It's so discouraging, nothing is for free…everybody wants money."

A few survivors mentioned having received mental health services directly from NGOs. These services were limited, however, and consisted primarily of counseling and home services. For some reason, though, these services were not utilized by many of our participants. It may have been the case that more basic needs, particularly housing, took precedence and that health and mental health care was postponed, as some providers suggested. At the time of our first interview with her, Jane Allison, a fifty-six-year-old African American female, had a room in a hotel that had been purchased by a nongovernmental organization that planned to convert the hotel into housing for homeless individuals and families. We mentioned this organization and its renovation project in Chapter 7. A counselor provided mental health services on site, but Allison seems not to have made use of them. She was clearly distraught and confided to the interviewer that since the storm, she had been having nightmares and difficulty sleeping. An excerpt from an interview illustrates her difficulties:

Interviewer: Do you feel like it would be beneficial to you at all to talk with somebody about the dreams you are having?
Jane: I think so.
Interviewer: You think so.... I would be happy to find out more about how they are scheduling those counselors if you think you might like to talk to somebody.
Jane: They have [a counselor] but we didn't have time. We didn't have time to get [therapy]. When we did get a chance to...get to it, [the counselor was] gone. We had so much running around....

We first met with Jackie Martin, an African American female in her early fifties, in January 2006. She suffered from disabilities and was depressed and anxious. Since the storm, she had been separated from the sister she used to care for. The loss of her home and the feeling of being homeless fueled her distress. She received both Medicaid and Medicare and was able to obtain mental health care at a clinic that provided services to the city's low-income population. Jackie told us that the mental health care she received had helped her. She also had received some mental health support at home, but it is not clear to us who had provided it. During our second interview in May 2006, she did not mention having received any further mental health care. During that interview, she talked about her spirituality and feeling more at peace with her situation. She was also preparing to move back to New Orleans.

Immediately after the storm, many free mental health services were available, but survivors were busy with more immediate needs. Many mental health professionals volunteered to work in the large shelters that housed evacuees in the first few weeks after their evacuation. As we have mentioned, mental health services were not an immediate priority for many of the evacuees and took a back seat to locating family members, finding housing, and getting medical care for previous or new physical problems, among many other problems. A year or so later, when those with mental health problems were ready to seek help, most of these free services were no longer available.

As is common with mental health problems, individuals needed intervention over long periods of time. Even those few social services agencies that provided basic counseling were able to provide only time-limited assistance. As we mentioned, Whitney Morris was in need of assistance for both physical and mental health problems. She had had great difficulty in obtaining health care coverage in spite of her many efforts. She told us that she had been experiencing severe symptoms of stress since the storm. During our first interview, she mentioned having contacted a large national organization's help line, but told us that she had problems getting any answer from them. During our second interview with her, Whitney had obtained some phone counseling that she had found helpful and she obtained some additional assistance from the same agency. Unfortunately, by the time of our third interview, Whitney told us that her counselor could no longer see her and that she would have to go elsewhere for services. He put her in contact with a case manager who might be able to provide information on other sources of care.

The counseling that Whitney obtained initially seemed to have helped her through some dark days. She reported that a counselor had come to her home three times. This assistance appears to have been a little inconsistent; she explained that the counselor had not been by for three weeks. She seemed confident, though, that the counselor would call back and she felt that they had a solid relationship. During a subsequent interview, she told us that her counselor had moved to another city. During that same interview, we found out that she had been seeing a psychiatrist after a visit to an emergency psychiatric clinic. She still had ongoing problems because of a lack of health insurance, but was hopeful that the problems could be resolved with the intervention of her psychiatrist, who appeared to have been ready to inquire on her behalf.

New ties with local helping professionals made early after her arrival in Austin proved useful in obtaining counseling for Jeri Anderson, a fifty-six-year-old African American female. She had met a volunteer nurse at the Austin Convention Center, who introduced her to a volunteer counselor who worked at a hospital during the day but provided therapy at individuals' homes in the evening. She told us about the therapy she received:

> I was getting to talk to her once a week. And she had gotten sick and I hadn't seen her in two weeks. And she was supposed to come back yesterday and I don't know what happened to her because remember I told you she was supposed to come on the tenth. She usually comes at five o'clock 'cause she leaves the [hospital]. And I know this past [inaudible] 'cause she is doing free, you know, helping me. She leaves the [hospital] and come give me my therapy on the third, so like I said, you know, I am so grateful for what they have done for me already because I came to a point I wouldn't be at if it wasn't for them. So I have got to be grateful for that.

Relatively few survivors received financial assistance for health care from nongovernmental organizations. In one case, Teri Chandler, a forty-one-year-old African American female, received physical therapy that was paid for by a private organization. Another survivor obtained money for glasses. Various organizations assisted other survivors, but this assistance was very limited and could hardly make a dent in the costs of prescriptions and other health care. In fact, very few interviewees mentioned financial assistance for prescription medications. As a result, some were not taking the medications they needed. Lynn Hughes, a white female in her early sixties who was caring for a friend with a chronic illness, obtained a voucher from a large NGO to cover part of the costs of her friend's medications. The amount provided, though, was insufficient to purchase the drugs. She applied for Medicaid and was waiting for an appointment, but her friend needed the medications immediately. In New Orleans, the medications had been provided free by a local clinic. Hughes told us of her dilemma:

...That's the thing. I am worried. Now last month when we were in the Convention Center, they filled her prescriptions...for one thing, it didn't occur to me that we would need medications the following month that we would still be in Austin....Well, last month it was [difficult] to get her meds. One of her medicines is three hundred and fifty dollars and when they told us that, I almost passed out. So we were trying to get vouchers. We got a partial voucher from [an FBO], but they wouldn't cover the whole thing, so we had to come up with almost two hundred dollars...which we did and got her medicine last month that way, so I said, "we will try to get you on [Medicaid]...get it established and set up correctly from the following month," but I don't know. We have started the process now, but whether or not we will be approved for Medicaid or not, I don't know. I really don't know. So I know she has got to have her medicine though....I don't know how that is going to work out...

Some local churches tried to assist with medical expenses, but this assistance was quite limited. Tyrell Booker, an African American male in his forties, had been issued a Medical Assistance Program (MAP) card at the resource center for the homeless and had been seen at a clinic for stomach problems. Unfortunately, he was unable to fill his prescriptions since he did not have the money for the co-pay that he had to cover since he was not technically homeless. He told us about a local nonprofit affiliated with a church that he had heard about from an acquaintance that might help: "...She told me...[that they are] supposed to be doing some[thing to] help you with your medicine but you got to get down there like six in the morning, yeah, and they got a line...she says they take like ten people...a day...."

Survivors who stayed in Austin for long periods needed assistance with prescriptions long after the initial crisis, during which prescriptions were often provided free. Tiffany Wilkins, the young African American woman with HIV we described earlier in this chapter, tried to obtain assistance to cover the costs of her expensive prescriptions from local social services but without success. She also tried to obtain assistance from a medical emergency program but did not meet the requirements. As she said,

> ...and I tried, like, I tried...but something [has] to be a real emergency and it has to happen within thirty days of when you call.... So when I tried them, they asked did I have any kind of medical emergency. I was like, "Well, yeah, I was diagnosed with HIV." She was like, "How long have you known?" And I'm like, "Well, a year." And she was like, "Well, it has to be thirty days."

CHURCHES AND CONGREGATIONS

As in other areas, churches and congregations provided some help to survivors in obtaining health care. Charlotte Hendricks, the fifty-one-year-old African American woman we first met in Chapter 4, had serious health problems. When she became ill early in 2006, she received assistance from a local congregation paying for medical care on two occasions. On the first occasion, it was in conjunction with a serious illness during which she received assistance from a family and others at her church. When we asked her how she found her doctor, she said, "...they [called] 911 and a family from that church...paid for me to go to the doctor...that's how sick I was...the congregation got together and paid my doctor bill, yeah, that's how sick I was...the ambulance had to come get me out of here."

On the second occasion, a case manager got her into an adopt-a-family program and a family responded and paid for medical tests. As Charlotte told us,

> ...I stayed with [a friend] for a while because I was sick, I told you I'm a cancer patient, so I was sick from maybe December [2005] to May [2006]....I was sick a long time...we tried to find some resources to try to get me in the hospital like MAP [Medical Assistance Plan] and stuff like that and it just didn't work. Remember I told you...the liaison...recommended a family to adopt me...[they got me into] the hospital...and to get my mammogram and all that done I got that done through [name] Wellness Clinic, so they did that and they found out that the polyps in my breast was, was benign....

Charlotte also had surgery at a local not-for-profit hospital. Her previous attempts at getting health care coverage had not succeeded and she had very few options.

As we mentioned in Chapter 6, Justine Betts and her husband had also been adopted by a family, whom she referred to as her "foster parents." In this case, the assistance did not last. Although individuals and families provided considerable help to some evacuees, that help was dependent on the resources and the continuing goodwill of the family. Betts was obviously resentful and told us that she felt she had been "used." As she said,

Now, my foster parents brought me to the dentist one time. When I went back, they [the dentist] wouldn't see me without them so I had been trying to get in touch with my foster parents. They seem like they just did it for the taxes, that's the way I look at it. That's the way I look at it 'cause…some of my people's foster family still sticking with them. And if you gonna be there for me, then you are supposed to be there for me all the way through. Everybody from Katrina is still not up on their feet yet. You don't just…jump back on [your feet] when you've lost everything. And you [are] in another city…you can't just snap back like that. It's not that easy. I'm thinking they are all doing it from the kindness of their hearts, but you all get something in return off of my tragedy. That's the way I looked at it.

In another case, a survivor family's relationship with a church was maintained over the long run. This family of five adults, whose members had a number of long-standing disabilities and chronic illnesses, was supported by a church group. Although our interviews with the family do not include specific discussions of health care, we know that a volunteer from the church put this family in contact with a state agency that dealt specifically with disabilities. This organization, in turn, was very helpful in getting the family established in Austin. With the division's assistance, family members were able to learn about the city and get help with paperwork to apply for social security and other programs.

Asking for assistance from churches was not easy for everyone. Tiffany Wilkins, for example, told us that she felt that asking for any assistance from churches meant that she had to open herself to too many questions. Another survivor told us that she did not feel ready to talk about her experiences, even to a pastor. During an interview in May 2006, Justine Betts, whom we have discussed earlier, confided to us that she was feeling depressed, but that she did not want to confide in a pastor even though she was religious. She preferred to keep to herself and felt that her depression was more a matter for her family to deal with. As she said when asked whether she had found a church with which to become involved,

…well, we had one [a pastor] but right now…I'm not ready just to open up to him…when my time comes, then I['ll] open up to him, but right now, I'm not ready to open up to the pastor. He always tells us whenever we need him…he [doesn't] care what time of night or day it is…just call him. But I'm not ready right now, not right now.

A LIMITED IMPACT

Given the fact that our sample was overwhelmingly impoverished and had lived in the most disadvantaged parts of New Orleans, often for generations before the storm, they had many of the physical and mental health problems common in impoverished communities. The ordeal of the storm and evacuation only worsened serious preexisting conditions. Facing lifelong health risks and with a generally unfavorable illness profile, this group of survivors was clearly in need of immediate, ongoing, and often intensive health care. Our interviews corroborate the findings of other studies that show that in the absence of a comprehensive health care delivery system, low-income individuals and families confront a mosaic of uncoordinated providers from whom they often receive incomplete and discontinuous care. Emergency rooms, free clinics, and charity are no substitute for a real medical home where one receives primary care and referral to more specialized medical treatment. Even when they are able to see a doctor, sick individuals with little income and no savings are often unable to pay for the drugs that their doctor prescribes.

As our case studies clearly reveal, for civil society organizations and even for governmental agencies, health care is only one of a wide range of problems brought on by disasters. As we mentioned in Chapter 7, survivors' health problems and difficulties accessing health care both contributed to and resulted from their problems with identification, housing, and employment. Survivors without identification faced more challenges in accessing health care. Those with untreated chronic physical and mental health problems were less likely to be able to work, and unemployment contributed to housing instability.

Some NGOs, civic groups, congregations, and even individuals made noble attempts to help survivors find and pay for health care. Often this assistance was in conjunction with help of other sorts, perhaps most importantly, housing. Yet our study leads us to conclude that civil society organizations are limited in what they can do in relation to the management of serious health problems or the financing of health care. These limitations are not confined solely to disaster situations, but apply, we suspect, to impoverished populations even in normal times. The health care needs of such populations are complex and difficult to manage. Modern medical care is sophisticated and expensive. Voluntary organizations can clearly engage in wellness programs or provide ill individuals who are isolated and have few social supports with companionship and perhaps transportation to clinics. Such organizations, though, are neither well equipped to provide complex and expensive medical care themselves nor are they in a position to replace the government or health insurance companies in paying for care.

Large nongovernmental organizations such as the Gates Foundation and Doctors without Borders provide vitally important services and care to low-income people worldwide, but they clearly cannot substitute for well-designed and fully funded national health systems. As health care consumes an ever-growing share of our gross domestic product, voluntary organizations may be looked to increasingly to provide the ancillary care that they are most capable of providing. Isolated low-income and elderly people would no doubt benefit greatly from companionship and assistance with the routine activities of daily life, such as cooking, cleaning, and basic home maintenance. These are as important to well-being as medicines and physical therapy. Voluntary organizations might also assist in illness management. Low-income and minority populations suffer disproportionately from diabetes and other diseases that require ongoing management. Assisting with diet, encouraging exercise, and monitoring compliance with prescription regimes are tasks that are neither expensive nor complex and technical. Our observations lead us to the conclusion that these sorts of health maintenance and assistance roles are where civil society can offer useful contributions in enhancing individuals' well-being.

9

The State, Civil Society, and the Limitations of Social Capital

In this book, we have focused on the response by federal and state agencies to the human crisis that resulted from Hurricane Katrina, as well as the role of civil society organizations in dealing with the short- and longer-term needs of individuals and families who were displaced by the storm. We are interested, though, in more than just this one disaster or even the role of civil society in responding to short-term crises. Rather, we focused on this particular event and the diaspora that it brought about for the survivors in order to address the question of whether local levels of government and especially civil society organizations can address the short-term and the longer-term structural vulnerabilities of marginalized groups. The question was motivated by the popular desire to shrink the federal government that has informed public policy in recent years. Our investigation revealed multiple legal, bureaucratic, logistic, and human barriers to a rapid and effective response to the crisis, and in particular it revealed deep-seated barriers to the longer-term return of certain individuals and groups to any semblance of self-sufficiency and stable community life. Civil society organizations, including secular nongovernmental and faith-based organizations, were active in multiple ways even before FEMA arrived in Austin, but their impact and effectiveness varied greatly depending on their structure, funding, staffing, and the tasks they addressed.

We end by asking what contributed to the mixed results and what might be done to make civil society organizations more central and effective contributors to the mission of crisis intervention, as well as the longer-term project of poverty alleviation and minority group empowerment. We also discuss factors that create or undermine social capital, a term that we have used to refer to the capacity of communities to act collectively to improve their members' life chances and well-being. Our focus in the previous chapters was not on the recovery and rehabilitation efforts in New Orleans. Rather, it was on those hurricane victims who evacuated to Austin, Texas, and who remained for some time. It became clear early in the study that some of the survivors whom we interviewed would never return to New Orleans and that they had, in effect, permanently relocated to Texas. A few of the survivors we interviewed were middle-class and possessed high levels of human and social capital. The couple in which both partners were physical therapists whose story leads off Chapter 2 quickly reestablished themselves in Austin, bought a new home, and began new careers. They were the clear exception. Because our study sample consisted primarily of low-income evacuees who were forcibly evacuated after the storm to one city, they are not necessarily representative of either residents of New Orleans who never left or who returned or those who were evacuated to other cities. Interviews with Katrina case managers in other parts of the country (Bell et al., 2010), in addition to research on survivors in other cities (Kromm & Sturgis, 2008; Stough & Sharp, 2008), indicate that our study participants did not return quickly to New Orleans because they had little to return to or they faced serious barriers to doing so. For some, their homes had been destroyed and they had no resources with which to rebuild; others had been renters who had no real property to draw them back; many simply did not have the resources to make the return trip. The majority of our participants were among those whose social ties to the old city and their old communities had been most completely severed by the storm.

In this final chapter, we discuss the implications of our study and the experiences of the survivors in terms of the overarching theme of the loss of community and the forces that contributed to their success or failure in reestablishing their lives in a new place. Again, one of our core theoretical questions had to do with the role of formal and informal civil society organizations in facilitating or impeding the survivors' success. It became clear early in the study that the community's response, as well as that of nongovernmental organizations, was affected in important ways by the public's perception of the moral worthiness of the victims of the storm. As we mentioned at the outset, the terms used to describe the victims evolved over time, largely in response to the desire of service providers and residents of the cities receiving survivors to avoid negative or stigmatizing labels. The term "survivors" was ultimately chosen since it implied resilience and avoided the negative stereotype that might be associated with terms such as "evacuees," "refugees," or even "victims." It was clear that public perceptions were an important aspect of the survivors' longer-term experiences and the willingness of the general public to assist. During the course of the study, and in fact rather quickly after the storm, the public's perceptions of the survivors changed. Immediately after the storm, the evacuees were welcomed by cities in Texas and elsewhere. The City of Austin, like Houston and other Texas cities, opened sports stadiums, convention centers, and other shelters to house survivors and to provide places where they could make contact with public and private relief agencies. Immediately following the evacuation, the survivors were treated as deserving victims who had suffered for reasons that had nothing to do with their own moral failures.

As time went on, though, the halo of victimization faded and many if not most of these low-income survivors joined the ranks of stigmatized long-term low-income people. The results of a poll reported in the *Houston Chronicle* revealed that seven months after the storm, three-quarters of those polled felt that the evacuees had put "considerable strain" on the community, and two-thirds felt that they were responsible for an increase in violent crime (Berger, 2006). This new stigma and suspicion no doubt undermined the willingness and ability of individuals, as well as of civil society organizations, to continue to respond to the survivors' needs. Rather quickly after the initial outpouring of assistance, both contributions and volunteers dried up. The experience of the faith-based ECSA, which we introduced in Chapter 6, is informative. The initial response was so extensive and generous that the organization found it necessary to move to a larger facility. The positive mood was such that the ECSA, based in a predominantly African American church, was joined by another congregation from the more affluent west side of the city, a collaboration that was not typical. Unfortunately, neither the generosity of volunteers nor the bridges to other congregations were maintained for long. Historically entrenched patterns reasserted themselves, and the organization moved back to its small headquarters and its previous mission. No permanent change had been made to the system of social stratification that placed the low-income African American victims of Hurricane Katrina at the bottom of the social hierarchy, except that, rather than finding themselves at the bottom of the social and economic hierarchies in Louisiana, they were at the bottom in Texas.

AGENCY AND STRUCTURE

One way of framing the forces that affected the ability of survivors to recover is in terms of the classic problem of structure and agency. As we mentioned in Chapter 3, in social theory, *agency* refers to the capacity of individuals or groups to control their physical and social environments and to act as autonomous agents to further their interests effectively (Ritzer, 2008; Ritzer & Gindoff, 1994). Structure, on the other hand, refers to all those factors that limit an individual's or a group's abilities to act as autonomous agents. These factors include social class, education, religion, gender, race, ethnicity, customs, norms, and much more. The question of the relative roles of agency and structure takes on particular salience when one's ability to control one's life is constrained by social class factors related to historical disadvantages based on race and ethnicity. The ability of the low-income victims of Hurricane Katina to avoid the devastation of the storm and their ability to recover were largely affected by historically based structural vulnerabilities related to the specific history of race and social class in New Orleans.

A problem arises when one focuses excessively on agency or individuals and attributes negative outcomes to aspects of their character. Such an attribution is referred to as "blaming the victim." Certain modern social theorists reject the notion that agency and structure can be treated in isolation from one another (Berger & Luckman, 1966; Bourdieu, 1977; Giddens, 1986). Agency and the capacity of individuals and groups to affect their fates are constrained by structure. As we discussed in the preceding chapter, many observers, including providers, attributed the survivors' difficulties in adapting to Austin to aspects of their own character, culture, and behavior. Such has been the case for chronically low-income people historically, as explanations of poverty have focused on the undeserving paupers whose plight is largely of their own making (O'Connor, 2002). The concept of "self-sufficiency," which was part of the language of personal responsibility ushered in by welfare reform, is the newest incarnation of this idea. A large body of research, as well as our own study, illustrates the ways in which deeply entrenched racial prejudices and structural racism limit the extent of and undermine the effectiveness of social capital for African Americans. These structural forces limited the options for effective agency of the residents of impoverished neighborhoods in New Orleans (Fussell, 2007; Somers, 2008).

THE CENTRAL ROLE OF THE STATE

Perhaps the most basic lesson that we learned from our study relates to the continuing importance of the welfare state. It ultimately defines the social, economic, and political structures within which citizens operate as agents. T. H. Marshall's view of the welfare state, which we outlined in the introduction, guarantees not only civil and political rights, but the material security that gives one the capacity to exercise one's civil and political rights. Our study and the large literature on civil society and social capital that we have reviewed make it clear that a vibrant and effective civil society requires a stable, powerful, efficient, and just state to function effectively (Esping-Andersen, 1999; Esping-Andersen et al., 2002). Individuals, even in groups, lack the knowledge or power to deal with major crises or bring about basic structural change on their own. Antonio Gramsci, who introduced the term "civil society," employed it to refer to what he saw as venues where the oppressed could collectively challenge the status quo (Gramsci, 1971). The hope for civil society among progressives is based on more than the potential utility of NGOs as subcontractors to the state or service providers in times of crisis, or even on their potential for dealing with the material needs of low-income people in the longer term. The hope is for the possibility of encouraging socially and politically effective collective action that can fundamentally improve the life chances of disadvantaged groups. That hope is based on the premise that self-help and autonomy are far superior to charity (Saegert, Thompson, & Warren, 2001; Silverman & Patterson, 2004).

Two decades ago, the collapse of the Soviet Union and the rather rapid restoration of democratic governments to the nations of Latin America fueled the hope that in previously oppressive societies grassroots and other local efforts would emerge to allow individuals to band together to further fully participatory democracies (Batliwals & Brown, 2006; Boli & Thomas, 1997; Eade, 2002; Michael Edwards, 2004; Edwards & Sen, 2000; Feinberg, Waisman, & Zamosc, 2006; Hudock, 1999). Twenty years later, that hope has been tempered by the reality of ongoing social inequalities and injustice and the apparent inability of the powerless to change the formal and informal rules of the game. Historically structured individual and group differences in access to economic and political power ensure that group differences in life chances and vulnerability to disasters remain large. The expectation that an emergent civil society would lead to radical change was probably unrealistic. Yet the proliferation of NGOs and the growth of voluntary activity all over the world continue to suggest that some basic change in citizen participation is possible, and that this participation holds the possibility of changing basic governance structures and systems of social stratification (Grzybowski, 2000).

In the end, we are back to interest group politics and the need for active participation by citizens and the groups that represent them in the political arena (Almond & Verba, 1963). In this concluding chapter, we return to some of the theoretical issues with which we began and ask what our study suggests about the potential of civil society to help bring about major social changes that improve the lives of the victims of short-term disasters and longer-term structured disadvantage. We frame the discussion in terms of social capital, organized political action, and the potential for civil society organizations to emerge from, or give rise to, new social movements aimed at changing the status quo and increasing civic participation and equity.

The recent fascination with the potential of civil society is not confined to the progressive left or the conservative right. As we discussed in Chapter 1, conservatives, communitarians, and anti–welfare state free-market purists place great faith in civil society primarily because it is not the state, with its power of regulation, control, and oppression (Etzioni, 1993, 1995, 2000; Hayek, 1944, 1976; Mead, 1986, 1997; Murray, 1994, 1996, 1999, 2006). From this perspective, small, local, and minimally regulated enterprises and organizations are morally and practically superior to big government and centralized market regulation. As we discussed in the first chapter, the philosophy of devolution espoused by Ronald Reagan, Margaret Thatcher, and others ushered in a new period of smaller government and a focus on greater self-sufficiency among citizens, particularly those who receive publicly funded services. Welfare reform in the United States and the New Third Way in Britain and elsewhere emphasized the philosophy of "no rights without responsibilities" and accepted the need for fundamental changes in the postwar welfare state.

Hurricane Katrina illustrates the inherent problem with excessive devolution and the belief that all social problems can be addressed at the local level. In modern economies and an increasingly globalized world, the forces that affect individuals and communities are often large and even international in scale. The global economic recession of 2008 is only the most recent example. Our study clearly reveals the useful contribution that civil society organizations can make to the short-term alleviation of suffering, but it also illustrates their clear limitations in the longer-term tasks of rebuilding lives and communities. The scale of the disaster was too large and the difficulties of coordinating a response too complex for individual civil society organizations or even groups of such organizations to address efficiently and effectively. Everyone looked to FEMA for assistance. The federal government was ultimately the only effective source of housing, income, health care, and other major assistance for the survivors. If the federal response was inadequate, there were no other organizations ready to step in. Local and state agencies were participants, but the ultimate authority and source of funding was the federal government. Without FEMA, the survivors' plight would have been far worse. As in the case of large-scale disasters in developing nations, they would have had to look to international relief agencies for assistance.

However, in the context of devolution of federal responsibility for many basic human services, we must think carefully about the nature of the federal role in addressing human needs. The experiences of the survivors we studied lead us to propose a larger federal role, even though we acknowledge that FEMA as it is currently (dis)organized was, in many cases, the single biggest impediment to survivors' recovery. A slow and bureaucratic response to crisis undermines faith in government and bureaucracy generally and feeds arguments to "starve the beast." The federal response to disaster must be adequately funded and staffed and designed to attend to the needs of those who are in greatest need. In the case of disaster, as we have seen, the majority of the victims are likely to be victims of long-term structural poverty and racism. This reality calls for a long-term commitment to addressing those structural challenges of affordable housing, employment for low-skill workers, and public transportation and infrastructure.

In addition to a more central command and control and adequate federal funding, better and more reliable partnerships with the localities are vital. Local governmental and civil society organizations are closer to the local reality than bureaucrats in Washington. In the case of FEMA, the federal government did not assign the determination of eligibility for assistance to localities. Greater coordination among different levels of government and nongovernmental organizations promises to reduce redundancy and the misallocation of resources and more quickly identify those most in need, as well as the most appropriate avenues for addressing those needs.

The organizations that responded to the immediate crisis represented the full range of federal, state, and municipal agencies. They also included the usual disaster-oriented nongovernmental actors such as the Red Cross. Many of these agencies and organizations stayed on after the immediate crisis and were involved in longer-term attempts to return the survivors' lives to some semblance of normality. Years after the storm, it is now clear that immediate relief and longer-term reintegration and community building, especially in a new city, are very different tasks. Our study leads us to ask under what conditions community building might be possible and what level of commitment it would require.

GEORGE MARSHALL AND REBUILDING WESTERN EUROPE AFTER WORLD WAR II

Nongovernmental civil society organizations have existed for centuries, but their number exploded after the Second World War (Boli & Thomas, 1997; Edwards & Sen, 2000; Fisher, 1997). Many NGOs were active during and after the war; they helped rebuild a war-ravaged Europe and represent a major force in development today (Edwards, 1999; Malhotra, 2000; Rahman, 2006). After the war, the economies of the nations of Western Europe, and that of Germany in particular, roared back from devastation and grew at phenomenal rates, partly as a result of the American European Recovery Program – known as the Marshall Plan, named after Secretary of State George Marshall – which provided huge amounts of redevelopment aid (Dulles, 1993; Milward, 1987; Sorel & Padoan, 2008). Comparisons of the Marshall Plan to the response to Hurricane Katrina or attempts to deal with chronic poverty more generally may be a bit strained, but they serve to emphasize the central importance of human and social capital in the form of an educated population that is ready to participate in a modern labor market, as well as the central role of an organized and efficient state in developing those skills. If Stalin had accepted the United States' offers to assist in the rebuilding of Eastern Europe, the result there would have probably been very different. Those nations did not have the human or social capital or the civic traditions of the West and languished in terms of economic and political progress for another half-century.

Rebuilding the lives of victims of Hurricane Katrina who had relatively few initial resources proved far harder than one might have expected. For all of the devastation of the war, the nations of Western Europe had high levels of human capital and other resources with which to rebuild (Sorel & Padoan, 2008). Some economic historians even doubt that the Marshall Plan was all that central to the recovery (Milward, 1987). The inherent strength of the Western European economies may have led to rapid recovery even without the assistance from the United States. In any case, it seems clear that given Europe's history of economic development, there was much to work with, whatever the ultimate contribution of the Marshall Plan and nongovernmental organizations. As we have shown in the case of Hurricane Katrina, those individuals and families with high levels of human, social, and material capital – a minority of our participants – recovered relatively quickly.

Of course, the size of the investment in our inner cities and FEMA's response to catastrophes has never been anything like a Marshall Plan. Social policy and investment have been inadequate to educate and train African Americans and Latinos to high levels, to transform failing educational systems into mechanisms for upward mobility, or to provide dignified, decently paid, and meaningful work to the residents of low-income communities. As we have discussed at length, the core philosophy of disaster case management is not to alter the status quo or move disaster victims into situations that are better than those in which they found themselves before the crisis; the purpose is only to return them to their previous state. Such an approach does not change fundamental social relationships or social structures, nor does it transform victims into powerful agents in control of their own lives.

CIVIL SOCIETY AND SOCIAL CHANGE

We return to the question of how effective NGOs, FBOs, and other civil society organizations and groups were, or could in principle have been, in assisting the impoverished victims of a disaster go beyond simple recovery to a situation that represents an improvement over what they had before. This question relates to the extent to which, and under what circumstances, such organizations can form the basis of effective social movements and move beyond charity to effective political action. From our experience, it is clear that accomplishing even the disaster case management goal of returning families with little human, social, or material capital to their pre-disaster situations is difficult enough. Going beyond that and improving the situations of survivors seems nearly impossible without some major social mobilization or some clear commitment by powerful political entities. In the end, our conclusion is that in widespread crises that affect thousands of individuals, or when dealing with historically marginalized populations, civil society is no substitute for the state and that its influence on the state is indirect, incremental, and short term.

In the short term, civil society organizations can serve as ancillary sources of social capital and assist victims of disaster and longer-term low-income people to make contact with whatever official state agencies are able to provide. If those agencies are nonresponsive, civil society efforts are only palliative and usually ineffective in terms of longer-term change. In the end, if they are to make fundamental improvements in impoverished communities, NGOs, FBOs, and other civil society actors have no choice but to engage in political action aimed at mobilizing public opinion to influence official policy and major state actors. In the contemporary economic and political climate, such mobilization and the likelihood of an effective defense of core welfare-state principles represent a major challenge.

The nature of aid provided by the Marshall Plan to Western Europe and that provided by NGOs to impoverished populations is vastly different, largely because of differences in the recipients of the aid. The Marshall Plan provided assistance to business and governments for rebuilding infrastructure and manufacturing capacity (Sorel & Padoan, 2008). That effort involved an educated workforce that had been industrialized before and during the war, and it was directed by stable and strong state systems. Western Europe was a developed, if destroyed, collection of nation-states at the war's end. Efforts of contemporary international nongovernmental organizations (INGOs) to deal with the problems of the developing world are very different. Rather than providing assistance to governments and organizations that have a history of effective functioning, charitable aid provided by or funneled through INGOs is focused on far more basic problems. This focus on sustainable development involves basic economic activity that is not aimed at creating large-scale productive capacity and high levels of human capital (Hopwood, Mellor, & O'Brien, 2005). For the most part, such aid is focused on subsistence. Such an approach does not attempt to achieve, nor is it likely to result in, fundamental and extensive social change.

RACE, CIVIL SOCIETY, AND SOCIAL CAPITAL

Throughout our discussion, the issue of race has remained at the forefront. We began with television images of individuals clinging to rooftops and stranded on bridges. The fact that most of these individuals were African American could not be ignored. Any discussion of the role of civil society organizations or anything else related to the situation of vulnerable Americans must deal with the issue of race. Because race is such a stark fact of life in most areas of social life, we might ask how it relates to civil society organizations and to our core themes. We, like many other observers, have pointed out the historically structured disadvantage that placed the African American community of New Orleans in ecologically vulnerable locations. The vulnerability to disasters was influenced not only by such historical factors as Jim Crow laws and labor market discrimination, but by government policies that created vulnerability in the name of economic progress (Burby, 2006; Stehr, 2006). Levee systems that are used to make dangerous locations supposedly habitable place residents in great danger if they are in fact inadequate. The failure of the levees in New Orleans was hardly an accident; it was the inevitable result of poor planning and even self-deception by government officials and state policy makers (Stehr, 2006). The race and social class of the victims illustrate the selective vulnerability of groups with little social, political, or economic capital.

Since William Julius Wilson published *The Declining Significance of Race* in 1978, an ongoing debate has focused on the question of whether race or social class is more important in accounting for the extreme vulnerability of certain individuals and communities such as those of the Lower Ninth Ward. Attempting to decide whether the African American community's vulnerability was the result of race or social class strikes us as pointless since the two are completely intertwined; being African American places one at elevated risk of poverty and marginality and that social class position reinforces individuals' and groups' vulnerability. Race and social class combine in a self-reinforcing double jeopardy. Clearly the low-income residents of New Orleans were autonomous human agents who were and are capable of making rational and informed choices. We do not wish to portray them as completely helpless victims or pawns of greater powers. Yet as we mentioned at the beginning of this story, humans' ability to act as autonomous agents is constrained by historically determined structural social realities. In the case of the African American residents of New Orleans, a long history of racist marginalization clearly limited the ability to evacuate or to return and rebuild after the storm (Elliott & Pais, 2006; Lavelle & Feagin, 2006). As we have shown, it also made resettling and rebuilding a new life in a new cultural and social environment difficult.

Yet we continue to ask what sort of progress has been made in improving the fundamental situation of the oppressed and how civil society has contributed to any improvement. We also ask how that role can be enhanced in ways that empower communities. A very real danger is that well-meaning outsiders fail to foster the autonomy of those that they would help and engage in what is really charity that does not build the community's own capacities for self-determination and empowerment. A very legitimate criticism of NGO activities in developing nations is that such organizations serve as what one author labels the "global soup kitchen" that reflects and reproduces the asymmetry between north and south, rich and poor (Malhotra, 2000). Although the intentions of those engaged in charity and good works may be noble, charity does not build sustainable capacity or empower vulnerable communities.

BACK TO BRIDGING AND BONDING TIES

We also began by introducing the concepts of strong and weak ties, also referred to as bonding and bridging ties, to emphasize their function and their relation to political power and the situation of the survivors of Hurricane Katrina (Agnitsch, Flora, & Ryan, 2006; Granovetter, 1973; Putnam, 2000). Strong, or bonding, ties characterize relationships among family members, close friends, and neighbors. These are the relationships that one relies upon on a daily basis and that provide essential emotional, social, and material support (Edin & Lein, 1997; Stack, 1974). The survivors' accounts of their local communities in New Orleans reflected strong bonding ties. Weak, or bridging, ties refer to less intimate relationships with individuals one interacts with less intimately or intensely, such as acquaintances, members of professional organizations, business contacts, or the friends of friends. Such ties are useful in making contacts with individuals and organizations at a distance. The survivors' accounts revealed relatively few such ties, and those who had them, such as the Johnsons, recovered much more rapidly. Among the most impoverished, this sort of social capital was completely absent.

The strong bonds that the survivors relied upon in New Orleans continued to exist but, uprooted and fragmented, they could not ensure day-to-day survival to all after the evacuation to a new location. This form of social capital turned out not to be transportable and remained largely tied to place. Individuals and families with few bridging ties had no one to whom they could turn, other than federal, state, and municipal governments and perhaps civil society organizations. The question that remains has to do with the extent to which civil society organizations can replace strong ties and provide the benefits of information-rich weak ties that can place one in contact with more powerful actors. Organizations or groups can have aspects of both bonding and bridging ties. African American religious congregations, for example, can bring together people of the same race but of different social classes. Even though it did not result in lasting change, the example of the African American ECSA that we introduced in Chapter 6 at least hinted at the potential of collective action. For a while, it served to bridge a less affluent eastside community with a more affluent westside community. It also attempted to connect low-income African American survivors from New Orleans to the African American community in Austin. It is the combination of bonding and bridging characteristics that has made the African American church so important in increasing the social capital of African American communities (Foley, McCarthy, & Chaves, 2001). Clearly there is far to go, but the sort of political action that characterized the civil rights movement shows that empowerment is not an easy goal to accomplish.

THE UTILITY OF THE CONCEPT OF SOCIAL CAPITAL

Let us return to a consideration of the concept of social capital which motivated the argument of the book. As we noted at the beginning, the utility of the concept of social capital is that like material capital, it represents a source of power that can be used to further individual and group interests. Social capital refers to the potential power inherent in social networks and the collective capacity of people to act together toward common goals (Coleman, 1988, 1990; Portes, 1998; Putnam, 1993, 1995, 2000; Warren, Thompson, & Saegert, 2001). As we noted, the utility of the concept of social capital for understanding the situation of vulnerable communities relates to the fact that it is a collective asset and not just an individual characteristic or attribute (Coleman, 1990; Warren, Thompson, & Saegert, 2001). Individuals do not possess social capital as individuals; they possess it by virtue of their group and community membership. Although many individuals object to the use of the term "capital" to refer to something that is not the result of investment, but rather that inheres in one's social location and is the result of one's birth, the use of the term in the context of differential group power emphasizes the instrumental importance of a group's capacity to act as a collective agent to further individual and group ends.

As we noted in our introduction, social capital is important in providing what individuals alone cannot acquire, including public safety and a healthy environment, political influence, and even material capital (Fukuyama, 2001; Guiso, Sapienza, & Zingales, 2004; Sampson, 1999; Sampson & Groves, 1989; Vieno et al., 2010; Zak & Knack, 2001). The social support that accompanies social capital can protect health (Berkman et al., 2000; Fujiwara & Kawachi, 2008; James, Schulz, & van Olphen, 2001). It keeps high school students from dropping out (Coleman, 1988) and it fosters individual occupational and social mobility (Burt, 1992; Lin, 1999). At the community level, it results in greater neighborhood stability and more effective rural community action (Agnitsch, Flora, & Ryan, 2006; Portney & Berry, 1997; Saegert, Thompson, & Warren, 2001; Silverman and Patterson, 2004; Temkin and Rohe, 1998). At the national level, it is associated with higher levels of economic development (Knack & Keefer, 1997; Portes & Landolt, 2000; Woolcock, 2002).

Yet the use of the concept of social capital is not without problems both theoretically and empirically, including a lack of precision concerning its major dimensions, a lack of clarity concerning its social origins, a lack of precision concerning its connection to economic and political resources and power, and doubt about its actual utility at the individual and collective levels (Bourdieu, 1986; Edwards, Foley, & Diani, 2001; Portes, 1998; Reimer et al., 2008; Wakefield & Poland, 2005; Woolcock, 2002, 2010). As we noted in the introduction, the term can obscure structural sources of power. Feminist scholars have criticized the failure of theorists and researchers to recognize the connection among gender roles, the family, and social capital (Rosalind Edwards, 2004). It is imperative, therefore, to understand the social, economic, and political contexts in which social capital functions for different groups. Theoretically and empirically, social capital and social class are mutually reinforcing (Bourdieu, 1986; Pichler & Wallace, 2009). Those social classes with greater material capital employ it to reinforce their class positions through their ability to leverage cultural and social capital.

Without understanding the mechanisms that make social capital an asset for individuals or groups, claims that a group lacks social capital are just another way of saying that they are disadvantaged, in which case little of intellectual or practical value has been gained. If social capital, material capital, and social class are so closely allied there may be no need for the concept. One might be better off focusing on social class and wealth and their ties to political power. Perhaps a group's relation to the means of production is where the story should lead.

Yet the term and concept remain immensely popular (Woolcock, 2010). The fact that most discussions of Robert Putnam's concept of social capital include serious criticisms does not diminish the concept's appeal. One wonders why such a contested and imprecise concept has such wide appeal. One plausible explanation is that the term *social capital* is useful specifically because of its global and nonspecific nature. As we have noted, the term has been employed in many disciplines to explain many different phenomena, from school success to health promotion and even development. It has an intuitive appeal since it draws attention to aspects of social life that are clearly important but that may be impossible to specify in a general sense that would apply to all contexts (Woolcock, 2010). There is probably no general theoretical or operational definition that is applicable everywhere and for all purposes. The utility of the concept and the term may be in fostering a general dialogue among individuals from very different backgrounds with perhaps a similar general objective of referring to the non-economic aspects of social interaction. What is necessary, therefore, is to specify the major dimensions of social capital that operate or do not in specific contexts and to be as precise as possible about the mechanisms whereby various forms of social capital benefit individuals and groups in those contexts. It is also necessary to identify those factors, such as race, ethnicity, gender, and social class, that foster or impede its development and effectiveness.

We have been clear to emphasize that social capital has value to the extent that it can be translated into material and social power. It can be understood only in terms of its association with cultural capital, financial capital, and human capital (Bourdieu, 1986; Light, 2004). It is also clear that social capital does not exist in an economic or political vacuum and that a highly developed welfare state with specific programs for fostering the development of and sustaining the activities of community organizations is necessary (Silverman & Patterson, 2004; Wakefield & Poland, 2005). Such political activity is necessary since, as our study and others clearly show, the lack of effective social capital in low-income communities is not a mere deficit; to a large extent, it reflects active interference by economically and politically powerful groups (Lopez & Stack, 2001; Peruzzotti & Smulovits, 2002; Portes & Landolt, 2000; Stahler-Sholk, Vanden, & Kuecke, 2008; Wacquant, 1998). The essence of oppression is the systematic exclusion of individuals and communities from access to political and economic power. One means of undermining the social capital of low-income communities and their ability for effective political action is to deny them material support (Cohen, 2001).

As we saw clearly among Katrina survivors, those with the greatest amount of social capital, in terms of networks outside of New Orleans, as well as human capital – including education, transferable skills, and a work history – recovered fastest. We also saw that among those with the least social capital, powerful structural obstacles in New Orleans – including poor schools, rampant crime, community segregation, and a local economy built on the tourist trade, characterized by low-skill, low-wage jobs – created powerful obstacles to the acquisition of social capital.

CHARITY VERSUS ADVOCACY

At the end of our study, we are forced to return to interest group politics and a consideration of the structural possibilities for effective civil society action (Cohen, 2001; Fuchs, Shapiro, & Minnite, 2001). In this study, we have taken a fairly general view of social capital as the ability to control important aspects of one's life associated with group membership. From the neo-Toquevillian perspective reflected in Putnam's writings, group membership and participation in and of themselves convey benefits, including greater political power (Putnam 1993, 2000). Logically, by contrast, individual or group isolation reinforces marginalization and weakness. It is clear from our study that group membership is a necessary condition for political power, but it is not a sufficient condition. We saw that the low-income African American survivors most often came from long-standing communities with dense social and kin networks. These networks made it possible for them to survive in New Orleans, but not thrive. It also made it almost impossible for them to survive outside of New Orleans. The group itself must have access to other groups and to sources of power. For that reason, we return to interest group politics and advocacy.

Civil society organizations occupy unique social positions and play potentially important roles in relation to the state and to the individuals they represent. In times of need, the most immediate task is to provide short-term material assistance in the form of shelter, food, water, and emergency health care. In the longer term, civil society organization can serve as intermediaries in terms of information flows. Perhaps the most important role of nongovernmental organizations in Austin was in helping survivors deal effectively with FEMA and other governmental agencies. Beyond these important tasks, though, nongovernmental organizations can act as advocates for the individuals they serve with the objective of empowering clients so that they are able to act as effective agents and improve their own lives. From this perspective, it is clear that civil society organizations combine service delivery and advocacy roles to varying degrees depending on their objectives (Pereira & Angel, 2009; Pereira, Angel, & Angel, 2009). These roles can conflict. As service providers, nongovernmental organizations often act as subcontractors to the state in providing goods and services to individuals and communities in need. In this role, the organization's goal is not to change the rules of the game, but rather to alleviate suffering while working within established social hierarchies. As we have elaborated repeatedly, disaster case management focuses on returning disaster victims to their pre-crisis state and does not focus on addressing their earlier disadvantaged position. Although sympathetic to the need for a political voice for survivors, the overwhelmed service providers were for the most part too focused on helping survivors manage crises to try to help them organize politically as well, and the cultural differences between the two groups would also make such an objective truly challenging.

Advocacy, on the other hand, refers specifically to attempts by organizations to change the rules of the game and to reduce the vulnerability of marginalized groups. It is almost by definition political and can threaten the status quo and existing power relations. In dictatorships, as was the case in Chile under Augusto Pinochet, civil society actors, including the Catholic Church, found it necessary to challenge aspects of authority in order to protect basic human rights (Pereira, Angel, & Angel, 2007). Organizations such as Amnesty International, Human Rights Watch, and many feminist NGOs direct their efforts at changing basic social relations, often rooted in culture and tradition, in order to protect human rights and overcome patriarchal oppression (Keck & Sikkink, 1998). Environmental NGOs attempt to influence nations and international bodies to introduce laws to protect the environment. Such roles can cause friction and lead to resistance by other groups or those in power.

Both service and advocacy are important and are often pursued jointly by specific NGOs, depending on the political and economic context. In the wake of Hurricane Katrina, as in those of other disasters, service in the form of rescue and attending to basic needs was of immediate importance, but with time many volunteers and organizations found themselves acting as advocates for particular individuals or families. Ultimately the experience may lead some of these individuals to advocate legislation aimed at changing the policies that increased the vulnerability of the victims of the hurricane. Our study clearly shows the need to streamline FEMA policies and provide real mechanisms for the coordination of voluntary efforts.

As important as providing services in times of need may be, providing an individual with food for a day does not teach her to fish or to obtain what she needs on her own. Advocates, on the other hand, can treat the victims of natural and man-made disasters as if they are helpless pawns. Ideally, the objectives of disaster case management and civil society actions in crisis situations should be to do more than simply return individuals to their prior marginal status. It should be to transform their situation into something better in which they are true agents with free will who are empowered to act in their own interests. Ultimately, this should be the objective of civil society organizations in dealing with all vulnerable groups, including chronically low-income people. As our study revealed, such an objective is truly difficult and often requires going against a history of structural race-based disadvantage and the social services that sustain that framework. Empowering communities is, of course, the objective of traditional community organization, and that objective is as important now as ever. Given the current economic climate and powerful anti-welfare sentiments among the electorate and those in power, immediate progress in improving the lot of the most vulnerable victims of Hurricane Katrina or of low-income people in general is probably quite low. But there is tomorrow and the day after and the day after that. Ultimately, a political culture that cuts large segments of the population loose is doomed.

The 2010 Census reveals that the majority of children in the country are now non-white (Frey, 2011). In twenty years, they will make up the majority of the labor force. If the productivity of a large fraction of this working-age population is compromised by poor health and low educational levels, our nation's global position will be placed in jeopardy and everyone's quality of life will decline. The generations that will soon be called upon to pay for Social Security, Medicare, and the rest of the middle-class welfare state have already been born. At the end of our journey, we once again call upon T. H. Marshall, whose vision of the welfare state we presented in the introduction. In the end, the conclusion that we arrive at is that an enlightened welfare state is the only guarantor of a nation's true well-being. Although nongovernmental and faith-based organizations, in conjunction with other civil society actors, are vital to a dynamic economy and a civilized and vibrant political culture, they are no substitute for a strong, functioning, and enlightened state. A vibrant and effective civil society and a strong and just state complement one another. In many parts of the world, we see nations that lack one or the other, or often both. Without strong states, societies descend into chaos; without strong civil societies, they descend into tyranny.

Bibliography

Agnitsch, Kerry, Jan Flora, and Vern Ryan. 2006. "Bonding and Bridging Social Capital: The Interactive Effects on Community Action." *Community Development: Journal of the Community Development Society* 37(1):36–51.

Aguilera, Michael B., and Douglas S. Massey. 2003. "Social Capital and the Wages of Mexican Migrants: New Hypotheses and Tests." *Social Forces* 82(2):671–701.

Almond, Gabriel L., and Sydney Verba. 1963. *The Civic Culture: Political Attitudes and Democracy in Five Nations.* Princeton, NJ: Princeton University Press.

Alston, Lee J., and Joseph P. Ferrie. 1993. "Paternalism in Agricultural Labor Contracts in the U.S. South: Implications for the Growth of the Welfare State." *American Economic Review* 83(4):852–76.

Amendola, Adalgiso, Maria Rosaria Garofalo, and Annamaria Nese. 2010. "Is the Third Sector an Emerging Economic Institution? Social Preferences versus Poverty Traps." *Nonprofit and Voluntary Sector Quarterly* 20(10):1–23.

American Red Cross. 2006. "From Challenge to Action: American Red Cross Actions to Improve and Enhance Its Disaster Response and Related Capabilities for the 2006 Hurricane Season and Beyond." Accessed March 25, 2011, at http://www.redcross.org/www-files/Documents/pdf/corppubs/file_cont5448_lango_2006.pdf.

Andrews, Geoff. 1999. "New Left and New Labour." *Soundings* (13):14–24.

Aneshensel, Carol S. 2008. *Neighborhood as a Social Context of the Stress Process.* Los Angeles: UCLA, California Center for Population Research.

Angel, Ronald J., Laura Lein, and Jane Henrici. 2006. *Poor Families in America's Health Care Crisis: How the Other Half Pays.* New York: Cambridge University Press.

Anheier, Helmut K., and Lester M. Salamon (Eds.). 1999. *Global Civil Society: Dimensions of the Nonprofit Sector.* Baltimore, MD: Institute for Policy Studies, Johns Hopkins University.

Appleseed. 2006. "A Continuing Storm: The On-going Struggles of Hurricane Katrina Evacuees: A Review of Needs, Best Practices, and Recommendations."

Accessed October 17, 2001, at http://appleseeds.net/Portals/0/Documents/Publications/KatrinaContinuingStorm.pdf.

Armada, Francisco, Carles Muntaner, and Vicente Navarro. 2001. "Health and Social Security Reforms in Latin America: The Convergence of the World Health Organization, the World Bank, and Transnational Corporations." *International Journal of Health Services* 31(4):729–68.

Arrow, Kenneth J. 2000. "Observations on Social Capital," in *Social Capital: A Multifaceted Perspective*, edited by Partha Dasgupta and Ismail Serageldin. Washington, DC: World Bank, pp. 3–10.

Bachelard, Gaston. 1957. *La poétique de l'espace*. Paris: Presses Universitaires de France.

Baiocchi, Gianpaolo, Patrick Heller, and Marcelo Kunrath Silva. 2008. "Making Space for Civil Society: Institutional Reforms and Local Democracy in Brazil." *Social Forces* 86(3):911–36.

Baldwin, Peter. 1990. *The Politics of Social Solidarity: Class Bases of the European Welfare State, 1875–1975*. New York: Cambridge University Press.

Barrientos, Armando, and Martin Powell. 2004. "The Route Map of the Third Way," in *The Third Way and Beyond: Criticisms, Futures, Alternatives*, edited by Sarah Hale, Will Leggett, and Luke Martell. Mancester and New York: Manchester University Press, pp. 9–26.

Barry, Norman P. 1999. *Welfare*. Minneapolis: University of Minnesota Press.

Barsky, Lauren, Joseph Trainor, and Manuel Torres. 2006. "Disaster Realities in the Aftermath of Hurricane Katrina: Revisiting the Looting Myth." Quick Response Research Report 184. University of Delaware, Newark: Disaster Research Center.

Basolo, Victoria, and Nai Thi Nguyen. 2005. "Does Mobility Matter? The Neighborhood Condition of Housing Voucher Holders by Race and Ethnicity." *Housing Policy Debate* 16(3/4):297–324.

Batliwals, Srilatha, and L. David Brown (Eds.). 2006. *Transnational Civil Society: An Introducation*. Bloomfield, CT: Kumarian Press.

Bea, Keith. 2010. "Federal Stafford Act Disaster Assistance: Presidential Declarations, Eligible Activities, and Funding." Washington, DC: Congressional Research Service.

Beausoleil, Julie, and Megan Reid. 2007. "Displaced and 'FEMAtized': Obstacles and Strategies of Katrina Survivors in Austin in Their Efforts to Secure Assistance from the Federal Emergency Management Agency (FEMA)." Society for the Anthropology of North America's Unnatural Disasters Conference, University of New Orleans, New Orleans, LA.

Bebbington, Anthony J., Michael Woolcock, Scott Guggenheim, and Elizabeth A. Olson (Eds.). 2006. *The Search for Empowerment: Social Capital as Idea and Practice at the World Bank*. Bloomfield, CT: Kumarian Press.

Bell, Holly. 2008. "Case Management with Displaced Survivors of Hurricane Katrina: A Case Study of One Host Community." *Journal of Social Service Research* 34(3):15–27.

Bell, Holly, Elissa Madden, Elisa Vinson Borah, Laura Lein, and Julie Beausoleil. 2010. "Case Management with Hurricane Katrina Survivors: Perspectives of Case Managers and Supervisors." *Journal of Social Service Research* 36(3):216–29.

Benhabib, Seyla. 2002. *The Claims of Culture: Equality and Diversity in the Global Era*. Princeton, NJ: Princeton University Press.

Berger, Eric. March 24, 2006. "Locals Evacuee-Weary; While Residents Are Proud of City's Response, They Feel a Growing 'Strain.'" *Houston Chronicle*, Section A, p. 1.

Berger, Peter L., and Thomas Luckman. 1966. *The Social Construction of Reality: A Treatise in the Sociology of Knowledge*. New York: Doubleday.

Berkman, Lisa F., Thomas Glass, Ian Brissette, and Teresa E. Seeman. 2000. "From Social Integration to Health: Durkheim in the New Millennium." *Social Science & Medicine* 51(6):843–57.

Berry, Jeffrey M. 1999. "The Rise of Citizen Groups," in *Civic Engagement in American Democracy*, edited by Theda Skocpol and Morris P. Fiorina. Washington, DC, and New York: Brookings Institution Press and Russell Sage Foundation, pp. 367–93.

Berube, Alan, and Bruce Katz. 2005. "Katrina's Window: Confronting Concentrated Poverty Across America." Brookings Institution Metropolitan Policy Program. Washington, DC: Brookings Institution. Accessed October 17, 2011, at http://www.brookings.edu/~/media/Files/rc/reports/2005/10poverty_berube/20051012_Concentratedpoverty.pdf.

Beveridge, Sir William. 1942. "Social Insurance and Allied Services." London: H.M. Stationary Office.

Beyers, Jennifer M., John E. Bates, Gregory S. Pettit, and Kenneth A. Dodge. 2003. "Neighborhood Structure, Parenting Processes, and the Development of Youths' Externalizing Behaviors: A Multilevel Analysis." *American Journal of Community Psychology*, Vol. 31, Nos. 1/2, March 2003:35–53.

Birnie, Sarah. 2009. "A Comprehensive Costing Analysis of Intensive Case Management for Individuals with Severe Mental Illness and a History of Homelessness, Including Cost-Effectiveness as Compared to Standard Care." Ottawa: University of Ottawa (Canada).

Boggess, Lyndsay N., and John R. Hipp. 2010. "Violent Crime, Residential Instability and Mobility: Does the Relationship Differ in Minority Neighborhoods?" *Journal of Quantitative Criminology* (2010) 26:351–70.

Boli, John, and George M. Thomas. 1997. "World Culture in the World Polity: A Century of Inernational Non-governmental Organization." *American Sociological Review* 62(2):171–90.

Bourdieu, Pierre. 1977. *Outline of a Theory of Practice*. New York: Cambridge University Press.

1986. "The Forms of Capital," in *Handbook of Theory and Research for the Sociology of Education*, edited by John G. Richardson. New York: Greenwood, pp. 241–58.

Braaten, Jane. 1991. *Habermas's Critical Theory of Society*. Albany: State University of New York Press.

Brasch, Walter M. 2006. *"Unacceptable": The Federal Response to Hurricane Katrina*. Charleston, NC: BookSurge.

Brinkley, Douglas G. 2006. *The Great Deluge: Hurricane Katrina, New Orleans, and the Mississippi Gulf Coast*. New York: HarperCollins.

Brodie, Mollyann, Erin Weltzien, Drew Altman, Robert J. Blendon, and John M. Benson. 2006. "Experiences of Hurricane Katrina Evacuees in Houston Shelters: Implications for Future Planning." *American Journal of Public Health* 96(8):1402–8.

Brown, David S., and Wendy Hunter. 1999. "Democracy and Social Spending in Latin America, 1980–92." *American Political Science Review* 93(4):779–90.

Brunsma, David L., David Overfelt, and J. Steven Picou. 2007. *The Sociology of Katrina: Perspectives on a Modern Catastrophe*. Lanham, MD: Rowman and Littlefield.

Building Oprah Katrina Homes. 2011. "Building Oprah Katrina Homes." Accessed May 30, 2011, at http://www.oprah.com/angelnetwork/Building-Oprahs-Katrina-and-Rita-Homes.

Burawoy, Michael. 1998. "The Extended Case Method." *Sociological Theory* 16(1):4–33.

Burby, Raymond J. 2006. "Hurricane Katrina and the Paradoxes of Government Disaster Policy: Bringing about Wise Governmental Decisions for Hazardous Areas." *Annals of the American Academy of Political and Social Science* 604:171–91.

Burcher, Jacqueline (Ed.). 2008. *México solidario: Participación ciudadana y voluntarado*. Mexico, D.F.: Limusa.

Bureau of Labor Statistics. 2006. "Hurricane Katrina Evacuees, October 2005." Accessed February 16, 2011, at http://www.bls.gov/katrina/2005 10status.htm.

Burt, Ronald S. 1992. *Structural Holes: The Social Structure of Competition*. Cambridge, MA: Harvard University Press.

Cabannes, Yves. 2004. "Participatory Budgeting: A Significant Contribution to Participatory Democracy." *Environment and Urbanization* 16(1):27–46.

Callaghan, William, Sonja Rasmussen, Denise Jamieson, Stephanie Ventura, Sherry Farr, Paul Sutton, Thomas Mathews, Brady Hamilton, Katherine Shealy, Dabo Brantley, and Sam Posner. 2007. "Health Concerns of Women and Infants in Times of Natural Disasters: Lessons Learned from Hurricane Katrina." *Maternal and Child Health Journal* 11(4):307–11.

Campanella, Richard. 2007. "An Ethnic Geography of New Orleans." *Journal of American History* 94(3):704–15.

Campbell, John L. 2004. *Institutional Change and Globalization*. Princeton, NJ: Princeton University Press.

Campbell, John L., and Ove K. Pedersen (Eds.). 2001. *The Rise of Neoliberalism and Institutional Analysis*. Princeton, NJ: Princeton University Press.

Carlisle, Kristin. 2004. "Recovery and Renewal for Survivors of Hurricanes Katrina and Rita in Texas." *Journal of Affordable Housing and Community Development Law* 4:365–76.

——— 2006. "It's Like You're Walking But Your Feet Ain't Going Nowhere," in *Shelterforce Online*, edited by National Housing Institute. Accessed October 17, 2011, at http://www.shelterforce.org/article/729/its_like_youre_walking_but_your_feet_aint_going_nowhere/.

Casserly, Michael. 2006. "Double Jeopardy: Public Education in New Orleans before and after the Storm," in *There Is No Such Thing as a Natural Disaster: Race, Class, and Hurricane Katrina*, edited by Chester Hartman and Gregory D. Squires. New York: Routledge, pp. 197–214.

Centers for Disease Control & Prevention. 2006a. "Illness Surveillance and Rapid Needs Assessment among Hurricane Katrina Evacuees – Colorado, September 1–23, 2005." *Morbidity and Mortality Weekly Report* 55(9):244–7.

2006b. "Rapid Assessment of Health Needs and Resettlement Plans among Hurricane Katrina Evacuees – San Antonio, Texas, September 2005." *Morbidity and Mortality Weekly Report* 55(9):242–4.

2006c. "Rapid Community Needs Assessment after Hurricane Katrina – Hancock County, Mississippi, September 14–15, 2005." *Morbidity and Mortality Weekly Report* 55(9):234–6.

Chamlee-Wright, Emily, and Virgil Henry Storr. 2009. "'There's No Place Like New Orleans': Sense of Place and Community Recovery in the Ninth Ward after Hurricane Katrina." *Journal of Urban Affairs* 31(5):615–34.

Chandra, Anita, and Joie Acosta. 2009. "The Role of Nongovernmental Organizations in Long-Term Human Recovery after Disaster: Reflections from Louisiana Four Years after Hurricane Katrina." Occasional Paper. Santa Monica, CA: Rand Corporation, Gulf States Policy Institute.

Charter, David. 2002. "Mandelson Tells Labour: We're All Thatcherites," in *Times* (London), June 10.

Cohen, Cathy J. 2001. "Social Capital, Intervening Institutions, and Political Power," in *Social Capital and Poor Communities*, edited by Susan Saegert, J. Phillip Thompson, and Mark R. Warren. New York: Russell Sage Foundation, pp. 267–89.

Coker, A. L., J. S. Hanks, K. S. Eggleston, J. Risser, P. G. Tee, K. J. Chronister, C. L. Troisi, R. Arafat, and L. Franzini. 2006. "Social and Mental Health Needs Assessment of Katrina Evacuees." *Disaster Management & Response* 4(3):88–94.

Coleman, James S. 1988. "Social Capital in the Creation of Human Capital." *American Journal of Sociology* 94(Special Issue):S95–S120.

1990. *Foundations of Social Theory*. Cambridge, MA: Harvard University Press.

Colten, Craig E. 2006. "Vulnerability and Place: Flat Land and Uneven Risk in New Orleans." *American Anthropologist* 108(4):731–4.

Comerio, Mary C. 1998. *Disaster Hits Home: New Policy for Urban Housing Recovery*. Berkeley: University of California Press.

Cooley, Charles Horton. 1922. *Human Nature and the Social Order*, Revised Edition. New York: Charles Scribner's Sons.

Cooper, Christopher, and Robert Block. 2006. *Disaster: Hurricane Katrina and the Failure of Homeland Security*. New York: Times Books, Henry Holt.

Danziger, Sheldon H., and Robert H. Haveman (Eds.). 2001. *Understanding Poverty*. Cambridge, MA, and New York: Russell Sage Foundation and Harvard University Press.

de Soto, Hernando. 2000. *The Mystery of Capital: Why Capitalism Triumphs in the West and Fails Everywhere Else*. New York: Basic.

De Vita, C. J., and E. Morley. 2007. "Providing Long-Term Services after Major Disasters," in *Charting Civil Society: A Series by the Center on Nonprofits and Philanthropy* 17. Washington, D.C.: Urban Institute. Accessed October 17, 2011, at http://www.urban.org/UploadedPDF/411519_major_disasters.pdf.

DeFilippis, James, and Elvin Wyly. 2008. "Running to Stand Still." *Urban Affairs Review* 43(6):777–816.

Delgado, Daniel García, and Luciano Nosetto (Eds.). 2006. *El desarollo en un contexto posneoliberal: hacia una sociedad para todos*. Buenos Aires: FLASCO Argentina: Coleccíon Transformacíon.

Díaz, Antonia, and María José Luengo-Prado. 2010. "The Wealth Distribution with Durable Goods." *International Economic Review* 51(1):143–70.

DiPasquale, Denise, and Edward L. Glaeser. 1999. "Incentives and Social Capital: Are Homeowners Better Citizens?" *Journal of Urban Economics* 45:354–84.

DiPerna, Paula. 2003. "Media, Charity, and Philanthropy in the Aftermath of September 11, 2001." Century Foundation. Accessed March 25, 2011, at http://tcf.org/publications/pdfs/pb78/diperna.pdf.

Doyle, Cathal, and Preeti Patel. 2008. "Civil Society Organisations and Global Health Initiatives: Problems of Legitimacy." *Social Science & Medicine* 66(9):1928–38.

Dulles, Allen W. 1993. *The Marshall Plan*. Oxford, UK: Berg.

Duncan, Cynthia M. 2001. "Social Capital in America's Poor Rural Communities," in *Social Capital and Poor Communities*, edited by Susan Saegert, J. Phillip Thompson, and Mark R. Warren. New York: Russell Sage Foundation, pp. 60–86.

Dwyer, Peter. 2004. *Understanding Social Citizenship*. Bristol, UK: Policy Press and the Social Policy Association.

Dyson, Michael Eric. 2006. *Come Hell or High Water: Hurricane Katrina and the Color of Disaster*. New York: Basic Civitas.

Eade, Deborah (Ed.). 2002. *Development, NGOs, and Civil Society*. Oxford, UK: Oxfam, GB.

Edin, Katheryn, and Laura Lein. 1997. *Making Ends Meet: How Single Mothers Survive Welfare and Low-Wage Work*. New York: Russell Sage Foundation.

Edwards, Bob, Michael W. Foley, and Mario Diani (Eds.). 2001. *Beyond Tocqueville: Civil Society and the Social Capital Debate in Comparative Perspective*. Hanover, NH: University Press of New England.

Edwards, Michael. 1999. "NGO Performance – What Breeds Success? New Evidence from South Asia." *World Development* 27(2):361–74.

2004. *Civil Society*. Cambridge, UK, Malden, MA: Polity Press.

2009. *Civil Society*, Second Edition. Malden, MA: Polity Press.

Edwards, Michael, and Gita Sen. 2000. "NGOs, Social Change and the Transformation of Human Relationships: A 21st Century Civic Agenda." *Third World Quarterly* 21(4):605–16.

Edwards, Rosalind. 2004. "Present and Absent in Troubling Ways: Families and Social Capital Debates." *Sociological Review* 52(1):1–21.

Ellickson, Robert C. 2009–10. "The False Promise of the Mixed-Income Housing Project." *UCLA Law Review* (4):983–1021.

Elliott, James R., and Jeremy Pais. 2006. "Race, Class, and Hurricane Katrina: Social Differences in Human Responses to Disaster." *Social Science Research* 35:295–321.

Elo, Irma T., Laryssa Mykyta, Rachel Margolis, and Jennifer F. Culhane. 2009. "Perceptions of Neighborhood Disorder: The Role of Individual and Neighborhood Characteristics." *Social Science Quarterly* 90(5):1298–1320.

Embry, Jason. September 4, 2005. "State Nearing Limit, Perry Says; with Hurricane Survivors Still Heading to Texas, Governor Urges Officials to Look to Other States." *Austin American Statesman*, Metro State, p. B1.

Esping-Andersen, Gøsta. 1990. *The Three Worlds of Welfare Capitalism.* Princeton, NJ: Princeton University Press.

    1999. *Social Foundations of Postindustrial Economies.* Oxford, UK, and New York: Oxford University Press.

Esping-Andersen, Gøsta, Duncan Gallie, Anton Hemerijck, and John Myles. 2002. *Why We Need a New Welfare State.* Oxford, UK, and New York: Oxford University Press.

Etzioni, Amitai. 1993. *The Spirit of Community: Rights, Responsibilities, and the Communitarian Agenda.* New York: Crown.

    (Ed.). 1995. *New Communitarian Thinking: Persons, Virtues, Institutions, and Communities.* Charlottesville: University Press of Virginia.

    2000. *The Third Way to a Good Society.* London: Demos.

Falk, William W., Matthew O. Hunt, and Larry L. Hunt. 2006. "Hurricane Katrina and New Orleans' Sense of Place: Return and Reconstruction or 'Gone with the Wind'?" *Du Bois Review: Social Science Research on Race* 3(1):115–28.

Farr, James. 2004. "Social Capital: A Conceptual History." *Political Theory* 32(1):6–33.

Faux, Jeff. 1999. "Lost on the Third Way." *Dissent* 46(2):67–76.

Feinberg, Richard, Carlos H. Waisman, and Leon Zamosc (Eds.). 2006. *Civil Society and Democracy in Latin America.* New York: PalgraveMacMillan.

FEMA. 2006. "Disaster Unemployment Assistance Extended for Additional 13 Weeks." Accessed May 22, 2011, at http://www.fema.gov/news/newsrelease. fema?id=24198.

    2010. "FEMA History." Washington, DC: Federal Emergency Management Agency, U.S. Department of Homeland Security.

Finley, Keith M. 2008. *Delaying the Dream: Southern Senators and the Fight against Civil Rights, 1938–1965.* Baton Rouge: Louisiana State University Press.

Fiorina, Morris P. 1999. "Extreme Voices: A Dark Side of Civic Engagement," in *Civic Engagement in American Democracy*, edited by Theda Skocpol and Morris P. Fiorina. Washington, DC: Brookings Institution Press, pp. 395–425.

Fisher, William F. 1997. "Doing Good? The Politics and Antipolitics of NGO Practices." *Annual Review of Anthropology* 26:439–64.

Fishkin, James S. 2009. *When the People Speak: Deliberative Democracy & Public Consultation.* New York: Oxford University Press.

Foley, Michael W., John D. McCarthy, and Mark Chaves. 2001. "Social Capital, Religious Institutions, and Poor Communities," in *Social Capital and Poor Cummunities*, edited by Susan Saegert, J. Phillip Thompson, and Mark R. Warren. New York: Russell Sage Foundation, pp. 215–45.

Fothergill, Alice, and Lori A. Peek. 2004. "Poverty and Disasters in the United States: A Review of Recent Sociological Findings." *Natural Hazards* 32:89–110.

Frailing, Kelly, and Dee Wood Harper. 2007. "Crime and Hurricanes in New Orleans," in *The Sociology of Katrina: Perspectives on a Modern Catastrophe*, edited by David L. Brunsma, David Overfelt, and Steve Picou. Lanham, MD: Rowman and Littlefield, pp. 51–68.

Franzini, Luisa, Margaret Caughy, William Spears, and Maria Eugenia Fernandez Esquer. 2005. "Neighborhood Economic Conditions, Social Processes, and Self-Rated Health in Low-Income Neighborhoods in Texas: A Multilevel Latent Variables Model." *Social Science & Medicine* 61(6):1135–50.

Fraser, Nancy, and Alex Honneth. 2003. *Redistribution or Recognition? A Political-Philosophical Exchange*. New York: Verso.

Fremont-Smith, Marion, Elizabeth T. Boris, and C. Eugene Steuerle. 2006. "Charities' Response to Disasters: Expectations and Realities," in *After Katrina: Public Expectation and Charities' Response*, edited by Elizabeth T. Boris and C. Eugene Steuerle. Washington, DC: Urban Institute, pp. 1–4.

Frey, William H. 2011. "America's Diverse Future: Initial Glimpses at the U.S. Child Population from the 2010 Census." Accessed April 6, 2011, at http://www.brookings.edu/~/media/Files/rc/papers/2011/0406_census_diversity_frey/0406_census_diversity_frey.pdf.

Frey, William H., and Audrey Singer. 2006. "Katrina and Rita Impacts on Gulf Coast Populations: First Census Findings." Metropolitan Policy Program. New York: Brookings Institution. Accessed October 17, 2011, at http://www.brookings.edu/~/media/Files/rc/reports/2006/06demographics_frey/20060607_hurricanes.pdf.

Fuchs, Ester R., Robert Y. Shapiro, and Lorraine C. Minnite. 2001. "Social Capital, Political Participation, and the Urban Community," in *Social Capital and Poor Communities*, edited by Susan Saegert, J. Phillip Thompson, and Mark R. Warren. New York: Russell Sage Foundation, pp. 290–324.

Fujiwara, Takeo, and Ichiro Kawachi. 2008. "Social Capital and Health: A Study of Adult Twins in the U.S." *American Journal of Preventive Medicine* 35(2):139–44.

Fukuyama, Francis. 2001. "Social Capital, Civil Society and Development." *Third World Quarterly* 22(1):7–20.

Fussell, Elizabeth. 2007. "Constructing New Orleans, Constructing Race: A Population History of New Orleans." *Journal of American History* 94(3):846–55.

Gajewski, Stephanie, Holly Bell, Laura Lein, and Ronald J. Angel. 2011. "Complexity and Instability: The Response of Nongovernmental Organizations to the Recovery of Hurricane Katrina Survivors in a Host Community." *Nonprofit and Voluntary Sector Quarterly* 40(2):389–401.

Galster, George C., Roberto G. Quercia, and Alvaro Cortes. 2000. "Identifying Neighborhood Thresholds: An Empirical Exploration." *Housing Policy Debate* 11(3):701–32.

Gary, Tiffany L., Sarah A. Stark, and Thomas A. La Veist. 2007. "Neighborhood Characteristics and Mental Health among African Americans and Whites

Living in a Racially Integrated Urban Community." *Health & Place* 13:569–75.

Gautam, Sandeep, Jonathan Menachem, Sudesh K. Srivastav, Patrice Delafontaine, and Anand Irimpen. 2009. "Effect of Hurricane Katrina on the Incidence of Acute Coronary Syndrome at a Primary Angioplasty Center in New Orleans." *Disaster Medicine and Public Health Preparedness* 3(3):144–50.

Germany, Kent B. 2007. "The Politics of Poverty and History: Racial Inequality and the Long Prelude to Katrina." *Journal of American History* 94(3):743–51.

Ghosh, Tista S., Jennifer L. Patnaik, and Richard L. Vogt. 2007. "Rapid Needs Assessment among Hurricane Katrina Evacuees in Metro-Denver." *Journal of Health Care for the Poor and Underserved* 18(2):362–8.

Giddens, Anthony. 1986. *The Constitution of Society: Outline of the Theory of Structuration.* Berkeley: University of California Press.

1994. *Beyond Left and Right: The Future of Radical Politics.* Cambridge, UK: Polity Press.

1998. *The Third Way: Renewal of Social Democracy (IGN European Country Maps).* Malden, MA: Blackwell.

2000. *The Third Way and Its Critics.* Cambridge, UK: Polity Press.

Glantz, Michael, and Dale Jamieson. 2000. "Societal Response to Hurricane Mitch and Intra- versus Intergenerational Equity Issues: Whose Norms Should Apply?" *Risk Analysis* 20(6):869–82.

Goldman, Karin Kunstler. 2006. "Nonprofits and Disaster: The Experience of New York State on September 11, 2001," in *After Katrina: Public Expectations and Charities' Response*, edited by Elizabeth T. Boris and C. Eugene Steuerle. Washington, DC: Urban Institute, pp. 19–22.

Government Accountability Office. 2002. "September 11: Interim Report on the Response of Charities." Accessed March 25, 2011, at http://www.gao.gov/new.items/d021037.pdf.

2005. "Hurricanes Katrina and Rita: Provision of Charitable Assistance." Accessed March 25, 2011, at http://www.gao.gov/new.items/d06297t.pdf.

2008. "Mass Care in Disasters: FEMA Should Update the Red Cross Role in Catastrophic Events and More Fully Assess Voluntary Organizations' Mass Care Capabilities." Washington, DC: Government Accountabilty Office. Accessed October 17, 2011, at http://www.gao.gov/new.items/d08117 5t.pdf.

2009. "Disaster Assistance: Greater Coordination and an Evaluation of Programs' Outcomes Could Improve Disaster Case Management." Accessed March 28, 2011, at http://www.gao.gov/new.items/d09561.pdf.

Gramsci, Antonio. 1971. *Selections from the Prison Notebooks.* New York: International Publishers.

Granovetter, Mark S. 1973. "The Strength of Weak Ties." *American Journal of Sociology* 78(6):1360–80.

Greenbaum, Susan. 2008. "Poverty and the Willful Destruction of Social Capital: Displacement and Dispossession in African American Communities." *Rethinking Marxism* 20(1):42–54.

Grzybowski, Cândido. 2000. "We NGOs: A Controversial Way of Being and Acting." *Development in Practice* 10(3–4):436–44.

Guiso, Luigi, Paola Sapienza, and Luigi Zingales. 2004. "The Role of Social Capital in Financial Development." *American Economic Review* 94(3):526–56.

Habermas, Jürgen. 1984. *The Theory of Communicative Action*. Boston: Beacon Press.

Habitat for Humanity. 2011. "Hurricanes Katrina and Rita Recovery Effort Fact Sheet." Accessed on May 30, 2011, at http://www.habitat.org/disaster/programs/details/Gulf_Recovery_Fact_Sheet.aspx.

Hacker, Jacob S. 2002. *The Divided Welfare State*. New York: Cambridge University Press.

Hale, Sarah, Will Leggett, and Luke Martell (Eds.). 2004. *The Third Way and Beyond: Criticisms, Futures, Alternatives*. Manchester and New York: Manchester University Press.

Hammer, Jeffrey, and Lant Pritchett. 2006. "Scenes from a Marriage: World Bank Economists and Social Capital," in *The Search for Empowerment: Social Capital as Idea and Practice at the World Bank*, edited by Anthony Bebbington, Muchael Woolcock, Scott Guggenheim, and Elizabeth A. Olson. Bloomfield, CT: Kumarian Press, pp. 63–90

Hartman, Chester, and Gregory D. Squires (Eds.). 2006. *There Is No Such Thing as a Natural Disaster: Race, Class, and Katrina*. New York: Routledge.

Hathaway, James C. 2007. "Forced Migration Studies: Could We Agree Just to 'Date'?" *Journal of Refugee Studies* 20(3):349–69.

Havemann, Paul. 2001. "No Rights without Responsibilities? Third Way and Global Human Rights Perspectives on Citizenship." *Waikato Law Review* 9(1):75–90.

Hayek, F. A. 1944. *The Road to Serfdom*. Chicago: University of Chicago Press.
   1976. *Law, Legislation, and Liberty*, Volume 2: *The Mirage of Social Justice*. Chicago: University of Chicago Press.

Henkel, Kristin E., John F. Dovidio, and Samuel L. Gaertner. 2006. "Institutional Discrimination, Individual Racism, and Hurricane Katrina." *Analysis of Social Issues and Public Policy* 6(1):99–124.

Herbert, Christopher E., and Eric S. Belsky. 2008. "The Homeownership Experience of Low-Income and Minority Households: A Review and Synthesis of the Literature." *Cityscape* 10(2):5–59.

Hero, Rodney E. 2003. "Social Capital and Racial Inequality in America." *Perspectives on Politics* 1(01):113–22.

Hill, Paul, and Jane Hannaway. 2006. "The Future of Public Education in New Orleans." Washington, DC: Urban Institute. Accessed October 18, 2011, at http://www.urban.org/UploadedPDF/900913_public_education.pdf.

Hill, Terrence, Catherine Ross, and Ronald Angel. 2005. "Neighborhood Disorder, Psychological Distress and Health." *Journal of Health and Social Behavior* 46(2):170–86.

Hoffman, Kelly, and Miguel Angel Centeno. 2003. "The Lopsided Continent: Inequality in Latin America." *Annual Review of Sociology* 29:363–90.

Holmwood, John. 2000. "Three Pillars of Welfare State Theory: T. H. Marshall, Karl Polanyi, and Alva Myrdal in Defence of the National Welfare State." *European Journal of Social Theory* 3(1):23–50.

Homedes, Núria, and Antonio Ugalde. 2005. "Why Neoliberal Health Reforms Have Failed in Latin America." *Health Policy* 71(1):83–96.

Homeland Security Institute. 2006. "Heralding Unheard Voices: The Role of Faith-Based Organizations and Nongovernmental Organizations during Disasters: Final Report." Accessed March 25, 2011, at http://www.homelandsecurity.org/hsireports/Herald_Unheard_Voices.pdf.

Hooghe, Liesbet, and Gary Marks. 2006. "Europe's Blues: Theoretical Soul-Searching after the Rejection of the European Constitution." *PS: Political Science & Politics* 39(02):247–50.

Hopwood, Bill, Mary Mellor, and Geoff O'Brien. 2005. "Sustainable Development: Mapping Different Approaches." *Sustainable Development* 13(1):38–52.

Horne, J ed. 2008. *Breach of Faith: Hurricane Katrina and the Near Death of a Great American City.* New York: Random House.

Hudock, Ann C. 1999. *NGOs and Civil Society: Democracy by Proxy?* Malden, MA: Polity Press.

Humphrey, Katie, and Emma Graves Fitzsimmons. September 1, 2005. "Survivors Surging into Texas: Austin Shelter Filling Up; Hospitals, School, Parks Opened." *Austin American-Statesman*, p. A13.

James, Sherman A., Amy J. Schulz, and Juliana van Olphen. 2001. "Social Capital, Poverty, and Community Health: An Exploration of Linkages," in *Social Capital and Poor Commuities*, edited by Susan Saegert, J. Phillip Thompson, and Mark R. Warren. New York: Russell Sage Foundation, pp. 165–88.

Jenner, Eric, Lynne W. Jenner, Eva Silvestre, and Maya Matthews-Sterling. 2008. "Final Evaluation of the United Methodist Committee on Relief: Katrina Aid Today, National Case Management Consortium." New Orleans: Policy and Research Group.

Jhung, Michael A., Nadine Shehab, Cherise Rohr-Allegrini, Daniel A. Pollock, Roger Sanchez, Fernando Guerra, and Daniel B. Jernigan. 2007. "Chronic Disease and Disasters: Medication Demands of Hurricane Katrina Evacuees." *American Journal of Preventive Medicine* 33(3):207–10.

Kapucu, Naim. 2007. "Non-profit Response to Catastrophic Disasters." *Disaster Prevention and Management* 16(4):551–61.

Katz, Bruce, and Margery Austin Turner. 2008. "Rethinking U.S. Rental Housing Policy: Build on State & Local Innovations." Washington, DC: Brookings Institution. Accessed October 18, 2011, at http://www.brookings.edu/~/media/Files/Projects/Opportunity08/PB_Housing_Katz.pdf.

Katz, Cindi. 2008. "Bad Elements: Katrina and the Scoured Landscape of Social Reproduction." *Gender, Place, and Culture* 15(1):15–29.

Kay, Alan. 2006. "Social Capital, the Social Economy and Community Development." *Community Development Journal* 41(2):160–73.

Keck, Margaret E., and Kathryn Sikkink. 1998. *Activists beyond Borders: Advocacy Networks in International Politics.* Ithaca, NY: Cornell University Press.

Kessler, Ronald. 2007. "Hurricane Katrina's Impact on the Care of Survivors with Chronic Medical Conditions." *Journal of General Internal Medicine* 22(9):1225–30.

Kessler, Ronald C., Sandro Galea, Michael J. Gruber, Nancy A. Sampson, Robert J. Ursano, and Simon Wessely. 2008. "Trends in Mental Illness and Suicidality after Hurricane Katrina." *Molecular Psychiatry* 13(4):374–84.

Kessler, Ronald C., Sandro Galea, Russell T. Jones, and Holly A. Parker. 2006. "Mental Illness and Suicidality after Hurricane Katrina." *Bulletin of the World Health Organization* 84(12):930–9.

Kim, Joongbaeck, and Catherine Ross. 2009. "Neighborhood-specific and General Social Support: Which Buffers the Effect of Neighborhood Disorder on Depression?" *Journal of Community Psychology* 37(6):725–36.

Knack, Stephen, and Philip Keefer. 1997. "Does Social Capital Have an Economic Payoff? A Cross-Country Investigation." *Quarterly Journal of Economics* 112(4):1251–88.

Kromm, Chris, and Sue Sturgis. 2008. "Hurricane Katrina and the Guiding Principles on Internal Displacement: A Global Human Rights Perspective on a National Disaster," Durham, NC: Institute for Southern Studies. Accessed October 18, 2011, at http://www.brookings.edu/~/media/Files/events/2008/0114_disasters/0114_ISSKatrina.pdf.

Kulkarni, Shanti, Holly Bell, Julie Beausoleil, Laura Lein, Ron Angel, and Johnnie Hamilton Mason. 2008. "When the Floods of Compassion Are Not Enough: A Nation's and a City's Response to the Evacuees of Hurricane Katrina." *Smith College Studies in Social Work* 78:399–425.

Kymlicka, Will. 1995. *Multicultural Citizenship: A Liberal Theory of Minority Rights*. New York: Oxford University Press.

2007. *Multicultural Odysseys: Navigating the New International Politics of Diversity*. Oxford, UK: Oxford University Press.

Kymlicka, Will, and Wayne Norman. 2000a. "Citizenship in Culturally Diverse Societies: Issues, Contexts, Concepts," in *Citizenship in Diverse Societies*. Oxford, UK, and New York: Oxford University Press, pp. 1–41.

(Eds.). 2000b. *Citizenship in Diverse Societies*. Oxford, UK, and New York: Oxford University Press.

Landphair, Juliette. 2007. "'The Forgotten People of New Orleans': Community, Vulnerability, and the Lower Ninth Ward." *Journal of American History* 94(3):837–45.

Langsdorf, Lenore. 2000. "The Real Condition for the Possibility of Communicative Action," in *Perspectives on Habermas*, edited by Lewis E. Hahn. Peru, IL: Open Court, pp. 21–50.

Larrance, Ryan, Michael Anastario, and Lynn Lawry. 2007. "Health Status among Internally Displaced Persons in Louisiana and Mississippi Travel Trailer Parks." *Annals of Emergency Medicine* 49(5):590–601.

Lavelle, Kristen, and Joe Feagin. 2006. "Hurricane Katrina: The Race and Class Debate." *Monthly Review* 58(3):52–66.

Lawrence, Robert Z. 2008. *Blue-Collar Blues: Is Trade to Blame for Rising US Income Inequality?* Danvers, MA: Peterson Institute for International Economics.

Lein, Laura, Ronald Angel, Holly Bell, and Julie Beausoleil. 2009. "The State and Civil Society Response to Disaster: The Challenge of Coordination." *Organization and Environment* 22(4):448–57.

Leventhal, Tama, and Jeanne Brooks-Gunn. 2000. "The Neighborhoods They Live In: The Effects of Neighborhood Residence on Child and Adolescent Outcomes." *Psychological Bulletin* 126(2):309–37.

Light, Ivan. 2004. "Social Capital for What?" in *Community-Based Organizations: The Intersection of Social Capital and Local Context in Contemporary Urban Society*, edited by Robert Mark Silverman. Detroit, MI: Wayne State University Press, pp. 19–33.

Lin, Nan. 1999. "Social Networks and Status Attainment." *Annual Review of Sociology* 25:467–87.

Lipsitz, George. 2006. "Learning from New Orleans: The Social Warrant of Hostile Privatism and Competitive Consumer Citizenship." *Cultural Anthropology* 21(3):451–68.

Lopez, M. Lisette, and Carol B. Stack. 2001. "Social Capital and the Culture of Power: Lessons from the Field," in *Social Capital and Poor Communities*, edited by Susan Saegert, J. Phillip Thompson, and Mark R. Warren. New York: Russell Sage Foundation, pp. 31–59.

Luft, Rachel E. 2009. "Beyond Disaster Exceptionalism: Social Movement Developments in New Orleans after Hurricane Katrina." *American Quarterly* 61(3):499–527.

Mair, Christina, Ana V. Diez Roux, and Jeffrey D. Morenoff. 2010. "Neighborhood Stressors and Social Support as Predictors of Depressive Symptoms in the Chicago Community Adult Health Study." *Health & Place* 16(5):811–19.

Make It Right. 2009. "Make It Right: Helping to Rebuild New Orleans' Lower 9th Ward." Accessed May 30, 2011, at http://www.makeitrightnola.org/.

Malhotra, Kamal. 2000. "NGOs without Aid: Beyond the Global Soup Kitchen." *Third World Quarterly* 21(4):655–68.

Marshall, Catherine, and Gretchen B. Rossmann. 2011. *Designing Qualitative Research*, Fifth Edition. Thousand Oaks, CA: Sage.

Marshall, T. H., and Tom Bottomore. 1950. *Citizenship and Social Class*. Cambridge: Cambridge University Press.

Martin, E. Davis, and Philip Browning. 2007. *Principles and Practices of Case Management in Rehabilitation Counseling*. Springfield, IL: Charles C. Thomas.

Mead, George Herbert. 1934. *Mind, Self, and Society: From the Standpoint of a Social Behaviorist*. Chicago: University of Chicago Press.

Mead, Lawrence M. 1986. *Beyond Entitlement*. New York: Free Press.

⸻ 1997. "Citizenship and Social Policy: T. H. Marshall and Poverty." *Social Philosophy and Policy* 14(2):197–230.

Meuleman, Bart, Eldad Davidov, and Jaak Billiet. 2009. "Changing Attitudes toward Immigration in Europe, 2002–2007: A Dynamic Group Conflict Theory Approach." *Social Science Research* 38(2):352–65.

Miller, Andrew C., and Bonnie Arquilla. 2008. "Chronic Diseases and Natural Hazards: Impact of Disasters on Diabetic, Renal, and Cardiac Patients." *Prehospital and Disaster Medicine* 23(2):185–94.

Mills, Mary Alice, Donald Edmondson, and Crystal L. Park. 2007. "Trauma and Stress Response among Hurricane Katrina Evacuees." *American Journal of Public Health* 97(Supplement 1):S116–23.

Milward, Alan S. 1987. *The Reconstruction of Western Europe, 1947–1951*. New York: Routledge.

Moore, Mark H. 2006. "Disasters and the Voluntary Sector: Reflections on the Social Response to Hurricane Katrina," in *After Katrina: Public Expectation and Charities' Response*, edited by Elizabeth T. Boris and C. Eugene Steuerle. Washington, DC: Urban Institute, pp. 23–7.

Morley, Elaine, Carol J. De Vita, and Jennifer Auer. 2006. "Findings from a Survey of 9/11-affected Clients Served by the American Red Cross September 11 Recovery Program." Washington, DC: Urban Institute. Accessed October 18, 2011, at http://www.urban.org/UploadedPDF/411335_redcross_survey.pdf.

Morris, John C. 2006. "Whither Fema? Hurricane Katrina and FEMA's Response to the Gulf Coast." *Public Works Management & Policy* 10(4):284–94.

Mueller, Elizabeth J., and Alex Schwartz. 2008. "Reversing the Tide: Will State and Local Governments House the Poor as Federal Direct Subsidies Decline?" *Journal of the American Planning Association* 74(1):122–35.

Munshi, Kaivan. 2003. "Networks in the Modern Economy: Mexican Migrants in the U.S. Labor Market." *Quarterly Journal of Economics* 118(2):549–99.

Murray, Charles. 1994. *Losing Ground: American Social Policy 1950–1980*. New York: Basic.

1999. *The Underclass Revisited*. Washington, DC: AEI Press.

2006. *In Our Hands: A Plan to Replace the Welfare State*. Blue Ridge Summit, PA: AEI Press.

Murray, Charles, and Ruth Lister (Eds.). 1996. "Charles Murray and the Underclass: The Developing Debate," London: IEA Health and Welfare Unit.

National Low-Income Housing Coalition. 2005. "Out of Reach 2005." Accessed May 25, 2011, at http://www.nlihc.org/oor/oor2005/.

National Voluntary Organizations Active in Disaster. 2004. "Long-Term Recovery Manual." Accessed February 3, 2011, at http://www.disasterrecovery-resources.net/VOAD-LTRecoveryManual.pdf.

Novy, Andreas, and Bernhard Leubolt. 2005. "Participatory Budgeting in Porto Alegre: Social Innovation and the Dialectical Relationship of State and Civil Society." *Urban Studies* 42(11):2023–36.

Nozick, Robert. 1974. *Anarchy, State, and Utopia*. New York: Basic.

OCHA. 2010. *Internally Displaced People: Exiled in Their Homeland*. New York: United Nations.

O'Connor, Alice. 2001. *Poverty Knowledge: Social Science, Social Policy, and the Poor in Twentieth-Century U.S. History*. Princeton, NJ: Princeton University Press.

Olsasky, Marvis. 2006. *The Politics of Disaster: Katrina, Big Government, and a New Strategy for Future Crises*. Nashville, TN: W Publishing Group.

Olsen, Edgar O. 2008. "Getting More from Low-Income Housing Assistance," *The Hamilton Project*, Discussion Paper 2008-13. Washington, DC: Brookings Institution. Accessed October 18, 2011, at http://www.brookings.edu/~/media/Files/rc/papers/2008/0923_housing_olsen/0923_housing_olsen.pdf.

Orlebeke, Charles J. 2000. "The Evolution of Low-Income Housing Policy, 1949–1999." *Housing Policy Debate* 11(2):489–520.

Orloff, Ann Shola. 1988. "The Political Origins of America's Belated Welfare State," in *The Politics of Social Policy in the United States*, edited by Margaret Weir, Ann Shola Orloff, and Theda Skocpol. Princeton, NJ: Princeton University Press, pp. 37–80.

Padgett, Deborah K. 2008. *Qualitative Methods in Social Work Research*, Second Edition. Thousand Oaks, CA: Sage.

Palier, Bruno (Ed.). 2010. *A Long Goodbye to Bismark? The Politics of Welfare Reform in Continental Europe*. Amsterdam: Amsterdam University Press.

Peacock, Walter Gillis, Betty Hearn Morrow, and Hugh Gladwin (Eds.). 1997. *Hurricane Andrew: Ethnicity, Gender and the Sociology of Disasters*. New York: Routledge.

Pereira, Javier, and Ronald Angel. 2009. "From Adversary to Ally: The Evolution of Non-Governmental Organizations in the Context of Health Reform in Santiago and Montevideo," in *Social Inequality and Public Health*, edited by Salvatore Babones. Bristol, UK: Polity Press, pp. 97–114.

Pereira, Javier, Ronald J. Angel, and Jacqueline L. Angel. 2007. "A Case Study of the Elder Care Functions of a Chilean Non-Governmental Organization." *Social Science & Medicine* 64:2096–2106.

2009. "A Chilean Faith-Based NGO's Social Service Mission in the Context of Neoliberal Reform," in *Bridging the Gaps: Faith-based Organizations, Neoliberalism, and Development in Latin America and the Caribbean*, edited by Tara L. Hefferan, Julie Adkins, and Laurie Occhipinti. Lanham, MD: Lexington, pp. 151–64.

Peruzzotti, Enrique, and Catalina Smulovits (Eds.). 2002. *Controlando La Política: Ciudadanos y medios en las nuevas democracias Latinoamericanas*. Buenos Aires: Temas Grupo Editorial.

Peters, David H., Anu Garg, Gerry Bloom, Damian G. Walker, William R. Brieger, and M. Hafizur Rahman. 2008. "Poverty and Access to Health Care in Developing Countries." *Annals of the New York Academy of Sciences* 11(36):161–71.

Pfeiffer, James, Wendy Johnson, Meredith Fort, Aaron Shakow, Amy Hagopian, Steve Gloyd, and Kenneth Gimbel-Sherr. 2008. "Strengthening Health Systems in Poor Countries: A Code of Conduct for Nongovernmental Organizations." *American Journal of Public Health* 98(12):2134–40.

Pichler, Florian, and Claire Wallace. 2009. "Social Capital and Social Class in Europe: The Role of Social Networks in Social Stratification." *European Sociological Review* 25(3):319–32.

Pierson, Paul. 1994. "Increasing Returns: Path Dependence and the Study of Politics." *American Political Science Review* 94(2):251–67.

2001a. "Coping with Permanent Austerity: Welfare State Restructuring in Affluent Democracies," in *The New Politics of the Welfare State*, edited by Paul Pierson. New York: Oxford University Press, pp. 410–56.

2001b. "Post-Industrial Pressures on the Mature Welfare States," in *The New Politics of the Welfare State*, edited by Paul Pierson. Oxford, UK, and New York: Oxford University Press, pp. 80–106.

Popkin, Susan J., Margery A. Turner, and Martha Burt. 2006. "Rebuilding Affordable Housing in New Orleans: The Challenge of Creating Inclusive Communities," in the series *After Katrina: Rebuilding Opportunity and Equity in the New New Orleans*. Washington, DC: Urban Institute. Accessed October 18, 2011, at http://www.urban.org/UploadedPDF/900914_affordable_housing.pdf.

Porter, Matthew, and Nick Haslam. 2005. "Predisplacement and Postdisplacement Factors Associated with Mental Health of Refugees and Internally Displaced Persons: A Meta-analysis." *Journal of the American Medical Association* 294(5):602–12.

Portes, Alejandro. 1998. "Social Capital: Its Origins and Applications in Modern Sociology." *Annual Review of Sociology* 24:1–14.

Portes, Alejandro, and Robert L. Bach. 1985. *Latin Journey: Cuban and Mexican Immigrants in the United States.* Berkeley: University of California Press.

Portes, Alejandro, and Patricia Landolt. 2000. "Social Capital: Promise and Pitfalls of Its Role in Development." *Journal of Latin American Studies* 32(2):529.

Portney, Dent E., and Jeffrey M. Berry. 1997. "Mobilizing Minority Communities: Social Capital and Participation in Urban Neighborhoods." *American Behavioral Scientist* 40(5):632–44.

Putnam, Robert D. 1993. *Making Democracy Work: Civic Traditions in Modern Italy.* Princeton, NJ: Princeton University Press.

1995. "Tuning In, Tuning Out: The Strange Disappearance of Social Capital in America." *PS: Political Science and Politics* 28(4):664–83.

2000. *Bowling Alone: The Collapse and Revival of American Community.* New York: Simon & Schuster.

Quadagno, Jill S. 1994. *The Color of Welfare: How Racism Undermined the War on Poverty.* New York: Oxford University Press.

Quarantelli, E. L. 1991. "Disaster Assistance and Socioeconomic Recovery at the Individual and Household Level: Some Observations." Newark: University of Delaware, Disaster Research Center.

1999. "The Disaster Recovery Process: What We Know and Do Not Know from Research." Newark: University of Delaware, Disaster Research Center.

Rae, Gavin. 2011. "On the Periphery: The Uneven Development of the European Union and the Effects of the Economic Crisis on Central-Eastern Europe." *Global Society* 25(2):249–66.

Rahman, Sabeel. 2006. "Development, Democracy and the NGO Sector." *Journal of Developing Societies* 22(4):451–73.

Rand Gulf States Policy Institute. 2008. "Road Home Program Leaves Many Homeowners Waiting." Rand Corporation. Accessed October 18, 2011, at http://www.rand.org/content/dam/rand/pubs/research_briefs/2008/RAND_RB9355.pdf.

Reich, Robert. 1999. "We Are All Third Wayers Now." *American Prospect* 10(43):46–51.

Reimer, Bill, Tara Lyons, Nelson Ferguson, and Geraldina Polanco. 2008. "Social Capital as Social Relations: The Contribution of Normative Structures." *Sociological Review* 56(2):256–74.

Reisch, Michael. 2009. "United States: Social Welfare Policy and Privatization in Post-Industrial Society," in *The Welfare State in Post-Industrial Society,* edited by Jon Hendricks and Jason Powell. New York: Springer, pp. 253–70.

Renz, Loren, and Leslie Marino. 2004. "Giving in the Aftermath of September 11: Final Update on the Foundation and Corporate Response." Accessed March 28, 2011, at http://foundationcenter.org/gainknowledge/research/pdf/9_11updto4.pdf.

Ridenour, M. L., K. J. Cummings, J. R. Sinclair, and D. Bixler. 2007. "Displacement of the Underserved: Medical Needs of Hurricane Katrina Evacuees in West Virginia." *Journal of Health Care for the Poor and Underserved* 18(2):369–81.

Riggirozzi, Pia. 2010. "Social Policy in Post-Neo-Liberal Latin America: The Cases of Argentina, Venezuela and Bolivia." *Development* 53(1):70–6.

Ritzer, George. 2008. *Modern Sociological Theory.* New York: McGraw-Hill.

Ritzer, George, and Pamela Gindoff. 1994. "Agency-Structure, Micro-Macro, Individualism-Holism-Relationism: A Metatheoretical Explanation of Theoretical Convergence between the United States and Europe," in *Agency and Structure: Reorienting Social Theory,* edited by Piotr Sztompka. Reading, UK: Gordon and Breach, pp. 3–23.

Roberts, Patrick. 2006a. "FEMA after Katrina." *Policy Review* (137). Accessed October 18, 2011, at http://www.hoover.org/publications/policy-review/article/7897.

2006b. "FEMA and the Prospects for Reputation-Based Autonomy." *Studies in American Political Development* 20(01):57–87.

Rocha, José Luis, and Ian Christoplos. 2001. "Disaster Mitigation and Preparedness on the Nicaraguan Post-Mitch Agenda." *Disasters* 25(3):240–50.

Rodriguez, S. R., J. S. Tocco, S. Mallonee, L. Smithee, T. Cathey, and K. Bradley. 2006. "Rapid Needs Assessment of Hurricane Katrina Evacuees – Oklahoma, September 2005." *Prehospital and Disaster Medicine* 21(6):390–5.

Rohe, William M., Roberto G. Quercia, and Shannon Van Zandt. 2002. "Supporting the American Dream of Homeownership: An Assessment of Neighborhood Reinvestment's Home Ownership Pilot Program," Chapel Hill: University of North Carolina. Accessed October 18, 2011, at http://www.issuelab.org/research/supporting_the_american_dream_of_homeownership_an_assessment_of_neighborhood_reinvestments_home_ownership_pilot_program.

Rohe, W. M., and L. S. Stewart. 1996. "Homeownership and Neighborhood Stability." *Housing Policy Debate* 7(1):37–81.

Rohe, William M., Shannon Van Zandt, and George McCarthy. 2002. "Home Ownership and Access to Opportunity " *Housing Studies* 17(1):51–61.

Rose, Kalima, Annie Clark, and Dominique Duval-Diop. 2008. "A Long Way Home: The State of Housing Recovery in Louisiana, 2008." Accessed May 25, 2011, at http://www.policylink.org/threeyearslater/.

Ross, Catherine E., and John Mirowsky. 2009. "Neighborhood Disorder, Subjective Alienation, and Distress." *Journal of Health and Social Behavior* 50(1):49–64.

Rudowitz, Robin, Diane Rowland, and Adele Shartzer. 2006. "Health Care in New Orleans before and after Hurricane Katrina." *Health Affairs* 25(5):393–406.

Sader, Emir. 2009. "Postneoliberalism in Latin America." *Development Dialogue* 51:171–9.

Saegert, Susan, J. Phillip Thompson, and Mark R. Warren (Eds.). 2001. *Social Capital and Poor Communities.* New York: Russell Sage Foundation.

Salamon, Lester M., and S. Wojciech (Eds.). 2004. *Global Civil Society: Dimensions of the Nonprofit Sector,* Volume 2. Bloomfield, CT: Kumarian Press.

Salmon, Jacqueline L. 2006. "Counterparts Excoriate Red Cross Katrina Effort," *Washington Post*, April 5, p. A14.

Sampson, Robert J. 1999. "What 'Community' Supplies," in *Urban Problems and Community Development*, edited by Ronald F. Ferguson and William T. Dickens. Washington, DC: Brookings Institution, pp. 241–79.

——— 2009. "Disparity and Diversity in the Contemporary City: Social (Dis)Order Revisited." *British Journal of Sociology* 60(1):1–31.

Sampson, Robert J., and Corina Graif. 2009. "Neighborhood Social Capital as Differential Social Organization." *American Behavioral Scientist* 52(11): 1579–1605.

Sampson, Robert J., and W. Byron Groves. 1989. "Community Structure and Crime: Testing Social-Disorganization Theory." *American Journal of Sociology* 94(4):774.

SAMSHA. 2008. "Impact of Hurricanes Katrina and Rita on Substance Use and Mental Health." in *National Survey on Drug Use and Health: The NSDUH Report*. Rockville, MD: Substance Abuse and Mental Health Services Administration (SAMHSA).

Schieman, Scott, and Stephen C. Meersman. 2004. "Neighborhood Problems and Health Among Older Adults: Received and Donated Social Support and the Sense of Mastery as Effect Modifiers." *Journals of Gerontology Series B: Psychological Sciences and Social Sciences* 59(2):S89-S97.

Schlozman, Kay Lehman, Sidney Verba, and Henry E. Brady. 1999. "Civic Participation and the Equality Problem," in *Civic Engagement in American Democracy*, edited by Theda Skocpol and Morris P. Fiorina. Washington, DC: Brooking Institution Press, pp. 427–59.

Schram, Sanford F., Richard C. Fording, and Joe Soss. 2008. "Neo-liberal Poverty Governance: Race, Place and the Punitive Turn in US Welfare Policy." *Cambridge Journal of Regions, Economy and Society* 1:17–36.

Shefner, Jon. 2008. *The Illusion of Civil Society: Democratization and Community Mobilization in Low-Income Mexico*. University Park: Pennsylvania State University Press.

Shroder, Mark, and Arthur Reiger. 2000. "Vouchers versus Production Revisited." *Journal of Housing Research* 11(1):91–107.

Sigerist, Henry E. 1999. "From Bismarck to Beveridge: Developments and Trends in Social Security Legislation." *Journal of Public Health Policy* 20(4):474–96.

Silverman, Robert Mark (Ed.). 2004. *Community-Based Organizations: The Intersection of Social Capital and Local Context in Contemporary Urban Society*. Detroit, MI: Wayne State University Press.

Silverman, Robert Mark, and Kelly L. Patterson. 2004. "Paradise Lost: Social Capital and the Emergence of a Homeowners Association in a Suburban Detroit Neighborhood," in *Community Based Organizations: The Intersection of Social Capital and Local Context in Contemporary Urban Society*, edited by Robert Mark Silverman. Detroit: Wayne State University Press, pp. 67–84.

Small, Mario Luis. 2009. "'How Many Cases Do I Need?' On Science and the Logic of Case Selection in Field-Based Research." *Ethnography* 10(1):5–38.

Smith, Steven Rathgeb. 2006. "Rebuilding Social Welfare Services after Katrina: Challenges and Opportunities," in *After Katrina: Public Expectation and Charities' Response*, edited by Elizabeth T. Boris and C. Eugene Steuerle. Washington, DC: Urban Institute, pp. 5–10.

Sobel, Joel. 2002. "Can We Trust Social Capital?" *Journal of Economic Literature* 40:139–54.

Somers, Margaret R. 2008. *Geneologies of Citizenship: Markets, Statelessness, and the Right to Have Rights*. New York: Cambridge University Press.

Somers, Margaret R., and Fred Block. 2005. "From Poverty to Perversity: Ideas, Markets, and Institutions over 200 Years of Welfare Debate." *American Sociological Review* 70(2):260–87.

Sorel, Eliot, and Pier Carlo Padoan. 2008. "The Marshall Plan: Lessons Learned for the 21st Century." Accessed April 2, 2011, at http://browse.oecdbookshop. org/oecd/pdfs/browseit/0108091E.PDF.

Soss, Joe, Richard C. Fording, and Sanford F. Schram. 2008. "The Color of Devolution: Race, Federalism, and the Politics of Social Control." *American Journal of Political Science* 52(3):536–53.

Souza, Celina. 2001. "Participatory Budgeting in Brazilian Cities: Limits and Possibilities in Building Democratic Institutions." *Environment and Urbanization* 13(1):159–84.

Spiegel, Paul B., Phuoc Le, Mija-Tesse Ververs, and Peter Salama. 2007. "Occurrence and Overlap of Natural Disasters, Complex Emergencies and Epidemics during the Past Decade (1995–2004)." *Conflict and Health* 1(2). Accessed October 18, 2011, at http://www.conflictandhealth.com/content/ pdf/1752-1505-1-2.pdf.

Stack, Carol B. 1974. *All Our Kin: Strategies for Survival in a Black Community*. New York: Basic.

Stahler-Sholk, Richard, Harry E. Vanden, and Glen David Kuecke (Eds.). 2008. *Latin American Social Movements in the Twenty-first Century: Resistance, Power, and Democracy*. Lanham, MD: Rowman and Littlefield.

Stake, Robert E. 1995. *The Art of Case Study Research*. Thousand Oaks, CA: Sage.

Stanton-Salazar, Ricardo. 1997. "A Social Capital Framework for Understanding the Socialization of Racial Minority Children and Youths." *Harvard Educational Review* 67(1):1–41.

Stehr, Steven D. 2006. "The Political Economy of Urban Disaster Assistance." *Urban Affairs Review* 41(4):492–500.

Sterba, James P. 2009. *Affirmative Action for the Future*. Ithaca, NY: Cornell University Press.

Steuerle, C. Eugene. 2002. "Managing Charitable Giving in the Wake of Disaster." Accessed March 25, 2011, at http://www.urban.org/uploadedpdf/310471.pdf.

Stockdale, Susan E., Kenneth B. Wells, Lingqi Tang, Thomas R. Belin, Lily Zhang, and Cathy D. Sherbourne. 2007. "The Importance of Social Context: Neighborhood Stressors, Stress-Buffering Mechanisms, and Alcohol, Drug, and Mental Health Disorders." *Social Science & Medicine* 65(9):1867–81.

Stough, Laura M., and Amy N. Sharp. 2008. "An Evaluation of the Impact of the National Disability Rights Network Participation in the

Katrina AID Today Project." Accessed March 25, 2011, at http://www.nationaldisabilityrightsnetwork.org/KAT/eval.pdf.

Strom, Stephanie. 2006. "Red Cross Sifting Internal Charges over Katrina Aid." *New York Times*, March 24, p. 1.

Taylor, Charles. 1994. "The Politics of Recognition," in *Multiculturalism: Examining the Politics of Recognition*, edited by Amy Gutman. Princeton, NJ: Princeton University Press, pp. 25–73.

Telford, J., J. Cosgrave, and R. Houghton. 2006. *Joint Evaluation of the International Response to the Indian Ocean Tsunami: Synthesis Report*. London: Tsunami Evaluation Coalition.

Temkin, Kenneth, and William M. Rohe. 1998. "Social Capital and Neighborhood Stability: An Empirical Investigation." *Housing Policy Debate* 9(1): 61–88.

Tennant, Margaret. 2009. "History and the Non-Profit Sector: Parish Pump Meets Global Constellations." *Kotuitui: New Zealand Journal of Social Sciences Online* 4(3):163–78. Accessed October 18, 2011, at http://www.tandfonline.com/doi/pdf/10.1080/1177083X.2009.9522452.

Texas Health and Human Services Commission. 2006. *Hurricane Katrina Evacuees in Texas*. Austin: Texas Health and Human Services Commission.

Thorp, Rosemary. 1998. *Progress, Poverty and Exclusion: An Economic History of Latin America in the 20th Century*. Baltimore: Johns Hopkins University Press for the Inter-American Development Bank.

Tulin, Leah J. 2007. "Poverty and Chronic Conditions during Natural Disasters: A Glimpse at Health, Healing, and Hurricane Katrina." *Georgetown Journal on Poverty Law & Policy* 14(1):115–54.

U.S. Census Bureau, 2005–7. "Population and Housing Narrative Profile: 2005–2007." Accessed May 29, 2011, at http://factfinder.census.gov/servlet/NPTable?_bm=y&-geo_id=16000US2255000&-qr_name=ACS_2007_3YR_Goo_NP01&-ds_name=&-redoLog=false.

U.S. Congress. 2010. *Disaster Case Management: Developing a Comprehensive National Program Focused on Outcomes: Hearing before the Ad Hoc Subcommittee on Disaster Recovery of the Committee on Homeland Security and Governmental Affairs, United States Senate, One Hundred Eleventh Congress, First Session, December 2, 2009*. Washington, DC: Senate Committee on Homeland Security and Governmental Affairs. Ad Hoc Subcommittee on Disaster Recovery.

U.S. Department of Housing and Urban Development. 2007. "Fact Sheet: HUD to Administer Continued Rental Housing Assistance for Residents Affected By Gulf Coast Hurricanes," in *Home and Community Website, Disaster Housing Assistance Program (DHAP)*. Washington, DC: Government Printing Office.

U.S. Department of Labor. 2011. "National Emergency Grants." Accessed February 16, 2011, from http://www.doleta.gov/neg/.

U.S. House of Representatives. 2006a. *A Failure of Initiative: Final Report of the Select Bipartisan Committee to Investigate the Preparation for and Response to Hurricane Katrina*, edited by Select Bipartisan Committee to Investigate the Preparation for and Response to Hurricane Katrina, U.S. House of Representatives. Washington, DC: U.S. Government Printing Office.

2006b. *A Failure of Initiative: Supplemental Report and Document Annex, March 16, 2006*, edited by Select Bipartisan Committee to Investigate the Preparation for and Response to Hurricane Katrina, U.S. House of Representatives. Washington, DC: U.S. Government Printing Office.

U.S. Senate, Committee on Homeland Security and Governmental Affairs, Ad Hoc Subcommittee on Disaster Recovery, 2009. *Far from Home: Deficiencies in Federal Disaster Housing Assistance after Hurricanes Katrina and Rita and Recommendations for Improvement*, edited by Department of Homeland Security. Washington, DC: Government Printing Office.

Valadez, Jorge M. 2001. *Deliberative Democracy, Political Legitimacy, and Self-Determination in Multicultural Societies*. Boulder, CO: Westview Press.

Van Deth, Jan W. 2003. "Measuring Social Capital: Orthodoxies and Continuing Controversies." *International Journal of Social Research Methodology* 6(1):79–92.

Van Heerden, Ivor, and Mike Bryan. 2006. *The Storm: What Went Wrong and Why during Hurricane Katrina – the Inside Story from One Louisiana Scientist*. New York: Viking.

Van Zandt, Shannon, and William M. Rohe. 2006. "Do First-Time Home Buyers Improve Their Neighborhood Quality?" *Journal of Urban Affairs* 28(5):491–510.

Vanden, Harry E. 2004. "New Political Movements and Governance in Latin America." *International Journal of Public Administration* 27(13, 14):1129–49.

Varady, David P., and Carole C. Walker. 2007. *Neighbourhood Choices. Section 8 Housing Vouchers and Residential Mobility*. New Brunswick, NJ: Center for Urban Policy Research Press.

Vieno, Alessio, Maury Nation, Douglas D. Perkins, Massimiliano Pastore, and Massimo Santinello. 2010. "Social Capital, Safety Concerns, Parenting, and Early Adolescents' Antisocial Behavior." *Journal of Community Psychology* 38(3):314–28.

Wacquant, Loïc J. D. 1998. "Negative Social Capital: State Breakdown and Social Destitution in America's Urban Core." *Netherlands Journal of Housing and the Built Environment* 13(1):25–40.

Wakefield, Sarah E. L., and Blake Poland. 2005. "Family, Friend or Foe? Critical Reflections on the Relevance and Role of Social Capital in Health Promotion and Community Development." *Social Science & Medicine* 60(12):2819–32.

Warren, Mark R., J. Phillip Thompson, and Susan Saegert. 2001. "The Role of Social Capital in Combating Poverty," in *Social Capital and Poor Communities*, edited by Susan Saegert, J. Phillip Thompson, and Mark R. Warren. New York: Russell Sage Foundation, pp. 1–28.

Washington Post. February 8, 2011. "Europe's Blues: Theoretical Soul-Searching after the Rejection of the European Constitution." Accessed April 29, 2011, at http://www.washingtonpost.com/wp-dyn/content/article/2011/02/08/AR2011020805443.html.

Watson, John T., Michelle Gayer, and Marie A. Connolly. 2007. "Epidemics after Natural Disasters." *Emerging Infectious Diseases* 13(1):1–5.

Weber, Rachel. 2002. "Extracting Value from the City: Neoliberalism and Urban Redevelopment." *Antipode* 34(3):519–40.

Weems, Curl F., Armando A. Pina, Natalie M. Costa, Sara E. Watts, Leslie K. Taylor, and Melinda F. Cannon. 2007. "Predisaster Trait Anxiety and Negative Affect Predict Posttraumatic Stress in Youths after Hurricane Katrina." *Journal of Consulting and Clinical Psychology* 75(1):154–9.

Weir, Margaret, Ann Shola Orloff, and Theda Skocpol. 1988. *The Politics of Social Policy in the United States.* Princeton, NJ: Princeton University Press.

Weisler, Richard H., James G. Barbee IV, and Mark H. Townsend. 2006. "Mental Health and Recovery in the Gulf Coast after Hurricanes Katrina and Rita." *Journal of the American Medical Association* 296(5):585–8.

Weiss, Thomas G. 2003. "Internal Exiles: What Next for Internally Displaced Persons?" *Third World Quarterly* 24(3):429–47.

White House. 2006. *The Federal Response to Hurricane Katrina: Lessons Learned.* Washington, DC: U.S. Government Printing Office.

Wilson, Rick K., and Robert M. Stein. 2006. "Katrina Evacuees in Houston: One-Year Out." Unpublished report. Houston: Rice University. Accessed October 18, 2011, at http://brl.rice.edu/Katrina/White_Papers/White_Paper_9_8_06.pdf.

Wilson, Thomas Charles. 2006. "Whites' Opposition to Affirmative Action: Rejection of Group-Based Preferences as Well as Rejection of Blacks." *Social Forces* 85(1):111–20.

Wilson, William Julius. 1978. *The Declining Significance of Race: Blacks and Changing American Institutions.* Chicago: University of Chicago Press.

  1987. *The Truly Disadvantaged: The Inner City, the Underclass, and Public Policy.* Chicago: University of Chicago Press.

Wineburg, Robert, Brian L. Coleman, Stephanie Boddie, and Ram A. Cnaan. 2008. "Leveling the Playing Field: Epitomizing Devolution through Faith-Based Organizations." *Sociology & Social Welfare* 35(1):17–42.

Winnick, Louis. 1995. "The Triumph of Housing Allowance Programs: How a Fundamental Policy Conflict Was Resolved." *Cityscape: A Journal of Policy Development and Research* 1(3):95–121.

Winston, Pamela, Olivia Golden, Kenneth Finegold, Kim Rueben, Margery Austin Turner, and Stephen Zuckerman. 2006. "After Katrina: Federalism after Hurricane Katrina. How Can Social Programs Respond to a Major Disaster?" Washington, DC: Urban Institute. Accessed October 18, 2011, at http://www.urban.org/UploadedPDF/311344_after_katrina.pdf.

Wolcott, Harry F. 2008. *Ethnography, a Way of Seeing,* Second Edition. Lanham, MD: AltaMira Press.

Wood, Lisa, Lawrence D. Frank, and Billie Giles-Corti. 2010. "Sense of Community and Its Relationship with Walking and Neighborhood Design." *Social Science & Medicine* 70(9):1381–90.

Woolcock, Michael. 2002. "Social Capital in Theory and Practice: Where Do We Stand?" in *Social Capital and Economic Development: Well-Being in Developing Countries,* edited by Jonathan Isham, Thomas Kelly, and Sunder Ramaswamy. Northampton, MA: Edward Elgar, pp. 18–39.

  2010. "The Rise and Routinization of Social Capital, 1988–2008." *Annual Review of Political Science* 13(1):469–87.

Wynn, Will. September 4, 2006. "How Best to Assist Neighbors in Need," *Austin American Statesman*, p. A4.

Yilmaz, Yesim, Sonya Hoo, Matthew Nagowski, Kim Rueben, and Robert Tannenwald. 2006. "Measuring Fiscal Disparities across the U.S. States: A Representative Revenue System/Representative Expenditure System Approach, Fiscal Year 2002." Occasional Paper 74. Accessed October 18, 2011, at http://www.urban.org/UploadedPDF/311384_fiscal_disparities.pdf.

Yin, Robert K. 2009. *Case Study Research: Design and Methods*, Fourth Edition. Thousand Oaks, CA: Sage.

Zak, Paul J., and Stephen Knack. 2001. "Trust and Growth." *Economic Journal* 111(470):295–321.

Zakin, Susan, Bill McKibben, and Chris Jordan. 2006. *In Katrina's Wake: Portraits of Loss from an Unnatural Disaster*. Princeton, NJ: Princeton Architectural Press.

Zedlewski, Sheila R. 2006. "Building a Better Safety Net for the New New Orleans," Washington, DC: Urban Institute. Accessed October 18, 2011, at http://www.urban.org/UploadedPDF/900922_safety_net.pdf.

Index